The Articulate Sailor

THE ARTICULATE SAILOR

Edited by James Tazelaar

Photography by Jan De Graff

John de Graff, Inc. 1973

Copyright © 1973 by James Tazelaar
ISBN Number: 8286-0058-9
Library of Congress Card Number: 79-185574

John de Graff Inc
34 Oak Avenue, Tuckahoe, N.Y. 10707

Copyright dates and owners are acknowledeged
in the reference section commencing on page 183.

Printed in U.S.A.

TO

MILLIE

my wife
companion
and secret sharer

PETE TAYLOR

friend
and sailing enthusiast
on whose Star it began

JOE RICHARDS

Masefield in paint
writer of a modern sea classic
shipmate on the high seas of
thought

RICHARD MAURY

sagacious mariner
articulate sailor
generous friend

Also by James Tazelaar,
Sea Verse in a Sailor's Locker

Contents

Introduction

A famous writer and small boat sailor once wrote that, waking or sleeping, he dreamt of boats. I share his condition for I, too, am boat-smitten.

Some years ago, removed because of work from the sail-active area that is Washington, D.C. and the nearby bay, I began to read the vast literature that sailors and other sea-oriented writers, ancient and modern, have written.

At first I read for evidence of literary merit, particularly for evidence of poetic merit. (Up to that point I had been unsuccessful in finding a collection of sailing poems that related to the modern sailing scene; thwarted, I read prose.) As I read I realized that certain writers were uncommonly expressive, their thoughts well-organized and articulate, and that their writings, if not exactly poetic in quality, were truly informative or genuinely entertaining. Happily, many of the writings had all of these qualities.

I began to collect from any book I could find excerpts that, in my opinion, had something of merit—literary, practical or humorous—and that were well-written. Ultimately my notes suggested a pattern, the pattern a book. I called it "The Articulate Sailor" in recognition of our heritage, as small boat sailors, of a literature that is expressive, clear and effective.

The sole purpose of good writing is to communicate with individuals. Editors of anthologies hope, in addition, to reach certain groups of individuals. My hope is to reach those who, like myself long ago in Kentucky's wild mountains, living in fields and hollows mute to the song of a ship's bell, dream of sailboats and shoreless seas. As the sea is ours, the book is theirs.

Having now come safely to port, we acknowledge the ancient cry, "Down killock!" The hook is down. Our thirst is up.

JT

Sloop *THE SPIRIT OF JOSHUA*
Hartge Yacht Yard
Galesville, Maryland

Why Sail?

I used to watch an old man, a retired judge, sail in the river near our house. When the airs were light he'd work his small sloop with main and genoa in and out of the narrow bays between the boat piers. Impressed with his skill, I once asked him why he continued to sail in an age of power. He became a sailor, he said, because of the pleasure that sailing promised. But first he had had to learn to respect fear. Then, he continued, the true pleasures of sailing became evident. Surprised, I asked what these pleasures were. He paused a few moments and then answered, "Patience, philosophy, and self-respect." Looking at me directly, with a twinkle in his denim-blue eyes, he added, "And Time!" He had mastered the pursuit of pleasure.

Douglas Phillips-Birt

To look for days upon an empty ocean impresses upon you the giant impersonality of the world. But when a long arm of that ocean creeps deep into the territory of man and ebbs and flows between his dwellings it becomes humanized and reduced to the human stature. Men do not feel small beside rivers.

John Hersey

"The river is a school," Su-ling said. "The greatest scholars of Peking come to learn from the river."

Herman Melville

. . . there never was a very great man yet who spent all his life inland . . .

Ralph Waldo Emerson

A great mind is a good sailor, as a great heart is. And the sea is not slow in disclosing inestimable secrets to a good naturalist. . . . But, under the best conditions a voyage is one of the severest tests to try a man. A college examination is nothing to it.

Charles Landery

The suggestion that I loved the sea walked coyly hand in hand with the "love of adventure" and was, I knew at once, false. That vast wetness cannot be loved; it can fascinate, impress and overpower; it can keep one eternally interested, hypnotized at times, but the salty sterility of the sea cannot summon so warm an emotion as love.

Rex Clements

Wherein lies the lure of the sea? What constitutes its superlative charm that has called man down the ages? It is customary to ascribe the growth of the sea-habit to the needs of economic development, the desire for riches, or the pressure of peoples from behind. Perhaps these played a part, but I will never believe they were sufficient in themselves to impel the first drenched barbarian to put off to sea in his hollowed tree trunk, or those old Egyptians to venture forth in their trussed and girded vessels to the land of Punt.

Something more than that was needed; it must have been the irresistible fascination to the spirit of man of the unknown, of what might lie between the tumbling expanse of water and the empty blue vault above.

Charles Violet

Love of the sea is a strange, unaccountable emotion.

Ray Kauffman

There was no answer. Pepe blew out the kerosene lamp and we lay in the dark security of the house, listening to the wind and rain as the storm raged over the mountain. I wondered why we were leaving that which we most sought. We had left home a year ago to get away from a streamlined life; and yet we were putting to sea in a small boat and would strive for twenty thousand more miles just to go back where we started.

Desmond Holdridge

The question that arises is why . . . but I am unable to supply an answer. I know only that the answer would be the answer to many other things. It would explain the enormous urge to have a little boat that dwells in many men. It would be the answer to why men go ocean racing, to why they spend money they need for clothes on coats of paint for fat little craft without beauty in any eyes but their own; it would be the answer to why, every year, a scattered fleet of small vessels steers south and out across the Pacific, manned by rapt dreamers in search of an island which cannot exist.

Charles Violet

To sail alone has always had a great appeal to me. Lurking in the dark corridors of my mind has been the idea that out alone on the wide wastes of the sea, it might be possible to lift a corner of the veil that keeps life a mystery to most of us.

Dwight Long

That is why I got a small boat of my own, so that I can poke along at my leisure, visiting remote corners of the earth and actually seeing how the other half of the world lives.

Rex Clements

On these windswept fields of infinity the sight of a vessel is a pleasant experience to eyes long accustomed to the empty ring of the horizon. In addition to that grace of line and motion which receives its most perfect expression in a sailing ship, particularly when running under full sail to a quartering wind, there is a sense of companionship, a flavour of romance, in the proximity of another little world, similar to one's own, yet inexorably sundered, that rises for a brief space out of the blue to fade therein again like an apparition from eternity.

Alain Gerbault

I wanted freedom, open air, adventure. I found it on the sea.

Farley Mowat

. . . as I stood in the dim and ancient store which was still redolent of Stockholm tar, oilskins and dusty canvas, something snapped within me.

Among the attitudes I acquired from my father was a romantic and Conradian predilection for the sea and ships. Like him I often had found surcease from the miseries I brought upon myself by spending hours immersed in books about the cruises of small boats to far-distant corners of the oceanic world. Ten years before . . . I had anchored myself to a patch of eroded sand hills in central Ontario, about as far from the sea as a man could get. There I labored to make grass, trees, vegetables, and mine own self take root. My labors had been in vain. Drought killed the grass. Sawflies and rabbits girdled the trees. Wireworms ate the vegetables. Far from rooting me into the Good Earth, a decade of servitude to the mingy soil only served to fuel a spirit of rebellion the intensity of which I had not begun to suspect until

I stood in the old ship chandler's store physically surrounded by a world I had previously known only in the imagination.

I bought. I bought and I bought and I bought. I bought enough nautical gear out of another age to fill an outbuilding on my parched little farm.

Charles Landery

The tide was out as the train pulled into my station; sailing ships were squatting comfortably in the mud, round-bottomed, sturdy, and scarcely listing. One of them might be *Bessie* and maybe she would be as glad to leave her soft, over-cushioned rut as I was to abandon mine.

Frank Wightman

. . . *Wylo* represented what I had lost after twenty years of working and scheming to escape from the triviality of the office chair, from the long littleness of a life of servitude to the God Routine, from the false coinage of the market place. Through the years I had waited stubbornly before the prison door, had saved and planned for the day I should have the funds and leisure to build my ship—and escape. I used to sit in my office chair in a room that had never known the sunlight, and hear in fancy the wind choiring through her rigging, feel her deck lift to the chasing seas, watch . . . flying fish spray from her bows.

Richard Maury

And Sail, sound and ageless, will float back on the first tide that brings simplicity into confusion, calm into chaos.

Humphrey Barton

The ideal cruise requires a good yacht, pleasant company, and a strange coast with plenty of islands and rocks. I love intricate navigation and islands fascinate me. I like to get under way soon after breakfast and spend all day threading my way through innumerable islands and rocks. At about 6 p.m. I look for a pleasant harbor or anchorage and I select it with great care. The evening is spent ashore, wandering about, having a meal or drinks, and then back to the yacht for a good night's sleep. That is my idea of a perfect day.

Hilaire Belloc

. . . an excellent strong memory of days calm, days windy, days peerless, days terrific, days humorous, days empty in long flats without a breath of wind, days beckoning, principally in the early mornings. . . .

William Robinson

. . . I took the pram and explored the numerous coves and inlets of this favorite hideout of the buccaneers. It was the place where Dampier had careened, and had lain in wait for passing Spanish ships. . . . Back aboard, I got out one of my treasures, an original edition of *A New Voyage round the World* by Dampier. The buccaneers who haunted these coasts were literary men as well. The accounts they wrote, in particular those of Dampier and Woodes Rogers, are a revealing commentary on what a small group of determined men can do in the face of incredible difficulties and overwhelming odds. The story of how they warped their vessels up the fast-running river to sack Quayaquil is an almost perfect blueprint of how to do the impossible. It seemed fitting, anchored here in their favorite rendezvous, to reread the parts about Lobos and the nearby coast.

William Robinson

There is something about island life. You can only get there by coming over the sea or through the air, which makes your piece of earth very special. The Japanese have a theory about what they call "island psychology" which applies just as well here, for it is quite true that one's whole attitude toward life changes when one lives on an island.

Frank Wightman

And then I sat down at the helm, the tiller in one hand, the coffee in the other. I was content. We were out on the wide Atlantic.

William Robinson

My dream was coming more and more true. It came to me with suddenness one evening at the wheel, as we slipped silently through the waters of the Koro Sea, bound for Suva. A thin curl of smoke drifted away from our stack into the night, and an appetizing aroma of browning fish came up to me as Etera prepared our evening meal.

Overhead, the white sails stretched their arms to catch the night wind. They were my sails—my wings—and they had brought me to the sea of my boyhood dreams.

I had always planned this, it seemed, but it had been almost too much to hope for. So now my heart was full.

Vito Dumas

I imagined that others, too, would be impelled to throw over the routine that stifles life and open their minds.

Alain Gerbault

Perhaps the comfort and luxury of early youth now asks for the counter-irritant of the plain life of a sailor with all its risks and adventure.

David H. Lewis

Of course, a security is necessary but security is only one aspect of life—man must also have things to fight and strive for, and so enhance the dignity of his life.

Humphrey Barton

This is far too much like hard work. The four hours on and four off, the long solitary night watches, the frequent sail changing and reefing down, the incessant motion, all combine to make it quite a strenuous life.

Alain Gerbault

. . . leading the plain life of a seaman, and bathing in the sun a body and mind not content to inhabit the houses of man.

Vito Dumas

What set me off, to throw off all my normal life and tempt fate? Was it to show that all was not lost after all, that dreamers propelled by their inward vision still lived, that romance somehow managed to survive? The young need examples; maybe, without being too self-conscious, I could provide one. I was torn between two alternatives: to stay, to lunch at a given hour, to wait for someone, receive guests, read newspapers, and tattle with friends outside work hours; the clock would go on telling the hours and I should be one of those creatures chained to the treadmill of today and tomorrow.

Rex Clements

It was fine to be at sea again with canvas a-stretch and the lipper of water overside. The hull lifted, the good sticks leaned and I realized then what later I grew heartily convinced of, that it's a grand thing to have a hand to the wheel, tops'ls sheeted home, and the world, the flesh and the devil fading out astern.

Sir Francis Chichester

As the years passed, this urge to circle the world alone lay dormant in me, like a gorse seed which will lie in the earth for fifty years until the soil is stirred to admit some air, or light, and the seed suddenly burgeons. And so it was with me.

Joshua Slocum

I had resolved on a voyage around the world, and as the wind on the

morning of April 24, 1895, was fair, at noon I weighed anchor, set sail, and filled away from Boston . . .

Herman Melville

Round the world! There is much in that sound to inspire proud feelings; but whereto does all that circumnavigation conduct? Only through numberless perils to the very point whence we started.

Stanley Smith and Charles Violet

We sigh for the clean, fresh smell of the open sea, an unobstructed horizon, more sun, snow, ice, mountains—anything to get away from the drab day-to-day scenes so devoid of romance and interest.

Then . . . we tremble within ourselves as we see a different life ahead of us. We wonder fearfully what demands will be made upon us. We try to measure the sea of uncerarity across which we are now committed to sail; we miss the thousand little comforts which accompany security; and realize that our very existence may depend upon it. If illness falls upon us there will be no days in bed to regain our strength for the elements are relentless and tireless. In this frame of mind we faced the prospect before us.

Yet we would not have changed places with anyone . . .

Robert Louis Stevenson

And they heaved a mighty breath, every soul on board but me,

As they saw her nose again pointing handsome out to sea;
But all that I could think of, in the darkness and the cold,
Was just that I was leaving home, and my folks were growing old.

Dennis Puleston

Conrad says that journeying in search of romance is much like trying to catch the horizon.

Carlton Mitchell

. . . for to be on water is a comfort to the soul of man.

Alan Villiers

There was much satisfaction in our leisurely wandering along, antiquated, primitive, and a hundred years behind the times as we were. I had a ship to sail; I was and am no philosopher. A pot had fallen on the cook's head in the galley, and I had to sew the cut.

Ann Davison

If anyone asked me and I was unguarded enough to reply, I would call it the pursuit of beauty, or truth, and if I were honest I would admit it was largely curiosity, the why and the what and the how at first hand.

Ernest K. Gann

This total security, coupled with the draining of his poison juices, promotes long life; which may be why people persist in going to sea in small vessels. In good weather the contentment simulates a return to the womb.

Joshua Slocum

To find one's way to lands already discovered is a good thing.

Bridget A. Henisch

"For thei that
sailen on the see, as we soth knowen,
in gret peril ben iput and perichen ful ofte"

Hilaire Belloc

Yet was I wise to beware, for if you give the strange gods of the sea one little chance they will take a hundred and drown you for their pleasure.

Hilaire Belloc

For one thing, I was no longer alone; a man is never alone with the wind—and the boat made three . . .

But far more than this is there in the sea. It presents, upon the greatest scale we mortals can bear, those not mortal powers which brought us into being. It is not only the symbol or the mirror, but especially is it the messenger of the Divine.

There, sailing the sea, we play every part of life: control, direction, effort, fate; and there can we test ourselves and know our state. All that which concerns the sea is profound and final. The sea provides visions, darknesses, revelations. The sea puts ever before us those twin faces of reality: greatness and certitude; greatness stretched almost to the edge of infinity (greatness in extent, greatness in changes not to be numbered), and the certitude of a level remaining forever and standing upon the deeps. The sea has taken me to itself whenever I sought it and has given me relief from men. It has rendered remote the cares and the wastes of the land; for of all creatures that move and breath upon the earth we of mankind are the fullest of sorrow. But the sea shall comfort us, and perpetually show us new things and assure us. It is the common sacrament of this world. May it be to others what it has been to me.

Joshua Slocum

The days passed happily with me wherever my ship sailed.

Jack London

The ultimate word is I LIKE.

William Snaith

. . . it is the kinetic loveliness of a sailboat working its way through the seas.

Frank Wightman

. . . in sail there is subtlety and flexibility—and mystery. The forces you are harnessing to your purpose are of infinite variety and incalculable complexity; the errant wind that knows no master, the sea that does not acknowledge man, the complex of weaknesses and strengths in a ship's design, and the frail fierce ghost of the ship herself, who is something more than the sum of her qualities. What engine can give you the surge and thrust of sail? A power at once curbing and urgent. The long, reluctant hull under the dominion of the silent sails . . .

William Robinson

How serene to be alone on a well-loved boat on an easy beam reach in smooth water!

Hilaire Belloc

. . . for, in truth, the *Nona* has spent her years, which are much the same as mine (we are nearly of an age, the darling, but she is a little younger, as is fitting), threading out of harbors, taking the mud, trying to make further harbors, failing to do so, getting in the way of more important vessels, giving way to them, taking the mud again, waiting to be floated off by the tide, anchoring in the fairway, getting cursed out of it, dragging anchor on shingle and slime, mistaking one light for another, rounding the wrong buoy, crashing into other people, and capsizing in dry harbors. It seemed to me as I considered the many adventures and misadventures of my boat, that here was a good setting for the chance thoughts of one human life; since all that she has done and all that a man does, make up a string of happenings and thinkings, disconnected and without shape, meaningless, and yet full: which is life.

Indeed, the cruising of a boat here and there is very much what happens to the soul of man in a larger way. We set out for places which we do not reach, or reach too late; and, on the way, there befall us all manner of things which we could never have awaited. We are granted great visions, we suffer intolerable tediums, we come to no end of the business, we are lonely out of sight of England, we make astonishing landfalls—and the whole rigamarole leads us along no whither, and yet is alive with discovery, emotion, adventure, peril and repose.

Alain Gerbault

On a sailboat one has to reckon with the wind. Why go against the wind towards certain islands if there are some equally beautiful ones to leeward?

Hilaire Belloc

To sail the sea is an occupation at once repulsive and attractive. It is repulsive because it is dangerous, horribly uncomfortable, cramped and unnatural: for man is a land animal. It is attractive because it brings adventure and novelty at every moment, and because, looking back upon it, a man feels a certain pride both in danger overcome and in experience. But is is also attractive in another and much more powerful fashion. It is attractive by a sort of appetite. A man having sailed the sea and the habit having bitten into him, he will always return to it: why, he cannot tell you. It is what modern people call a "lure" or a "call." He has got it in him and it will not let him rest.

That, I think, is the best answer in the long run to the question I put myself whenever I come back from sailing the sea. It is a beckoning from powers outside mankind.

Sir Francis Chichester

What bliss to be in the cockpit with the sun and the warm breeze on one's skin, just watching the sea, and the sky, and the sails. . . .

Charles Landery

I wriggled into my sleeping-bag and gave the wood by my ear an approving pat. Damning all hotel rooms, I went to sleep.

Vito Dumas

. . . "It's out there at sea that you are really yourself."

Joshua Slocum

To young men contemplating a voyage I would say go.

The Boat

Very few boat designers have written expressively about their boats. Even fewer boat builders have done so. Quite naturally, the persons who have written most sensitively of boats have been the men and women who've sailed them. To write about one's boat after a notable or difficult voyage, however, doesn't ensure the reference has merit other than as a footnote to marine history. Before me as I write are paintings of three famous sailor-writers, one of whom completed a circumnavigation. Only one, however, wrote with feeling about his craft, though all wrote expressively and with great feeling about other aspects of voyaging and the sailor's life.

Boats have a chemistry and, according to some writers, a soul. Some boats reportedly have charisma, others a feminine mystique. These facets, the more pragmatic problems and pleasures of ownership, and the almost mystical relation between man and boat, have given us some of the finest writing in yachting literature.

Joshua Slocum

The seasons came quickly while I worked. Hardly were the ribs of the sloop up before apple trees were in bloom. Then the daisies and the cherries came soon after. Close by the place where the old *Spray* had now dissolved rested the ashes of John Cook, a revered Pilgrim father. So the new *Spray* rose from hallowed ground. From the deck of the new craft I could put out my hand and pick cherries that grew over the little grave.

Alfred Loomis

Up went her arm, down went the bottle and again the words "I christen thee *Hotspur*," smote the atmosphere. This time the glass came into violent collision with brass, and good liquor wet the deck of the little cutter, trickling down to gladden for a short moment the sad life of the Saugatuck River.

Ray Kauffman

The day for the launching arrived. Everyone who had anything to do with the construction of the boat was on hand. The blacksmith who had made the ironwork, tall and gaunt with huge ears bracing up a wide-brimmed hat, strode around the yard in a long, black frock coat. So long were his legs and so high his waist that the ship chandler down from Mobile for the launching said that he was split up the middle like a pair of dividers. The engineer who had rebuilt the old tractor engine and the plumber who had installed the tanks were on hand in their Sunday clothes to sample the "la'nching whisky." The spar-maker was there; and the old caulker with the long flowing white mustache, who had kept us in suspense while caulking the decks, fearful lest his mustache would become mixed with the cotton and he would hammer himself fast to the deck seams. The Krebs family was there in full force; the women folk in Sunday clothes and the small children romping in the sawdust pile; but the four shipyard hands were in work clothes, standing by to knock the wedges out from behind the bilge blocks. Even Nigger, the little dog who had grown up with the ship, was there, hungrily licking the tallow off the ways.

Friends, neighbor and in-laws, the curious and the loafers, regular hands at funerals, births, weddings and launchings, gathered on the yard and circulated around the pump under the huge live oak tree festooned with gray moss where the "la'nching whisky" was kept cool in gallon stone jugs. Spirits rose as the jug passed around and the tide came in. The bayou would soon be deep enough. An old river tug backed up at the foot of the ways and with her nose against a piling churned up the muddy bottom to increase the depth.

By the time the tide was in and the bayou pronounced deep enough the crowd was hilarious; but, at the sound of the heavy mall striking the hardwood wedges, they quieted down and formed a semicircle around the bow for the christening. No champagne foamed over the sturdy stem. She was not that kind of ship but a child of the cypress swamps and the tidewater marshes. She was gently baptized with a conservative amount of Mississippi corn whisky poured from a stone jug, properly anointed with a liberal amount of tobacco juice, and named the *Hurricane*.

As the wedges were driven out, she rocked uneasily in her cradle, moved slowly backwards a foot or so, then gathering momentum, rushed down the greased ways and plunged into the muddy bayou. The cheering of the spectators drowned the noise made by twenty tons of wood and iron being born into a ship. Floating high like a duck, she sailed backwards across the stream and fetched up in the saw grass on the other side.

E. A. Pye

We had been told how roughly the local schooners were built, but . . . on the beach at Bequia, we saw the skeleton of one, started two years previously. We stood and gazed at her in wonder. Her ribs were whole branches of trees with the bark stripped off, but no attempt had been made to square them or to alter the shape that nature had given them. A few planks were in position, joined with ungalvanized fastenings from which brown rust trickled down. I wouldn't have believed that such a ship could float, and yet they say the average age of a schooner is thirty years . . . so there she lies, being fast devoured by termites.

Richard Hughes

For a schooner is in fact one of the most mechanically satisfactory, austere, unornamented engines ever invented by Man.

Hilaire Belloc

My boat was the best seaboat that ever sailed upon the sea. The reason of this was that her lines were of the right sort, belonging as they did, to the day when England was England; and my boat was so English that if you had seen her in any foreign port you would have known at once that you had seen an English thing. But, indeed, nowadays, what with their boats made like spoons and their boats made like tableknives, and their boats made like tops, and their boats made like scoopers, and their boats made like half-boats, cut away in the middle, no one can tell whether a boat is Choctaw, Eskimo, or Papuan. For boats have nowadays fallen into chaos, like everything else.

John MacGregor

We came upon a nest of twelve English yachts, all in the basin of this port, so my French comrade spent the rest of this time gazing at their beauty, their strength, their cleanliness and that unnamed quality which distinguished English yachts and English houses, a certain fitness for their special purposes. These graceful creatures (is it possible that a fine yacht can be counted as an inanimate thing?) reclined on the muddy bosom of the basin, but I would not put the *Rob Roy* there, it seemed so pent up and torpid a life . . .

Charles Landery

Round-bottomed and broad-beamed, *Bessie* was a matronly ketch which had shopped the Bristol Channel and the Irish Sea for years, as salty, wooden, and tarry-sided as we could wish—and maybe just a little more tarry than was altogether necessary.

We found her in the West of England; and we upset the shipyard's watchman when we asked him where she lay.

"Little *Bess-eye!*" he exclaimed, astounded at our ignorance. "Why, everyone do know the little *Bess-eye!* She be one o' us'n."

And so she was, a citizen in a sea-going community where ships and men matured together, where the adventures of the local craft were as interesting as the affairs of the neighbors, and generally more so. But a locally-owned *Bessie* was one thing; *Bessie* with Samual Barclay *captain* and Charles Landery *mate* was a boat of a very different color. We were foreigners. Orientals almost, since we came from the east coast. Our purchase brought displeased frowns to Devonshire foreheads. Their normal curiosity was whipped to gale-force and the town was tantalized, searching suspiciously for our motives.

We were not seamen, that they knew for sure; nor were we traders, and if we were yachtsmen then what did we want with their craft? Theirs were working boats, not fancy bits for gaddin'.

Nevertheless, there lay *Bessie,* primping and preening for foreign parts, and her forty-six if she was a day! Up to no good they'd be bound.

Since we were reluctant to answer questions, they answered for themselves. We were going to smuggle, or do something similarly, and acceptably, dishonest. This decision restored *Bessie,* and us, to favor. . . .

Marco Polo

The vessels built at Ormus are of the worst kind, and dangerous for navigation, exposing the merchants and others who make use of them to great hazards. Their defects proceed from the circumstance of nails not being employed in the construction; the wood being of too hard a quality, and liable to split or to crack like earthenware. When an attempt is made to drive a nail, it rebounds, and is frequently broken. The planks are bored, as carefully as possible, with an iron auger, near the extremities; and wooden pins or trenails being driven into them, they are in this manner fastened. After this they are bound, or rather sewed together, with a kind of rope-yarn stripped from the husk of the Indian nuts, which are of a large size, and covered with a fibrous stuff like horsehair. This being steeped in water until the softer parts putrefy, the threads or strings remain clean, and of these they make twine for sewing the planks, which lasts long under water. Pitch is not used for preserving the bottoms of vessels, but they are smeared with an oil made from the fat of fish, and then caulked with oakum. The vessel has no more than one mast, one helm, and one deck. They have no iron anchors, but in their stead employ another kind of ground tackle; the consequence of which is, that in bad weather—and these seas are very tempestuous—they are frequently driven on shore and lost.

Joshua Slocum

Good work in the building of my vessel stood me always in good stead.

Charles Landery

You could sense her lines, their round practicality, and get pleasure from the sensation, in knowing, somehow, despite lack of experience, that they were "just right."

Ray Kauffman

Islanders have the same respect for the sea as sailors, for what is an island but a huge moored ship breasting the blue water stream, the ebb and flow of the tide.

John Hersey

Last winter with the help of old Burkett's disenchanted eye Tom had found out the cause of the dry rot. In a moment of laziness, or carelessness, or making-do in the old Yankee way to save a few pennies, the boatbuilder had made an unforgivable choice of wood for the keelson. *Harmony* and her gear were exquisitely assembled, like a masterwork of parquets and inlays, from great woods from the corners of the earth. Honduran mahogany for wheel and coaming, seats and decks of teak from Burma, Norway-pine planking, a dinghy of Port Orford cedar, spars of spruce from Nova Scotia, hackmatack knees, white-ash battens, honey locust cabin bulkhead, cherry-faced drawers against butternut cabinetwork—and timbers and frames of white oak, as hard as the screws that bound them. But when it came to the biggest piece of wood of all, the keelson, running like an inoperable backbone all along the hull, the builder had settled for a timber of cheap wood from round-about his shipyard—a piece of local red oak. Burkett, on his hands and knees, reaching with the oilstone-narrowed blade of his clasp knife down into the bilges to chip at the big timber, had shaken his grizzled head and said, "Knew bettuh. He knew bettuh." There just wasn't any doubt. It was a lousy piece of red oak, Quercus borealis—notorious for checking and cracking and harboring insidious spores.

You can be sure the builder had not told the man for whom he had built the boat.

Charles Landery

"Soft here!" he continued, digging the wood with a knife while Sam groped absentmindedly for his—"And here! and here!"

"Nail sickness, too, not serious. Flood tide: couldn't see all the bottom but saw enough. Pretty sound. Keel's been repaired, by the way; split running forward to aft. Couldn't tell if they'd put on a sand-bar though: better check later, else you're in for trouble if you go aground.

"Bulwarks are poor in quite a few places, but that's not very important. Want a whole new strake port side; quite a bit of new planking altogether . . . lead patches in the stern . . . ought to replace them. Engine's pretty good though, and the masts. Need scraping and oiling, though. . . ."

Piece by piece, he was taking *Bessie* apart, showing her false teeth, wig, and wooden-leg, as well as her ragged underwear. It was scarcely polite; I left him to depress Sam, my spirits having sunk again. Cursing his ability to deflate, I went on deck where I resented the evening just because it happened to be there and unruffled. I watched some no doubt happy gulls, although they seemed as querulous as ever, swooping hungrily on *Bessie* and glaring angrily back at me. A crow swooped with them, pretending to be a gull, but eventually embarrassed by his own amateurishness, he perched on a nearby tree and made iconoclastic croaks. What might have been a good day had reached its close, and I wished this stranger could have stayed away, if only for twenty-four hours; I would, at least, have had that long as a potential and happy shipowner. As usual, I told myself there were other ships but it was still *Bessie* I wanted and not a facsimile, reasonable or otherwise.

The surveyor drove us back to the hotel, three sad bodies although why *he* should have been sad I could not say; he was a paid depressant. Having joined us in a drink he relaxed and forgot his crime, grew expansive, and even said that *Bessie* was a good buy. . . .

Alfred Loomis

. . . and I learned to my regret that the sloop was a whited and red-leaded sepulcher. She was good superficially, but the heart was false, and she could almost be guaranteed to open up when the nearest land was directly underneath me.

Ernest K. Gann

. . . other sailors' castoffs—elderly yachts scrofulous with rot . . .

Ray Kauffman

. . . Wet moldy canvas drooped over the main boom, but the stiff new foresail was as conspicious as a white flag.

Dwight Long

I loved that little tub. But I recognized her limitations, and after a while I painted her and sold her for a profit.

Farley Mowat

A true schooner hull in miniature, she measured thirty-one feet on deck with a nine-foot beam and a four-foot draft. But she was rough! On close inspection she looked as though she had been flung together by a band of our paleolithic ancestors—able shipbuilders perhaps, but equipped only with stone adzes.

Her appointments and accommodations left a great deal to be desired. She was flush-decked, with three narrow fishing wells in each of which one man could stand and jig for cod, and with two intervening fisholds in each of which the ghosts of a million long-dead cod tenaciously lingered. Right up in her eyes was a cuddy two feet high three feet wide, and three feet long, into which one very small man could squeeze if he did not mind assuming the fetal position. There was also an engine room, a dark hole in which lurked the enormous phallus of a single-cylinder, make-and-break (but mostly broke) gasoline engine.

Her rigging also left something to be desired. Her two masts had apparently been manufactured out of a couple of Harry Lauder's walking sticks. They were stayed with lengths of telephone wire and cod line. Her sails were patched like Joseph's coat and seemed to be of equivalent antiquity. Her bowsprit was hardly more than a mop handle tied in place with netting twine. It did not appear to me that the Hallohans had sailed her very much. I was to hear later that they had

never sailed her and shared the general conviction of everyone in Muddy Hole that to do so would probably prove fatal.

She was not a clean little vessel. In truth, she stank. Her bilges had not been cleaned since the day she was built and they were encrusted with a glutinous layer of fish slime, fish blood, and fish gurry to a depth of several inches. This was not because of bad housekeeping. It was done "a-purpose," as the Muddy Holers told me *after* I had spent a solid week trying to clean her out.

"Ye see, Skipper," one of them explained, "dese bummers now, dey be built o' green wood, and when dey dries, dey spreads. Devil a seam can ye keep tight wit' corkin (caulking). But dey seals dersel's, ye might say, wit' gurry and blood, and dat's what keeps dey tight." . . .

The tide was out and she lay on her side, half in the water and half out of it, amid a rich collection of broken bottles, rotting kelp, dead fish, and nameless slimy objects. I picked my way out along the cod-oil soaked sticks of the stage and stood beside my dream ship.

Her hull had not been touched since I had seen her last, and the remains of her green paint hung in scrofulous tatters from her naked planking. Her belly, bare of the last trace of copper paint and smeared with bunker oil, gleamed greasily. Her decks were a patchwork of gaping holes, open seams, rough pieces of new plank, and long black rivulets of tar, where someone had been doing some perfunctory caulking. Her mainmast was broken off ten feet above the deck and her foremast, unstayed, swayed at a weird angle importuning the unheeding skies.

The most appalling thing about her was an enormous unpainted box-like structure that appeared to have been roughly grafted to her decks. It was huge, stretching from the steering well forward to the foot of the foremast. It looked like a gigantic sarcophagus. It was as if the little ship, feeling herself to be dying of some incurable and loathsome disease, had taken her own coffin on her back and gone crawling off to the graveyard, but had not quite been able to make it and had died where she now lay.

The sight of her left me speechless, but it had the opposite effect on my snuffy-nosed little guide. He spoke for the first time.

"Lard Jasus, sorr!" he said. "Don't she be a wunnerful quare sight?"

Richard Maury

A makeshift craft will not do. Long-voyage crews are influenced above all by the temperament of the boat they sail, adjusting themselves to her living spirit. That a cruiser can be but a machine-like convenience for reaching new and alluring lands, is an illusion. She must be more. She must live, and she must be made to live. She must have the character, the turn of temperament, the high spirit to dwell in salt water—with the flow of a wave, with something of the wind captured in her own bones. Perhaps all things touching the elements so completely must have this conforming character, and this flame, in order to exist. At any rate, once off soundings, the sea can make or break the spirit of any venture by making or breaking the spirit of the craft, and in turn, that of the crew. The craft

herself must also be an adventurer in the real sense—a living spirit. And that spirit is more vital than vague, emanating in a good craft directly from the integral spirit of her designer; a symbol revealing his science, but more important, his art, and even before these, his ideals, loyalties, faiths. And there is nothing mystical here, for those contemplating a voyage, merely a hint that the craft chosen be approved by the heart as well as by the mind; that she be designed by one who goes beyond to the feel of ships, striving to find Truth in his creation; not by one who is a scientist only, and lastly, never by a layman, for never yet has a happy home-designed cruiser sailed the seas.

Ernest K. Gann

Suppose you took a house and tossed it in the air, then twisted it back and forth after it had slammed back in its original position, then tipped it from 30 to 40 degrees or even more from side to side and constantly pounded it with tons of force while propelling it through a resistant mass. And you repeated this torture at least once a month, hour after hour, day after day, year after year. How long would a house last before it collapsed?

E. A. Pye

. . . She must have a metacentric shelf like a mountain range.

Ray Kauffman

I no longer had the sensation of traveling but a feeling of living an isolated life on an island forty-five feet long.

Arthur Ransome

Houses are but badly built boats so firmly aground that you cannot think of moving them. They are definitely inferior things, belonging to the vegetable not the animal world, rooted and stationary, incapable of gay transition. I admit, doubtfully, as exceptions, snailshells and caravans. The desire to build a house is the tired wish of a man content thenceforward with a single anchorage. The desire to build a boat is the desire of youth, unwilling yet to accept the idea of a final resting place.

Charles Landery

I was at sea again, this time with a very lovable assembly of teak, oak, canvas, and companions.

William Snaith

. . . bounding wooden island . . .

Stanley Smith and Charles Violet

At sea in a small boat one can imagine all the ominous creakings and groanings, betokening heaven knows what weakness in stringer, timber, floor, planking or fastening. But it is comforting to recall the desperate hopelessness we may have known in the past when a bigger boat suddenly springs a leak; water mounting up over the cabin sole, through inaccessible seams down in the darkness of a flooded bilge: deep below the waterlines water under pressure forcing itself in so that soon it is impossible either to keep it down or find where the trouble lies. No, not for us. We prefer the safety of a small boat.

Joshua Slocum

. . . but she was stiff as a church.

Dennis Puleston

The Sabans think of their island as a mighty ship, sometimes riding before the steady blow of the trades, sometimes lying lazily in a calm, and sometimes battling into the teeth of a hurricane.

Alfred Loomis

. . . my idea of comfort in a small cruising yacht had undergone a complete transformation. I no longer thought of boat comfort as the ability to stand up and take anything—and keep on taking it until the wind shifted. A comfortable boat, it now seemed to me, was one which, in offshore cruising, would round a headland with a certain amount of discomfort and be snug in harbor while the beamy family boat was still slogging into it. For more amiable conditions of wind and sea, the boat must have a tall rig to catch vagrant breezes which do not kiss the surface of the water. In short, I expressed to Rigg my preference for a fast, Marconi-rigged, windward-working cutter . . .

Herman Melville

You never saw such a rare old craft as this same rare old *Pequod*. She was a ship of the old school, rather small if anything; with an old-fashioned claw-footed look about her. Long seasoned and weather stained in the typhoons and calms of all four oceans, her old hull's complexion was darkened like a French grenadier's, who has alike fought in Egypt and Si-beria. Her venerable bows looked bearded. But to all these her old antiquities, were added new and marvelous features. She was appareled like any barbaric Ethiopian emperor, his neck heavy with pendants of polished ivory. She was a thing of trophies. A cannibal of a craft, tricking herself forth in the chased bones of her enemies. All round, her unpaneled, open bulwarks were garnished like one continuous jaw, with the long sharp teeth of the sperm whale, inserted there for pins, to fasten her old hempen thews and tendons to. Those thews ran not through base blocks of land wood, but deftly traveled over sheaves of sea ivory. Scorning a turnstile wheel at her revered helm, she sported there a tiller; and that tiller was in one mass, curiously carved from the long narrow lower jaw of her hereditary foe. The helmsman who steered by that tiller in a tempest, felt like the Tartar, when he holds back his fiery steed by clutching his jaw. A noble craft, but somehow a most melancholy! All noble things are touched with that.

William Robinson

I must say a word for the junks. First of all, whoever named these remarkable Chinese craft junks was crazy. Disreputable they may be, barge-like even, with masts like Harry Lauder's stick grown to the thickness and length of a telephone pole, and sails consisting of various pieces of vegetable matter, old clothing, canvas, or what have you. But give them a little breeze and they sail like witches. We were passed by one, one day as we ploughed at top speed, power and sail, trying to make the last mile or so to a port before dark. She lumbered by awk-wardly, to all appearances standing still but actually doing about eight knots. She was rolling serenely at anchor when we got in.

Joseph Conrad

The fore-and-aft rig in its simplicity and the beauty of its aspect under every angle of vision is, I believe, unapproachable. A schooner, yawl, or cutter in charge of a capable man seems to handle herself as if endowed with the power of reasoning and the gift of swift execution.

Alan Villiers

When I first boarded her they were hauling up clean water in goatskins from her well, bailing her constantly, though she lay then in the quiet waters of Ma'alla Bay, and they bailed almost the whole way to Gizan. Of all the dhows in port she was undoubtedly the meanest, though none of her people thought so. She was dreadfully small, horribly overloaded, and she stank frightfully. She had no accommodation of any kind, and there was never much to eat. A matting of loosely woven palm leaves, lashed above her bulwarks along both sides, served to keep out most of the sea when she rolled, but one angry sea breaking on board would have been the death of her. She was a low, rakish little thing, green-painted with a white limed mouth where her sweet cutwater bit the sea, and a pattern of triangles in reds and blues round the railing at her sharp stern. She sat prettily in the water, and her lines were excellent. She had a graceful and fleet little hull, and her high raking mainmast grew from her gracefully. Her latten yard was constructed from the branches of two trees, lashed together end for end, and her one sail was a loosely seamed piece of cheap Japanese cotton, roped with coir made from Indian coconut fiber. Her rudder seemed balanced precariously on one pintle, from which it threatened every moment to break adrift, and even in the quiet waters of the harbor she seemed in imminent danger of foundering.

I voyaged in that little ship 600 miles, and I enjoyed every mile of it and was sorry when the time came to leave her. Mean and incredibly poor as she was, she was a ship, and there was a spirit aboard her rare in these days and never found in liners.

E. A. Pye

She was fifty-two years old, fastened with iron, her planking unsheathed. To sail in her would be to ask for the attentions of the toredo, an unpleasant worm-creature, which lives in the warm waters of the tropics. On its head is a borer, a replica of a modern drill, and this is so hard that no shipwright will risk his saw upon wood suspected of having the dead worm in it. The worm enters a plank through a hole the size of a pin's head, turns at right angles and bores along the length of it. In six weeks the wood will be riddled, and, most treacherously, the damage will not show from the outside. Wood covered with paint is safe, but if the paint is scraped off it is immediately in danger, so that the only safe course is to sheath the underwater hull with copper. If this is done in an iron-fastened ship galvanic action may set up between the copper and the iron. As the iron is destroyed before the copper, there is nothing to hold the planks to the timbers.

Alfred Loomis

. . . and we put in only to take the ground and scrub our sides with sand to cleanse them . . .

Dennis Puleston

Removing her ballast, the crew take tackles from her mastheads over to the sturdy mangrove roots. Then they heave away until the ship is well careened on the sandbank, when they can get to work with sections of coconut husk, which make the best scrubbing brushes.

Edward H. Dodd, Jr.

A great deal of weed was growing to the boot top—the four-inch band on the waterline which had been painted green. Below it the copper paint was clean, but we had been worried for some time about toredo worms in this strip. It was now just four months since we had left Panama . . . and sure enough, after the weed and green paint had been scraped off, there appeared several clusters of minute holes. And when we scorched the planks with the blow torch a flock of worms came out to protest. The boat was left heeled over two days, supposedly enough to kill the worms. Copper paint was then lavishly applied. It took another three days to do the other side.

Woodes Rogers

July 8, 1710. This Day . . . the *Marquiss* began to careen . . . but the Carpenters having view'd her betwixt Wind and Water, finding her very bad, and that she had but a single bottom, eat to a Honey-comb by the worms, they judg'd her altogether unfit to go to Europe . . .

Warwick Charlton

I think they perceive in our little ship—Mayflower II— a glimpse of man before the atom age, when he was less complicated, had fewer doubts, both about himself, and the world around him; an age of ignorance, perhaps, but also an age of faith and courage.

Richard Henry Dana

I was so lost in the sight that I forgot the presence of the man, until he said, half to himself, still looking at the marble sails—"How quietly they do their work!"

Charles Landery

This was a very soothing period after the chaos of storing and refitting, and I spent most of my off-hours with my back against the mainmast staring at the blue sea and sky (when they were visible), their brightness emphasized by the yellow line of our gunwale, the worn tan of our jib and mizzen, and the green and white of our bulwarks; only ships, barges, and caravans can get away with such gaiety; once they are on board these colors even though traditional enemies become friends.

Ernest K. Gann

The more we studied the sail the worse it appeared. It had been stretched without mercy, several inches of the leech flapped uselessly no matter how we trimmed it, and the great bulbous area which presumably was the principal driving force of the sail was so low in relation to the remainder that it often plopped into the sea and collapsed. There was absolutely no scientific reason why the *Henrietta* should move in anything less than a gale, much less go dancing along like a racer in hot pursuit. Coagli had no explanation . . .

Frank Wightman

. . . her dew-darkened sails . .

Ernest K. Gann

. . . and we glided rather sluggishly over the sea. I took the helm and studied the sail, which was made of coffee and flour bags sewn together with heavy twine. Poor Jesus. There was a hole the size of a football halfway up the leech of his sail and I could see streaks of the glittering sea through many of the seams joining the various bags. My compassion increased as I saw into his eyes and realized that here was a moment which far transcended what little financial reward he would receive from my few hours' rental of his awkward craft.

Arthur Ransome

Racundra, shaking waters from her beloved nose . . .

Jack London

To touch that bow is to rest one's hand on the cosmic nose of things.

Francis Herreshoff

Most everyone who has inherited a love of the sea feels that the clipper bow is a befitting finial to a sailing vessel, as a beautiful head of hair is to a woman. Perhaps neither the long hair nor the bowsprit is necessary, but when either is removed there is a loss of character that is hard to replace.

Edward H. Dodd, Jr.

As we crept up on the buoy, the waves grew larger. The bowsprit, jib and all, would spear a big one, tossing a lather of spray on the foredeck, would jump high in the air to take aim for the next.

Richard Hughes

. . . the narrow milky deck sloped up to the foreshortened tilt of the bowsprit, which seemed to be trying to point at a single enlarged star just above the horizon.

Frank Wightman

I loved the ageing clippers, but I gave my heart also to . . . that legendary company of figureheads—kings and queens and allegorical beings—that leaned urgently over murky quaysides. To me it was fitting that a ship should have a Presence beneath her bows.

Rex Clements

The barque was now beginning to look shipshape and Bristol fashion and, by way of a finishing touch, the old man determined to paint the figurehead as it should be painted . . . *Arethusa* boasted an exceptionally fine one. It represented her namesake of old rising out of the waves, with long streaming hair and arm outstretched ahead. Hitherto this work of art had been hidden under a coat of dull mast-colored paint. Now justice was to be done to it and the saucy sea maiden trimmed up with our best skill.

For this purpose we rigged a platform of stages under the bow and commenced operations. At about the twelfth attempt the bosun succeeded in mixing a flesh-color paint to his satisfaction and we gave her three coats of this. Then, with the expenditure of much pains, just the right tints were obtained for eyes, hair and lips and the nails of her fingers. The sea waves were painted a light blue, edged with silver, and the scroll work above the cutwater crimson and gold. When it was done the saucy *Arethusa* looked her beauteous self and we were not a little proud of her. Indeed when we got to port she came in for a good deal of admiration.

In the olden days a fine figurehead was the pride and glory of a ship's company. Many were designed and carved by good artists and the utmost care and attention was lavished upon them. To mutilate one was an unpardonable crime, punished in the merchant service by transportation and in the Royal Navy by death.

Ernle Bradford

She went by with a lift and a swagger some twenty yards away. The helmsman was standing up balancing the tiller between his thighs, the oarsman was working away in a slow steady rhythm, and two others were busy amidships hauling down on the tackle at the foot of the sail. A fine rain of spray drifted over them all the time and there was a rainbow over the bows. She looked as if she had sailed off a Greek vase.

Richard Maury

. . . she was of an able model, sweet of line, amply masted.

Richard Baum

The ship lifted a saucy transom to the afterglow behind her . . .

Ernest K. Gann

As each swell overtook us, the little *Fred Holmes* lifted her stout butt just enough and in time to avoid being pooped. A cunning, knowing hand had fashioned her well below the water where style really counted.

John Hersey

. . . as the gentle glazed swells rhythmically lifted the boat's little metal anus out of the water awhile, then put it under awhile.

E. A. Pye

She might prove faster than her fat little hull suggested.

Charles Landery

All that day and night we kept up the pace, *Bessie* shoving the seas out of her path with a fat sort of joy.

Richard Maury

Hull lines, not sail power, had brought about the unexpected.

Hilaire Belloc

She was built by Ratsey of Cowes in 1864, so she is rather an ancient vessel; but she was constructed in a much stronger fashion than is usual in these days of thoroughly seasoned teak. . . . there is not a weak spot in her, and she is in fact a far more reliable craft than a newer vessel would have proved; for, even as a human life is more secure after it has safely passed through the period of infantile disorders, so a vessel, if she does not develop dry rot within a few years of her launching, is not likely to do so afterwards.

Joseph Conrad

There had been at that time a great rise of waters, which retiring soon after left the old craft cradled in the mud, with her bows grounded high between the trunks of two big trees, and leaning over a little as though after a hard life she had settled wearily to an everlasting rest.

Ernest K. Gann

. . . a vessel fit for a man with an expanse of deck to accommodate his stride. Her mainmast was gone and there was only a stump of a foremast on which a hoisting boom had been rigged. Her jibboom had been sawed off by an extraordinarily clumsy carpenter and long threads of dry oakum protruded from most of her seams. But the basically fine lines of

her transom were still apparent and a splendid taffrail extended nearly to her waist. She had once been painted a green which time and neglect had faded to a lime-yellow, and there were great splotches of bare wood, scrofulous undercoating, and bubbled areas of paint festooning her hull everywhere. She was such a colorful hag that I was taken with her as I might have been with a dockside harlot who though long past her prime had contrived to keep her jollity.

Frank Wightman

The schooner was not flying, but she was certainly ploughing through it. At her bows the sea piled up in a solid mound, then dipped down in a great smooth hollow as it creamed past her sides and welled up again under the heavy quarters. As she drew away she looked beset, but thoroughly in command of the situation—like an old body being blown along in front of a gale, holding on to her hat, her clothes, and her parcels.

Rudyard Kipling

But the best fun was when the boys were put on the wheel together and she cuddled her leerail down to the crashing blue, and kept a little homemade rainbow arching unbroken over her windlass. Then the jaws of the boom whined against the masts, and the sheets creaked, and the sails filled with roaring; and when she slid into a hollow she trampled like a woman tripped in her own silk dress, and came out, her jib wet half-way up, yearning and peering for the tall twin-lights of Thatcher Island.

Rex Clements

A ship, unlike the majority of her sex ashore, always wears her best clothes in bad weather, and when skies are soft and winds gentle changes into her oldest and most worn attire.

Edward H. Dodd, Jr.

The man at the wheel swayed easily, feeling his way through every wave and puff. The ship was a live being full of strange wiles and impulses. A joyous spirit in her was communicated to everyone on board.

Joseph Conrad

High aloft, some dry block sent out a screech, short and lamentable, like a cry of pain. It pierced the quietness of the night to the very core.

Edward H. Dodd, Jr.

A ship is certainly a thief of privacy as no other thing is, yet there is no more perfect isolation than to sit with the stars at the top of the boat. Aloft you are completely separated from it. Two hazy squares of yellow light that mark the forward hatch and sky-light, a flash of red from the port running light, and a flickering ray from the binnacle only emphasize its snug independence. If it were not for slender ripples at the bow and a boiling trail of phosphorus behind, you would scarcely realize that it is moving across the smooth black surface around it. . . . You suddenly feel a strong kinship of motion—this gallant, gliding movement that is sweeping everything on to the unattainable ho-

rizon. A vague elation makes you clasp one arm around the mast and cling to the stay that you shall not lose this eagerly joyous ship and its gay company of winds and stars.

The deck is a sluggish place, another life with all things in their due proportion. The heavens are above, not around you, and the horizon seems to bind close. You are soon pulling out a blanket to make your bed on the deckhouse.

Bridget A. Henisch

"For when that we shall go to bedde,
The pumpe was nygh our beddes hede,
A man were as good to be dede
As smell therof the stynk."

Richard Maury

. . . an air of strict, almost puritanical simplicity was retained about the craft. And if simplicity ruled on deck where the three modest working sails, all inboard, were free of topping lifts and lazy jacks, then also it ruled below . . . the after cabin was devoted to the engine, tanks, and bulk stores. The main had its bunks, its well-filled lockers, a stove—no more.

Jack London

The food was rough but good, and the smack of the salt air and the seafittings around him gave zest to his appetite. The cabin was clean and snug, and, though not large, the accommodation surprised him. Every bit of space was utilized. The table swung to the centerboard case on hinges, so that when not in use it actually occupied no room at all. On either side, and partly under the deck, were two bunks. The blankets were rolled back, and the boys sat on the well-scrubbed bunk boards while they ate. A swinging sealamp of brightly polished brass gave them light, which in the daytime could be obtained through the four deadeyes, or small round panes of heavy glass which were fitted into the walls of the cabin. On one side of the hood was the stove and woodbox, on the other the cupboard. The front end of the cabin was ornamented with a couple of rifles and a shotgun, while exposed by the rolled back blankets of French Pete's bunk was a cartridge-lined belt carrying a brace of revolvers.

Samuel Eliot Morison

Possibly this love for a small cabin was atavistic, derived from our remote ancestors for whom a cave was the only safe, indeed the only possible dwelling.

Ernest K. Gann

In little boats such thoughts are possible and the dreams of ordinary men can become realities. In little vessels there is joy. In large vessels there is travail and perplexity.

Frank Wightman

I slid down the companion ladder into the world of man.

Ernest K. Gann

As it is for all sailors, my bunk is my home at sea and now I have a leak in the roof. I have tried to persuade myself this is meant to be, since the area occupied by my head is to the total area of the *Albatross* as a single star is to the universe, and yet there, right there above my left ear, is the *only* leak in the entire deck. The seas are eternal, but so are deck leaks . . .

Frank Wightman

Then I lifted the dropslide from the hatch so that the cabin light would show to anything coming up from astern, and went up to the foredeck. This was a favorite haunt of mine at night when conditions allowed *Wylo* to sail herself. I glanced back for a moment, and across the dark deck I could see the cockpit with all its sea furniture. Lit dimly from below by the glow from the cabin, it looked like something seen on a stage; a picture small, neat and authentic. Suspended against the night in its own faint radiance, isolated and without supporting or corroborative scenery, it had the authenticity of something final; and the poignancy of the deserted. An ocean fane lit by the candle of faith.

Hilaire Belloc

For a bell is a land thing, and even in salt water we think of it as sounding upon a buoy near shore, or as the companion and regulator of human things, like the bell aboard ship.

Arthur Ransome

Fine copper sidelights they were too, prewar, bought last year and horribly expensive . . .

All winter they had lain in my room beside

compass and lead-line, log, sea anchor, sextant and cabin lamp, and, shining there with the promise of the summer's cruise, had warmed me with an inward glow what time the snow was deep in the garden outside and the thermometer stood resolutely at zero or considerably below.

Erling Tambs

The whole ship was dark save for an inoffensive riding light, which I used to hang in the windward rigging and which made noble efforts to shine for the double purpose of attracting flying fish and of indicating our presence to other ships that might have lost their way. However, it generally went out before midnight, and I never relit it.

Ernest K. Gann

The *Thetis* proved to be about as charming a vessel as any man ever loved and I was a fool to have sold her. I should have kept her until the day I died and even after that my descendants should keep her in a bottle. For she was the only siren of them all who was utterly without fault.

The *Thetis* was only 28 feet long, which gave her the status of a bird feather upon the open oceans. She was the only maiden I had ever possessed who could honestly lay claim to the class of yacht. Perhaps as some unkind gossips said, she was too plain of line, and it was true that she lacked sheer; yet somehow this lover of sheer found her lack of it a part of her special appeal. She drew five feet of water, which is very small for so small a craft, but both her draft and the design

of her underbody gave her a remarkable stability without crankiness. She rode the big Pacific swells like a brave little petrel and though we never challenged a gale together, there was rarely a time when it was not possible to slip below to her tiny cabin and sleep or eat a meal in comparative comfort. In smooth water she sailed so smartly and maneuvered so easily in tight quarters that I often forgot she had an engine beneath her cockpit deck.

Richard Maury

At times she maddened us, at times she interested us by her repertoire of tricks, and then again she would amuse us by sporting gestures, stubborn, and all her own. She had a kind of humble gallantry, and she was heroic—but only as simple fishing folk are heroic.

William Snaith

Each boat seems to contain a personality which manifests itself in the way she takes a sea. She may snap-roll back after being pressed down by a gust, or be soft in her movement of recovery. She may bang through the top of a sea or work smoothly over it. She may steer like a willful though speedy bitch on a run or a reach, leaving the helmsman with aching arms after a half-hour stint at the tiller or wheel, or she may be balanced and track like a proper lady, lacking the sense of danger and excitement of the speedy bitch but communicating the certainty that you will get there in one piece. But above all, her identity as a living creature, invested with personality, becomes apparent to the men who guide her in their separate watches as

they weary and change. Untouched by the cyclically flagging strengths of her human masters and by the differing qualities of the hands that handle her, she plunges tirelessly on. Unchanged, unflagging, meeting each sea eagerly, she goes on hour after hour, day after day.

Rex Clements

Ships, particularly sailing ships, have a character of their own. One cannot say precisely whence it springs, but weatherliness, handiness, speed and seaworthiness all play a part in it. Some ships are awkward brutes and can't go about without getting in irons; some are hard-mouthed and take a wicked amount of labor to steer; while others again seem to have a suicidal tendency and never make a passage without losing a man. The *Arethusa* was none of these, but without being a record breaker was a handy little barque, easy to steer and to work. It was a pleasure to watch her in heavy weather and see how gamely she battled with sea and wind. She would tack like a witch, or again, with a t'gallant breeze on the quarter, would lay down to it and scamper like a colt.

Richard Maury

We would regard her with disparagement, compassion, ill humor; patience, reverence, intolerance. She was the pivot of action to each of our lives. Nothing on ten thousand miles of water was so important. We knew her every weakness, the last ounce of her strength, her will, her small failings, jaunty enthusiasms, her occasional melancholy—and concerned ourselves primarily with her destiny.

Joshua Slocum

As she rode at her ancient, rust-eaten anchor, she sat on the water like a swan.

Joseph Conrad

And on the smooth water of the Straits, the little brig lying so still seemed to sleep profoundly, wrapped up in a scented mantle of starlight and silence.

Frank Wightman

Wylo seemed to sleep on the black water, her furled sails like closed eyes.

Joshua Slocum

I carried on sail to make the harbor before dark, and she fairly flew along, all covered with snow, which fell thick and fast, till she looked like a white winter bird.

Frank Wightman

Her bows were buoyant and finely drawn. Her quarters were a delight. She rested on the water like a gull in all that gloom of smoke and oily sludge, and she was out of Liverpool.

Rex Clements

The bird has a soul and so has the windjammer.

John MacGregor

. . . and nothing in front but sea, sea, sea. Then the little boat you are in, and know in every plank, and love too, becomes more than ever cherished as a friend. It is your only visible trust, and, if it is a good boat, you trust it well, for indeed it seems to try its very best, like a horse on a desert plain that knows it must go on if it is ever to get to the other side. Then as the cliffs that looked high behind you, dwindle into a line of deep blue, the compass by your knees becomes a magic thing, with no tongue indeed to speak, but surely a brain it must have to know the way so well.

Edward H. Dodd, Jr.

A passerby would have been amazed to see this little schooner, shortly after leaving, begin to sail in huge circles, jibbing and coming about as if puzzled by its course. After all this coquetry we had the deviation checked on all points . . .

Frank Wightman

. . . I drew the dinghy alongside and stepped down into it. As I sculled it round her stern there occurred one of those moments to epitomize a whole episode: I caught sight of her name in black letters on the slim counter—*Wylo.* It had the startling effect of a word uttered in silence: as though she had spoken her name to me. I let the dinghy idle to a stop.

Charles Landery

With a black sky louring at her masthead and a green swell lurching under her hull, *Bessie* wrenched savagely at the sheets, crashing her booms and swearing that no parasitic barnacle was going to rob her of a single inch of rolling, whatever it might do to her headway.

Ernest K. Gann

"You old bitch!" I whispered. "Your butt is covered with barnacles and your bosum sags with weeds. Your limbs are scarred with wear and your hair is dyed with rust. You are demanding and expensive and uncomfortable to live with . . ."

Suddenly, as if my rebellion could have been heard, I switched with chameleon ease from scorn to finding excuses or cures for all of her imperfections. And in moments I was so re-enchanted I allowed the jolly boat to drift under her counter where I sat in the shade bemused at my facile self-deception. This absurd relationship between a man and his vessel would be better called a fetish than love, yet what in the end was the difference?

Hilaire Belloc

She had her mortalities; but in a seaway she is magnificent. With her few inches of freeboard, her old-fashioned straight stem, her solid grip upon the water, she takes the sea as though she belonged to it, and so she went that day, riding in high-bred fashion, worthy of all praise, and praise she received from me as she leaned over and took the combers one after the other. I gave her perpetual encouragement: for no boat will do her best unless she is sufficiently flattered.

Ernest K. Gann

My esteem as a sailor also took a drubbing. When would I ever learn that vessels were as deceptive as people and that pounding and slapping one on her rump declaring what a stout craft she seemed to be by no means confirmed her structural health.

Richard Maury

. . . these seemed the fairest thoughts as I saw her last, even as I saw her first, three years before, swaying airy and buoyant as though of fragile porcelain . . .

William Snaith

To begin with, she is very pretty. Just as beauty in woman creates allure and inspires affection, so it does in a boat. In a boat, that beauty also rests in a rare combination of form and proportion. In this case it is the shape and relationship of her bow to her transon; in the spring of her sheer; the height and rake of her spars; and in the placement and size of her deckhouses. In *Figaro,* these all come out to mean beauty.

Frank Wightman

In full view of the yacht club I circled my arms around her mizzen mast and flattened my nose against it. A Creole voice lilted across the water: "Do you want to be alone with her?"

Vito Dumas

After sunset I went below; alone in my boat after more than a month—I could not help kissing a panel in a surge of affection for my shipmate.

William Snaith

At times, the sense of exhilaration and response on the part of the crew to the magnificent way she is behaving erupts into a simultaneous and spontaneous exchange of glowing opinions. Then the cockpit conversation seems to be that of men speaking of a magnificent creature. And, ridiculous as it may seem, I have—on more than one occasion while at the wheel and having become filled with an excess of joy in response to her sea-kindly movement—leant over and planted a kiss on her deck, as becomes a lover to his lass.

Ralph Stock

A mother on the subject of her child is almost derogatory compared with an owner concerning his ship . . .

E. A. Pye

There was a sudden cry from Anne as she glanced over the side, then a grinding, jarring sound as *Moonraker* went on a reef, listing over to port, her stern nearly two feet above its normal level. For a moment time stood still. I saw *Moonraker* wrecked on this lonely island and our venture ended in ignominy, and all for lack of that extra care. I never knew till then how much I loved our ship.

Erling Tambs

Never has a finer craft existed. Graceful were her lines, ever pleasing to the eye, because she was the embodiment of usefulness. Like a true masterpiece, she stood above the fickle taste of fashion. She was fast and she was safe. She was an able boat. During the thirty-five years when she served as a pilot boat, surely many a ship's crew and many a valuable cargo would have been lost but for the staunch ability of this boat.

Now she has gone. I have cried over her like a child, wept over her as over the loss of a dear friend. Heartsick have I stumbled about amongst the wreckage washed ashore on Challenger Island the day after the disaster, picking up odd bits of timber and pressing them to my heart. Each piece I recognized, each spoke to me, each told me a tale.

In a hidden cove a square piece of planking had driven ashore. I sat down on it to rest, caressing those planks with sorrowing hands, and then, glancing warily around lest someone should see me, I bent down and kissed those planks goodbye. Oh, I am not ashamed of that now.

She has gone, our boat, our home for nigh on four years. Splendid as had been her career as a pilot boat, she ended her days as the plaything of a foolish seeker of happiness, a fool, however, with a great love for the boat that carried him as near as it is given mortals to come to ever elusive happiness. Can you wonder that I loved her?

Hilaire Belloc

The patching up had got more and more difficult. It had had to be renewed more and more often. The expense was nothing. We will always pay for doctors when it is a matter of those we love. But off the Norman coast the other day she gave me that look which they give us before they leave us, and she started a plank. It was high time. Had she not been near the piers it might have gone hard with those on board. But she got us through, though the Channel was pouring in, and she reached the basin within, her cockpit half full, and then lay up upon the mud. And there she did what corresponds in man to dying. She ceased to be a boat for the purposes of a boat any longer. She was no longer patch-up-able. She had fulfilled her task. It was all over. She had taken to her repose.

Very soon she with hammer and wedge was dissolved into her original elements—all that was mortal of her—and the rest is on the seas of paradise.

I wish I were there—already: now: at once: with her.

Rex Clements

Yet there is something to be said for the out-of-date windjammer. If the simple joy of living is what makes life worthwhile, and not merely the amount of work and worry crowded into the twenty-four hours, then assuredly the old canvas wings cannot pass without a sigh of regret. Was the life hard?—one slept the sounder for it. The food poor?—salt pork tastes better to a man in Fifty South than a banquet to an epicure. The pay paltry?—there is other wealth, thank God, than that of gold.

The sailing ship was an exacting mistress to serve. She was all that; she was a heartbreaking wench at times, yet none the less a Cleopatra among the sisterhood of the sea, inspiring an affection the lady-like liner is powerless to evoke. Her passages were made by the sea-cunning of men, not by the strength of machinery. Her sail plan had the complexity of a woman's character and, woman-like, "her infinite variety" would respond to every thought and act of one who understood and loved her.

Ralph Stock

Is there anything more wearisome than a steamer voyage—after sailing your own ship? You sleep throughout the night instead of breaking the twenty-four hours into the sensible segments of four on and eight off. You are called by a smug-faced steward instead of being gently squeezed or roughly shaken into life by the previous watch; and instead of commanding your own destinies at the tiller under the stars, you watch others doing it in brass buttons and electric light from a bridge.

Richard Maury

The survey of our schooner had shown her red coppered surfaces blending well with the white, that the slight apple to the bows gave way at the waterline to a fine-cut entrance beneath; that bilges were hard, while the run, noticeably fine, and forming the only concave lines, extended an unusual distance forward. What we had seen was the form of a wellknit model, small, slight, strong, embodying besides the stout science of boatbuilding, something more rare: the art that had taken a bundle of wood and tubs of metal fasteners to create an object at-

taining poise, balance, and, yes—something of beauty—the simple beauty of utility; no other.

John MacGregor

The perfection of a yacht's beauty is that nothing should be there for only beauty's sake.

Francis Brenton

. . . I hated to go ashore, for the boat looked smaller every time I left. Then one fine morning I awoke, looked more closely at my floating home, and saw everything in its true perspective: the *Nengo* wasn't small, she was compact.

Alan Villiers

There is little man has made that approaches anything in nature, but a sailing ship does. There is not much man has made that calls to all the best in him, but a sailing ship does. There is little man has done, these modern days of rush and nerve-wrack—when beauty is sacrificed to Epstein hideousness and art to the monstrosity of daubers, when books were churned out as soulessly as their presses, and theater is given up to bawling shadows—there is little that man has made to inspire the future and carry on loveliness and sweetness of glorious and efficient beauty. The sailing ship does these things; even old, battered sea-worn and a little unsafe, there is inspiring loveliness and grand pursuit of difficult and dangerous duty about her, and loyal devotion, and steadfast noble carrying-on through all obstacles and difficulties.

Rex Clements

But these first days of fine weather were above all a revelation to us first voyagers in the knowledge of the ship. When first I had seen her, embayed amid the cranes and warehouses of the East End, she looked grimy and unkempt from her long stay in port. So too in the bewilderment and physical weariness of wild romp down Channel and battering across the Bay I had hardly taken in any details of my surroundings.

But now I looked about me and found I was in a different world. The ship was the same, yet utterly different. She was alive now instead of dead; clean, scrubbed and burnished; neat and orderly aloft and alow where before had been a disreputable confusion. The stately fabric of her seemed to possess a life of its own. She leaned or dipped to every gust of the breeze and every surge and undulation of the sea. There was a place for everything and everything was in its place.

The third mate's boast about the decks, which were scrubbed night and morning, had come true. The racks of capstan bars, the rows of polished buckets, the rails with their long lines of pins and neatly coiled ropes, the tightly battened hatches and the glint of sunshine on the brasswork—all looked seamanlike, shipshape and Bristol fashion.

Now, too, she was peopled by a little company who understood and skillfully tended her. On the poop was always a controlling intelligence in the shape of the captain or officer of the watch, and at the wheel leaned the alert figure of the helmsman. Amidships the galley funnel smoked and Tommy bustled about with much clattering of pans and superabundance of energy. And on deck and aloft the men moved and worked and lent a familiar air of purposeful activity.

And how glorious, I often thought, the barque looked as she curtseyed her way to the southward! To stand at the break of the poop and, looking forward, watch the sweep of her bows as they rose and fell against the deep indigo of the sky was a sheer delight. Or, again, to glance aloft and see the great swaying pyramids of snow-white canvas towering up into the blue was to behold a picture of insurpassable beauty.

Every fresh initiation into the mysteries of a sailor's duties gave me a keener pleasure in the ship and I soon learnt the names of all the ropes and could find them in the dark, recognizing them by means of a gentle pull or even by the feel of the rope. I listened too with more and more interest to Paddy's yarns and began to share his pride in the ship.

Ernest K. Gann

But I could not turn away, because I knew this would be the last time I would see the *Albatross* as mine again. What sentimental foolishness! I condemned to hell the unknown romanticist who originated the ridiculous fancy that a man might fall in love with a thing. And what else was a vessel but a thing? Yet long before my time men ensnared by this same suspect fetish had lavished both affection and fortune on ships in which to sail the seas. So doughty and yet so amorous a man as Nelson referred to his great ungainly flagship *Victory* as his "little darling." Drake was nearly maudlin about his awkward, roly-poly little *Golden Hind* . . . It was as if they lived.

Desmond Holdridge

Seem to be carefree, light of heart and gay—the very elements will love you. Call your ship *Daisy* or *Bouncing Bess*—and the sun of life will sparkle on that course where fair winds drive her laughingly along.

Edward H. Dodd, Jr.

. . . we waived the luxuries and comforts of a well-appointed yacht and concentrated on seaworthiness and a reasonable price. The lure of a seagoing ship, of tarred ratlines, and a hand winch was a strong one. Later on we learned that an ounce of ice was worth a pound of romance . . .

Frank Wightman

. . . yielding stiffly and humming with purpose she put her cheek down on the ink-blue sea . . .

Hilaire Belloc

He who had designed the lines of her approached the power of a creator, so perfect were they and so smooth and so exactly suited to the use of the sea.

Frank Wightman

At her weather bows the seas were running eagerly. As she dipped slowly—her motion was damped and controlled by the pressure of her sails—they caught her near the stem, licked swiftly up her side in a circular sweep, clear as a sheet of glass, and fell back into the sea. As I looked, one more eager than the others topped her rail and flashed whitely across the foredeck. It was so like the quick, warm swipe from a dog's tongue that I burst out laughing. The sea was greeting her.

Rockwell Kent

And pitch! How she would lift and ride those short, steep seas! Climb to their tops till, overbalanced there, she'd pitch head foremost to the trough with the resounding smash of her broad cheeks and thirteen tons on water. And from my forecastle I thought: "The keel is an iron casting weighing three tons. It is secured to the boat by vertical iron bolts. On the end of these are nuts screwed upon slender threads. It is these threads that hold that iron to the boat. God, is that all!"

Rex Clements

A sailing ship is so absolutely at one with her environment. She adapts herself and responds to every mood of the sea, every undulation of its surface, and the winds of heaven are her very life-blood. Skill, courage and long experience are required to handle her and to a master hand she responds like a living creature. No more beautiful thing artist ever created. A steamer, driving its brute way through the indignant seas, under or over no matter so long as course is kept, may be a triumph of human skill and ingenuity, but grace, glamor and romance—it "vanished with the coal they burn!"

Desmond Holdridge

. . . we listened to the blows of the sea against the long bows, listened to the creaking of the great timbers as they were forced against the storm by half an acre of canvas . . .

Rockwell Kent

There was no crash—that time. Ever so gently, just as we seemed to draw away again, our stern post touched the ledge; so lightly touched it that it made no sound, only a little tremor. And the tremor ran through the iron keel and the oak, and through the ribs and planking, and through every bolt and nail, through every fibre of the boat and us. Maybe we had not known that the end had come; now, as if God whispered it, we knew.

So for a third time we were floated back.

Then, as if the furies of the sea and wind were freed at last to end their coquetry, they lifted us—high, high above the ledge—and dropped us there. And the impact of that shock was only less than those that followed for that half an hour until *Direction* sank.

Desmond Holdridge

Something had to give. The sail had to burst, the schooner had to collapse, crushed between the upper stone of the wind-filled canvas and the nether stone of the boulders on which she lay, or she had to drag herself off.

Robbie hoisted the jib and she dragged herself off.

Ray Kauffman

Cold and wet from the sea, we clung to the rigging and waited for the blessing of sunlight. The tide was receding and the sea broke only under the counter. With each sickening thud, I involuntarily cringed as her unprotected ribs pounded painfully into the sharp rock. Then the boat lay quite still. She had given up her struggle with the sea. The nightmare of shipwreck had come true. The bleak spars of the *Hurricane* canted across the starry sky. She was a dead thing and all the beauty had gone out of her.

Values

Many of the authors whom I've read have sensed a deepened awareness, when at sea, of man's niche in the grandness of nature. At times intensely poignant, at times intensely personal, this awareness has placed the sailor a bit closer than most landsmen to life's meaning. And it seems probable that the sailor's increased awareness springs from the most valuable quality of sea life, simplicity. Faced with discovery of life's true simplicity, faced as it must be on a small seaborne craft, articulate sailors have provided us insight into spiritual facets of life as real as those more tangible.

Edna St. Vincent Millay
INLAND

People that build their houses inland,
People that buy a plot of ground
Shaped like a house, and build a house there,
Far from the sea-board, far from the sound

Of water sucking the hollow ledges,
Tons of water striking the shore,—
What do they long for, as I long for
One salt smell of the sea once more?

People the waves have not awakened,
Spanking the boats at the harbour's head,
What do they long for, as I long for,—
Starting up in my inland bed,

Beating the narrow walls, and finding
Neither a window nor a door,
Screaming to God for death by drowning,—
One salt taste of the sea once more?

Hilaire Belloc

The sea is the consolation of this our day, as it has been the consolation of the centuries. It is the companion and the receiver of men. It has moods for them to fill the storehouse of the mind, perils for trial, or even for an ending, and calms for the good emblem of death. There, on the sea, is a man nearest to his own making, and in communion with that from which he came, and to which he shall return. For the wise men of very long ago have said, and it is true, that out of the salt water all things came. The sea is the matrix of creation, and we have the memory of it in our blood.

Ernest K. Gann

It is said we came from the sea, beginning as unicells; our sperm tastes of the sea, our tears are of salt water. As embryos we resemble fish, and the mammals of the ocean are our underdeveloped cousins. Noah reduced our species by putting to sea, and only at sea may the complete mixture of all the grand elements best be sensed and comprehended.

Joshua Slocum

I was born in the breezes, and I had studied the sea as perhaps few men have studied it, neglecting all else.

Frank Wightman

Perhaps the lure of sea is that it is a life without pretense—and there are no rackets.

Joseph Conrad

Lingard . . . contemplated the sea. He had grown on it, he had lived with it; it had enticed him away from home; on it his thoughts had expanded and his hand had found work to do. It had suggested endeavor, it had made him owner and commander of the finest brig afloat; it had lulled him into a belief in himself, in his strength, in his luck . . .

Frank Wightman

For the sea knows nothing of man. It carries none of his monuments. It bears no testimony to the "human incident."

Through the ages the faithless sea has spoken imperiously to the audacity that sleeps in the heart of man; has lured him away from the land, that she may know the measure of his awareness, and test the staunchness of his heart. The sea has known so many races, and bears testimony to none. The transient pomp of nations, the resounding names of men, have left no trace on this ageless face.

Joseph Conrad

It is not an individual, temperamental achievement, but simply the skilled use of a captured force, merely another step forward upon the way of universal conquest.

Charles Landery

I suppose I wanted freedom mainly, and a small ship could, I thought, give geographic freedom, although at the same time I realized that a population of two in a world reduced to ketch dimensions meant an increase in restraint, a greater need for self-discipline. Crowded together with no other companions, for weeks at a time, we could depend on angry seconds when one's tic would be the other's torture, a twitching eyebrow, the way a nose was blown, anything at all, might be enough to end friendship and make murder a logically desirable solution to all differences.

Richard Maury

. . . the sea, the isolating sea, confines one to one's own resources.

Ernest K. Gann

It is remarkable how quickly a good and favorable wind can sweep away the maddening frustrations of shore living.

Alan Villiers

Always we sailed with beauty; the form of the little world that held us was beautiful, and its name was grace . . . and that is why when he reaches the restraining ugliness that exists in most ports he seeks to drown his sense of beauty in beer.

Ann Davison

But the sea is an alien element. One cannot live in it or on it for long. One survives by one's own wit, judgment and the Grace of God. When a man says he loves the sea, he loves the illusion of mastery, the pride of skill, the life attendant on seafaring, but not the sea itself. One may be moved by its beauty or its grandeur, or terrified by its immensity and power of destruction, but one cannot love it any more than one can love the air or stars in outer space.

Frank Wightman

As I stood at the hatch before going down to the cabin, the day was breaking. On the curved cabintop the great beads of dew reflected the growing light, so that they looked like opals strewn over the deck, and on each there was sketched a minute picture of the mainmast with all its rigging. One of them moved mysteriously and broke its bonds. It claimed a

fellow with a quivering excitement that shimmered into stillness. Wobbling now with amplitude, it started a hesitant, zig-zag course down the slope, raced suddenly for the edge—and fell into the sea with a tinkle. The jeweled cloak that was spread over the deck now showed a dark tear. Soon minute cascades were falling into the sea all round the hull with a tiny carillon that was startling in the stillness.

Joseph Conrad

With her anchor at the bow and clothed in canvas to her very trucks, my command seemed to stand as motionless as a model ship set on the gleams and shadows of polished marble. It was impossible to distinguish land from water in the enigmatical tranquility of the immense forces of the world. A sudden impatience possessed me.

"Won't she answer the helm at all?" I said irritably to the man whose strong brown hands grasping the spokes of the wheel stood out lighted on the darkness, like a symbol of mankind's claim to the direction of its own fate.

Frank Wightman

The sea does not assail you with the nagging little fears of the city: loss of position, loss of caste—of face, of income. At sea your "position" is on its surface—or not. It is just as simple as that—and there will be no malicious pleasure when you are not. Your caste at sea is one without opprobrium: one who lives by his wits. Face does not figure among the sea's

verities. Your income at sea acquires a primal simplicity: you are working for your living. It will be rendered scrupulously, without deductions, as long as you earn it. Perhaps because your claim to it is less presumptuous that it is in the city—and your toil for it is more exacting—it is granted in full measure. When it is forfeit there is a certain finality about it, and it is not by act of parliament; it is by act of God.

William Robinson

Svaap seemed to be imbued with the spirit of a song, a carefree, never ending rhythm that was a part of the rhythm of the sea, perhaps of the universe itself.

Hilaire Belloc

As I looked at the rope I further considered how strange it was that ropes had never been worshiped. Men have worshiped the wall, and the post, and the sun, and the house. They have worshiped their food and their drink. They have, you may say, ceremonially worshiped their clothes; they have worshiped their headgear especially, crowns, mitres, ta-ra-ras; and they have worshiped the music which they have created. But I have never heard of any one worshiping a rope. Nor have I ever heard of a rope being made a symbol. I can recollect but one case in which it appears in a coat of arms, and that is, I think, in the case of the County or City of Chester, where, as I seem to remember, the Chester knot is emblazoned. But no one used it that I can remember in the Crusades, when all

coat of arms were developing. And this is odd, for they used every other conceivable thing—windmills, spurs, boots, roses, staffs, waves of the sea, the crescent moon, lions and leopards and even the elephant, and black men's heads, birds, horses, unicorns, griffons, jolly little dogs, chessboards, eagles—every conceivable thing human or imaginary they pressed into service; but no ropes.

Ray Kauffman

But I felt we were embarked on a useful purpose and it was an inspiring contrast from the two years of utter useless wandering in a yacht; and I wished that with wood and canvas and sweat we could produce something more than a passage to the westward. As yachtsmen or tourists, we were a sideshow, taking no part in life; and I thought seriously of rebuilding the *Hurricane* for a purpose in life; hauling cargo, diving for trochus shells or trading among the islands.

John Masefield

Men in a ship are always looking up, and men ashore generally looking down.

Rex Clements

Of all that salt-scarred host, sea captains and seamen, the Horn, it seems to me, is the fitting memorial, the emblem of their exploits and the measure of their valor. The grim old Cape is the Valhalla of seamen. Nowhere else in this old world do the giant forces of nature walk with so unabashed and imperative a stride.

There may be many conquests for the spirit of man to make, and far superior to bloody enslavements of one's fellow men, second only to the heroisms of the soul, is the splendor of the triumph of man's heart and arm over the awakened powers of nature. Given a floating plank and a web of flax, for brain and sinew to win their way through all that winds and waters of the untamable waste can do—is not this something worth living for?

Richard Maury

The elements, and especially the sea, demand the respect of the conservative side of one's nature. And yet the same sea tends to draw out any duality in a voyager's nature, to bring forth his defiant, his carrying-on side, so that his life is one of constant conflict between these two opposing, contradictory impulses.

Hilaire Belloc

I ought, I suppose, to have stopped in Port Madoc and renewed the memories of my childhood. But a fig for the memories of my childhood, at six o'clock in the morning: At six o'clock of a May morning, and a nice little leading breeze, all cold and merry! The memories of childhood and the contemplation of the Divine are for the evening; they go with candlelight and with a wine I know, and with friends of twenty years. But, so help me He that made me, when I find the morning wind blowing well for the salt and myself freshly roused from a good sleep, I am full of nothing but the coming of the course and an eagerness for the line of the sea against the sky and the making of a further shore.

Desmond Holdridge

I was master of the *Dolphin,* five tons, no guns, British-built, and bound for Hudson Strait and other places beyond the seas.

E. A. Pye

At sea the children were harnessed on deck with a bucket of sea-water handy to play with; if the weather got bad, they went below and lay in their bunks or sat on the wooden floor drawing pictures with chalks. They didn't know the meaning of the word "fear." They loved the life. In mid-Atlantic Robin said to his father, "Daddy, I hope I go on sailing until I go up to God."

Harry Pidgeon

I liked my way of seeing the world best.

Ralph Stock

I had no wish to be a yachtsman, being rather too fond of the sea.

E. A. Pye

. . . I'm not a good yachtsman. I don't put a white top on my hat on May first, nor do I bother very much with flags. I am so proud of my club burgee that it goes up on the first day of the cruise and comes down on the last. One day Captain Hudson said to me, "You know, Pye, I've known men keep their ensigns up all night!"

John MacGregor

He must have good health, and good spirits, and a passion for the sea. He must learn to rise, eat, drink, and sleep, as the water or winds decree, and not his watch. He must have wits to regard at once the tide, breeze, waves, chart, buoys, and lights; also the sails, pilot book, and compass; and more than all, to scan the passing vessels, and to cook and eat, and drink in the midst of all. With such pressing and varied occupations, he has no time to feel "lonely," and, indeed, he passes fewer hours in the week alone than many a busy man in chambers.

Joshua Slocum

The acute pain of solitude experienced at first never returned.

Frank Wightman

The sea life is singularly free of the nagging worries man has to support in the cities. There is a peace at sea of a quality that is unknown on land. On the occasions when there is no peace at sea, your powers are so extended that, when you do have time to register, the scale of the forces arrayed against you bring about an acceptance that is the spirit of resignation. When there is no alternative to your lot, the sense of "injustice" is lacking that is such a characteristic of misfortune on land. At sea, what is coming to you (and you can usually see it coming) must be faced. The absence in your world of others who are more "fortunate" robs you of whining comparisons, and the size of the stage on which your capers for survival will take place is such that your sense of self-importance is extinguished. With it goes that sense of "what is owing to me"—with all its miseries.

Ralph Waldo Emerson

I find the sea life an acquired taste, like that for tomatoes and olives. The confinement, cold, motion, noise, and odor are not to be dispensed with. The floor of your room is sloped at an angle of twenty or thirty degrees, and I waked every morning with the belief that someone was tipping up my berth. Nobody likes to be treated ignominiously, upset, shoved against the side of the house, rolled over, suffocated with bilge, mephitis, and stewing oil. We get used to these annoyances at last, but the dread of the sea remains longer. The sea is masculine, the type of active strength. Look, what eggshells are drifting all over it, each one like ours, filled with men in ecstacies of terror, alternating with cockney conceit as the sea is rough or smooth. Is this sad-colored circle an eternal cemetery? In our graveyards we scoop a pit but this aggressive water opens mile-wide pits and chasms and makes a mouthful of a fleet. To the geologist, the sea is the only firmament; the land is in perpetual flux and change, now blown up like a tumor, now sunk in a chasm, and the registered observations of a few hundred years find it in a perpetual tilt, rising and falling. The sea keeps its old level; and 'tis no wonder that the history of our race is so recent, if the roar of the oceans is silencing our traditions. A rising of the sea, say an inch in a century, from east to west on the land, will bury all the towns, monuments, bones and knowledge of mankind, steadily and insensibly. If it is capable of these great and secular mischiefs, it is quite as ready at private and local damage; and of this no landsman seems so fearful as the seaman.

Ralph Stock

It is best for the mariner, if he can manage it, not to think too deeply during time of stress.

William Robinson

I had read too much. I remember too well all those sailors' stories of the great gales and seas and tragedies of the Roaring Forties. It was all very romantic to want to experience it too, in theory; but in practice, confronted by the real thing, I was not so sure. Perhaps the moral is: Don't read—stick to the pilot chart for your technical information, and let it go at that.

Hilaire Belloc

Read less, good people, and sail more . . .

John Hersey

He picked up the ball of twine and put it to his nose and drew in the smell of boats, caulking smell, rope-locker smell—the smell which, savored in deepest gloom of wintertime, had the power of evoking faraway sunlit wavetops, a canted mast, splashing bow-waves, a warm summer breeze on a helmsman's cheek.

John MacGregor

Now, there are two sensations which after experience at sea seldom deceives you as to what they prognosticate, though it is impossible to give reasons for their hold upon the mind. One is the feeling, "I am drifting," another, "The water is shoaling," and the third, "Here comes a breeze." Each of these may be felt and recognized even with your eyes shut.

Alfred Loomis

I may be hopelessly wrong in my opinion, but I believe that the difference between riding out a storm and scurrying for a strange harbor in the dead of night is just this: When you're getting a drubbing off soundings the worst is yet to happen; but when you miss the entrance to a harbor and find yourself in the breakers your cup is full and running over.

Ernie Bradford

The deep-etched squalor of the mountain villages, the harsh life of the land, and the sun-dried earth washing into the gullies with the autumn rains (because the trees have gone)—these were not part of our world. People who live on, or by, the sea always have the sight and sound of it to make up for poverty and squalor. As the old man said who took our lines in Messina: "I have no work for nearly two months. But the day is good and the sea is beautiful. This afternoon I go and fish from the breakwater."

Alain Gerbault

After months of isolation it was a strange sensation to find other ships on the sea. Evidently the world of water was no more my own and in consequence I felt a little sad as I watched . . .

Sir Francis Chichester

. . . three months' solitude is strong medicine. One may behave as usual, but for a while one's feelings are changed. The beauty and magic of nature is as if seen under a magnifying glass, and life seems lived to the full. Anyway, to live life to the full is to do something which depends both on physical action and on the senses and also, at the same time, on the man-developed part of the brain.

Ernest K. Gann

The death of desire is linked directly to deepwater needs which are very simple. Soap is needed for cleanliness, and desire is born again if it is long unavailable. Some passing thought must be given to clothing, an old piece of cloth here and there for modesty and, according to the vessel's latitude . . . body warmth. Since high fashion is hopelessly impractical at sea, a vicious pair of human frailties is

dropped overboard. Vanity and envy will not be retrieved until the sailor steps ashore again.

Soon more subtle influences commence to make themselves known and further soothe the unavoidably troubled personality who only a few days previously had striven to survive in the complex of shoreside existence. According to his political persuasion, status, or social conscience, the voyager may have been distressed by racial problems, international threats, or merely by the gyrations of the market; now suddenly he realizes they are continuing without his vicarious supervision, and while at first he may experience a sense of futility and uselessness, these frustrations will soon be canceled by the citizen duties of his new world, which is now measured in feet and inches . . .

Once rid of such debilitating influences, man stands in the new danger of discovering himself, and for a while the cure can be as ravaging as the disease . . .

Vito Dumas

. . . So one goes on expecting less and less; and any trifle may become a source of satisfaction. Perhaps this is truly living.

Sir Francis Chichester

During the next week's sailing I came to terms with life. I found that my sense of humor had returned; things which would have irritated me or maddened and infuriated me ashore made me laugh out loud, and I dealt with them steadily and efficiently.

Rain, fog, gale, squall and turbulent forceful seas under grey skies became merely obstacles. I seemed to have found the true values of life. The meals I cooked myself were feasts, and my noggins of whiskey were nectar. A good sleep was as valuable to me as the Kohinoor diamond. All my senses seemed to be sharpened; I perceived and enjoyed the changing character of the sea, the colors of the sky, the slightest change in the noises of the sea and wind; even the differences between light and darkness were strong and a joy. I was enjoying life, and treating it as it should be treated—lightly. Tackling tough jobs gave me a wonderful sense of achievement and pleasure.

Ernest K. Gann

We were very much alone in a world that had no time for the problems of sailing ships. Very well, then the challenge was all the more stimulating.

Arthur Ransome

"Master and owner of the *Racundra*." Does any man need a prouder title or description? In moments of humiliation, those are the words that I shall whisper to myself. I ask no others on my grave.

John Hersey

There lay *Harmony*, as they swung in from the channel line, ahead, in profile, a white statement of sturdiness and endurance. Her mild sheer rose toward the dark bowsprit thrust out over an old-fashioned clipper bow, with trailboards above the cutwater in lieu of a figurehead, light blue panels with carved gilt scribing and letters. In pride Audrey pointed her out to Flick. Tom looked at his face and saw the immediate disappointment. This martini-time swab didn't want to be on a powerful, waisty, hard-bilged, wide-quartered old girl that would stand up like a church in a blow; he wanted to lollop on some sweet-lined yacht, a money boat. Yet Flick raised himself in the bows of the launch and lied with fabulous bravery, "Oh, she's a honey, Tom! She's really a sexpot. I *like* her." Then he began to grind his teeth.

Joseph Conrad

To him she was as full of life as the great world. He felt her live in every motion, in every roll, in every sway of her tapering masts, of those masts whose painted trucks move forever, to a seaman's eye, against the clouds or against the stars. To him she was always precious—like old love; always desirable— like a strange woman; always tender—like a mother; always faithful—like the favorite daughter of a man's heart.

For hours he would stand elbow on rail, his head in his hand and listen—and listen in dreamy stillness to the cajoling and promising whisper of the sea, that slipped past in vanishing bubbles along the smooth black-painted sides of his craft . . .

No doubt he, like most of us, would be uplifted at times by the awakened lyricism of his heart into regions charming, empty, and dangerous. But also, like most of us, he was unaware of his barren journeys above the interesting cares of this earth.

Yet from these, no doubt absurd and wasted moments, there remained on the man's daily life a tinge as that of a glowing and serene half-light. It softened the outlines of his rugged nature; and these moments kept close the bonds between him and his brig.

He was aware that his little vessel could give him something not to be had from anybody or anything in the world; something especially his own. The dependence of that solid man of bone and muscle on that obedient thing of wood and iron, acquired from that feeling the mysterious dignity of love. She—the craft—had all the qualities of a living thing: speed, obedience, trustworthiness, endurance, beauty, capacity to do and to suffer—all but life. He—the man—was the inspirer of that thing that to him seemed the most perfect of its kind. His will was its will, his thought was its impulse, his breath was the breath of its existence. He felt all this confusedly, without ever shaping this feeling into the soundless formulas of thought. To him she was unique and dear, this brig of three hundred fourteen tons register—a kingdom!

Erling Tambs

Among the visitors who came to see the boat was a British colonel. He wanted to buy *Teddy*.

"I love your boat," he said.

"So do I," I responded.

Then followed an offer amounting to three times the price I had paid, including repairs and outfitting.

No response.

"I am a very rich man," observed the colonel with considerable dignity.

"Not rich enough to buy this boat!"

That concluded the interview.

But day after day the colonel returned to the quay.

He, too, had fallen in love with our boat and he coveted her.

Frank Wightman

She was running heavily before a westerly gale somewhere south of Kerguelen. I was sitting out at the end of her bowsprit looking down at her figurehead, a woman in classical draperies, on her head a fillet of gold. From a back-thrown head her widely gazing eyes stared at the far horizon, and she strained forward in white immobility over the tumult of waters beneath the shearing bows. On her lips was a secret smile.

To me, her significance was confusing and disturbing. In heavy weather, I watched her soaring with smiling abandon over great flashing seas; poised giddily, a small, trance-like figure beneath the ship's storming bows, high above the havoc of the racing swells. Then she would plunge with glacial composure into a valley that was combed and furrowed by the gale. A leaping sea would hurl itself to meet her downward plunge, and there would be a breathy roar of waters split asunder as she tore a white furrow through the seas. Then she would fly smoothly upward in a soaring flight that was full of stillness and violence, the waters streaming raggedly from her smiling lips.

I used to reflect that for forty years, on all the oceans of the world she had leaned forward in that posture of strenuous repose, her wide and sightless eyes on countless horizons. In smoky docks, over roadways where men toiled, she held her leaning poise, as though she were about to take flight from the groaning swarms of the cities.

What did that wooden and imperturbably smiling figure do to my twenty-three years? No doubt she was quite remarkable as sailing-ship figureheads went in those days. To the man who fashioned her in Londonderry in 1882 she was probably just "another job." But to me she was a symbol of enormous significance. I thought she revealed the sea to me. She converted me; and with all the ardor of the newly converted, I closed my eyes to reason and took my vows.

Joshua Slocum

There are no poetry-enshrined freighters on the sea now.

E. A. Pye

"However," he grinned, "the smaller the boat, the better it is for one's soul."

Hilaire Belloc

The cruiser, the strong little, deep little boat . . . is a complete satisfaction for man . . .

Frank Wightman

. . . the music of the scuppers . . .

John MacGregor

The *Rob Roy* was very pleasant lodgings when moved down to the lovely bend at St. Cloud. Sometimes she was made fast to a tree, and the birds sang in my rigging, and gossamers spun webs at the masts, and leaves fell on the deck. At other times we struck the anchor into soft green grass, and left the boat for the day, until at night returning from . . . a pleasant and cool walk "home" by the river side, there was the little yawl all safe on a glassy pool, and her deck shining spangled with dewdrops under the moon, the cabin snug within—airy but no draughts, cool without chill, and brightly lighted up in a moment, yet all so undisturbed, without dust or din, and without any bill to pay.

Joseph Conrad

Lingard's love for his brig was a man's love, and was so great that it could never be appeased unless he called on her to put forth all her qualities and her power, to repay his exacting affection by a faithfulness tried to the very utmost limit of endurance. Every flutter of the sails flew down from aloft along the taut leeches, to enter his heart in a sense of acute delight; and the gentle murmur of the water alongside, which, continuous and soft, showed that in all her windings his incomparable craft had never, even for an instant, ceased to carry her way, was to him more precious and inspiring than the soft whisper of tender words would have been to another man. It was in such moments that he lived intensely, in a flush of strong feelings that made him long to press his little vessel to his

breast. She was his perfect world full of trustful joy.

The people on board the yacht, who watched eagerly the first sail they had seen since they had been ashore on that deserted part of the coast, soon made her out, with some disappointment, to be a small merchant brig beating up tack for tack along the inner edge of the reef . . .

Arthur Ransome

For the first time and not on paper and in dreams, I had the little ship alone in my hands in a night of velvet dark below and stars above, pushing steadily along into unknown waters. I was extremely happy.

John Hersey

He lifted the seatboard over the lazaret and took from a canvas bucket hanging there among spare lines a round head of true sponge (for he despised, at least on boats, the multicolored, square-edged, synthetic saucepan cleaners), and he held the lovely once-living form, still nearly alive to the touch, in his two hands, kneading it, and he thought of the slowness with which it had shaped its myriad cavities and vacuoles just for him, of its years of growth in a warm sea so that now, on this foggy morning in Edgartown harbor, he, Tom Medlar, could perform a ritual, could sweep it over the glistening brightwork and brass in and around the cockpit of his beloved boat, squeezing the moisture overboard now and then, performing the sacred morning wipe-down of the semi-circular expanse of the old Friendship cockpit that was his special pride—his outdoor throne room, he called it, though Audrey had another name for it: his playpen. The hooded binnacle, the deeply varnished wheel with a white cord Turkshead on the midships spoke, the wide teak seats and narrow teak deckboards, especially the high coaming, as upright as a church pew, reaching aft in a noble and generous curve from side to side of the cabin trunk—every detail contributed to a sense of an old-fashioned quality, a homely elegance. *Harmony* had a broad-beamed grace; a crew of eight could daysail and picnic in comfort in her cockpit. It was fashionable—"sea going"—in the big boats these days to let brass and bronze darken with verdigris, and to paint out coamings and handrails, but Tom called that sort of fashion mere laziness; he still polished and varnished all summer—and the cockpit sparkled under the sponge even in fog.

Frank Wightman

I filled the coffee pot and stuck my head out of the hatch into the sooty night. It closed over my face in a smothering blackness. Then I looked down at the deck. In the faint light of the binnacle the tiller pointed at me like the arresting finger of the advertisement. It was a finger bejewelled on its underside with raindrops, and the compass light had turned them into a row of cairngorms. *Wylo* raced down the face of a sea, the finger trembled, and the jewels fell into the cockpit without a sound.

Desmond Holdridge

For boats, even the uglier ones, are among the loveliest creations of man's hands, and though owning them brings a train of debts, hangnails, bruises, bad frights, and all kinds of worries not experienced by those who content themselves with the more practical vices, the relation between a man and his boat is as personal and intimate as the relation between husband and wife.

Richard Maury

The testing of a craft goes on forever, there is no end of it, but a point is reached where finally the spirits of ship and men to some degree reflect of one another; where often the weakness of one becomes the weakness of the other, the strength of one, the other's strength.

John MacGregor

... and somehow I became more cautious as to exposing my little craft to danger the more experience I acquired; certainly also she was valued more and more each day. This increase together of experience and of admiration, begetting boldness and caution by turns, went on until it settled down into a strange compromise—extreme care in certain circumstance, and undue boldness at other times.

William Robinson

When I think of it now in retrospect—the calmness with which we went blithely sailing across all the oceans there are—I have to laugh. It simply got to be a habit.

E. A. Pye

I am an optimist about things in general, but I look upon the sea as the ancients viewed their gods, with superstition; and I propitiate the monster in little ways like never filling my destination in the log book till I get there. If I ever became sure of myself, I should expect the sea to swallow me up, as, no doubt, it would.

Hilaire Belloc

Then in despair I prayed to the boat itself . . . "Oh, Boat . . . bear me safe round this point, and I will scatter wine over your decks." . . . that night we scattered her decks with wine as I had promised and lay easy in deep water . . .

Thor Heyerdahl

The closer we came into contact with the sea and what had its home there, the less strange it became and the more at home we ourselves felt. And we learned to respect the old primitive peoples who lived in close converse with the Pacific and therefore knew it from a quite different standpoint from our own. True, we have now estimated its salt content and given tunnies and dolphins Latin names. They had not done that. But, nevertheless, I am afraid that the picture the primitive peoples had of the sea was a truer one than ours.

William Robinson

Something makes me want to fight the elements, and to endure hardships, to feel the great luxury of sailing into a strange and beautiful port when it is all over. I am always seeking beauty: in the storm itself, in the sunrise, in the scintillating sea and far places—always beauty and nature. And so the ship strained on, the seas crashed overhead, and I lay there and knew that I loved it.

Alain Gerbault

I was happy at the thought of the difficulties to be overcome.

Edward H. Dodd, Jr.

The mid watch continues, a silent watch immersed in its own thoughts. Surrounded by elements whose limits are too far removed to comprehend, isolation is complete. Size and position lose all significance. One might be a star or an atom a thousand light years from the earth instead of a pensive human a thousand miles from land. Detached from their environment, events and theories are sweepingly revalued. An objectivity never before so complete leads one to conclusions so comprehensive that they soon lose all meaning. And yet they are accepted and discarded like the petty plans and inspirations of daily life. The mind has a new environment and, ever elastic, it stretches to the farthest constellations until it is on the verge of being cramped by space itself.

Alain Gerbault

At such time, alone upon the sea, gazing . . . I often pondered at the smallness of man . . .

Desmond Holdridge

. . . the chart gave a disappointingly accurate idea of the bays we wished to explore.

E. A. Pye

"Shall we give this up and go to the West Indies in *Moonraker?*" I said.

She walked over to the window, watching a steady stream of trams and lorries going down our road. "You mean . . . sell everything we've got and take a chance on what happens if we come back?"

"Yes," I replied.

She sat down in front of the fire, her shoulders against my knees. "It seems a big venture in so small a boat, but it might be a good thing, a complete break from our old life. Let's try it."

Richard Maury

Her stern sinks, the furious little bow slashes, noses, lifts; drops, and the stern rises high: Do or Die!

Hilaire Belloc

It is not an accident that the tall ships of every age of varying fashions so arrested human sight and seemed so splendid. The whole of man went into their creation, and they expressed him very well; his cunning, and his mastery, and his adventurous heart. For the wind is in nothing more capitally our friend than in this, that it has been, since men were men, their ally in the seeking of the unknown

and in their divine thirst for travel which, in its several aspects—pilgrimage, conquest, discovery, and, in general, enlargement—is one prime way whereby man fills himself with being.

Alan Villiers

If one is always to be overawed by the circumstances which may arise against one—why full-rigged ships would never have been built!

L. Francis Herreshoff

Miss Prim then spoke up: "Pa, just what do you mean by a boat being romantic?"

"Why, Prim," he replied, "when a thing is out of the usual and pleasing to contemplate it is romantic. When an object is nicely proportioned and has retained some well-proven ancient quality, it is romantic-looking. I suppose to a sailor a romantic vessel is one that looks like a good sea boat, one which has a good sheer and nicely proportioned ends: in short, a vessel that he falls in love with at first sight . . ."

Frank Wightman

. . . This is the life man was meant to live but he has got all confused. In this life he could believe in God . . .

William Snaith

But the rarest pleasure of all is that, in this lonely immensity, you are not alone. Though the dark magnitude isolates you in your own sensations, you are conscious of your shipmates.

Arthur Ransome

Then began a wild but, in a curious way, rather enjoyable night. No misfortunes at sea are enjoyable in themselves. He is a liar who says they are and he is a fool who courts them. But when misfortune has come against your will, when it is there, when you have shaken hands with it, realized it thoroughly, and done what you think is the best possible thing to do, there comes a sort of release from further worry which is quite sensibly pleasant.

Hilaire Belloc

But as for you, sailing ordinarily upon the sea, be quite content if she does her duty with the wind halfway between beam and bow. It is here as it is with most things in life, be content with the sound average, keeping the limits which God has set all round. Do not wish for too long a life, for too large a fortune, or for too much honor. Eat your peck of dirt before you die; take the rough with the smooth; consider that it is all in a day's work; expect rain and fine. In general, write out a list of all the Commandment-proverbs and learn that list by heart. Then break them.

E. A. Pye

How typical of sailing this was—hours of calm, then a tearing wind, sailing blind, looking for an opening in a coast we couldn't see, for a light that might or might not be lit!

Vito Dumas

It is said that solitude is best shared with another. These seas offer joy to anyone who is capable of loving and understanding nature. Are there not people who can spend hours watching the rain as it falls? I once read somewhere that three things could never be boring: passing clouds, dancing flames and running water. They are not the only ones. I should add in the first place, work.

E. A. Pye

The wide loneliness of a great ocean breeds a humility that is good for the soul.

Hilaire Belloc

I have often thought that a boat running snug, and properly reefed to suit the wind, is a model of the virtue which the theologians call temperance . . . for temperance does not mean doing things half-heartedly, still less does it mean doing or not doing things extremely. It means suiting your implements to your motive power, and not carrying on at a risk. It is not unconnected with dignity, and there is something profound about it; I will call it the contralto among the virtues and leave it go at that.

Erling Tambs

. . . We had no spare sails, and a few other things were missing which to some people would seem indispensable. But, among the various possessions there figured a bag of potatoes and a fishing line . . .

John MacGregor

A boat's mop is, of course, well known to be always fair spoil to him who can take it, and whatever other article the yachtsman leaves loose on an unguarded deck, he never omits to hide or lock up the mop, for a mop is winged like an umbrella; it strays, but seldom returns. The usual protection for mops is their extreme badness, and it is on this account, no doubt, that you never can find a good mop to buy. The *Rob Roy's* mop was the only bad article on board, and I left it out loose in perfect confidence. Often and often it had evidently been turned over, but on examination it was found supremely bad, worse than the thief's own mop, and not worth stealing. At last, however, and in Cowes, too, the focus of yachting, if not of honesty, my mop was stolen. The man who took it is to be pitied, for, clearly, before he coveted a bad mop, he must have been long enduring a worse one.

Alain Bombard

Under the boiling sun, I had returned to the primitive life. The solitude was becoming increasingly oppressive and the log was my substitute for a human companion. I was worried that I might run out of paper. When it was necessary to sacrifice a book for purposes of my natural functions, I finally decided that the most appropriate was the Rabelais.

Edward H. Dodd, Jr.

By this time all cigarettes had gone and the last remnants of moldy tobacco were being rolled in cigarette papers cut from the blank pages of the *Oxford Book of English Verse.*

Joshua Slocum

As for the jib, let it go; I saved pieces of it, and, after all, I was in want of pot-rags ...

Erling Tambs

We were moored in the Bassin de Commerce, in the very heart of the City, amongst a number of the finest yachts in the world. A few yards away lay—like a palace of gold and ivory—Baron Rothschild's exquisite steam yacht. When we went ashore, we would leave our dinghy at the steps right under her stern.

One day, on our returning from a stroll ... a fine old gentleman, whom I suspected to be the great financier himself, spoke to me from the yacht. He had seen some boys playing around with my dinghy, he said, and had chased them away.

Subsequently, I used to amuse myself when disembarking, by telling my wife: "Baron Rothschild will look after the dinghy."

Harry Pidgeon

While the *Islander* was resting in Honolulu Harbor, the British cruiser *Renown* came in with the Prince of Wales on board, so they had the two of us there at the same time.

E. A. Pye

It is pleasant to take your ship alongside a quay with every stitch of canvas set, and pleasanter still if you have an audience.

Erling Tambs

We managed to scrape past the boom end with half an inch to spare and were greeted with applause by the public who seemed to think that I was doing tricks—a nautical looping the loop—for their amusement.

E. A. Pye

On the day we left, Anne, who had been presenting Watty with a long list of last-minute ideas, suddenly had another one. "Mr. Watty, could you make us a double bed on the port side?"

"What d'you want a double bed on a boat for?" he demanded, his face crinkling at so outrageous a suggestion. "I've never heard of such a thing." I burst out laughing and the poor girl blushed furiously. Watty turned away, muttering something under his breath, but the bed was made.

John MacGregor

Is it right to moralize at all in a logbook? and will not the reader say, that when there is not a storm in the yawl, or a swamp, there is sure to come a sermon?

Frank Wightman

When you are so close to the sea that you can reach out your hand and touch the face of the deep itself, there is an intimacy about the experience that is immediate and urgent ... Perhaps it is the love of ships that casts out fear at sea.

Hilaire Belloc

Once out on the Looe with an ugly thunderstorm glowering and lumbering down from the north, full of zigzags of lightning, I, in this same boat, was shortening sail rapidly to meet the gust when it should come. Even as I did so, I saw a fierce red light beating upon the Seven Sisters and Beachy Head, more than forty miles away. You could see every detail of those chalk cliffs. You could have touched them with your hand; yet the sea in between was vague; and that was a vision of the unseen. I say that the sea is in all things the teacher of men.

Frank Wightman

... out there you seem to understand that death is as much a function of life as birth ... At sea you seldom think of death, even when it is imminent. Like the runner, you are not thinking of losing, but you hope to win. A life that is lived in hope is not a bad life.

Charles Violet

Everyone has read from time to time of ships sailing down a silvery path of moonlight. At midnight I switched on my faithful little radio in the middle of a violin concerto. I went on deck to glance around, and there was the *Nova* really sailing a silvery moonpath. The strains of an exquisite slow movement helped to bring additional beauty to the scene. All too seldom can we feel completely detached from the prosaic pettiness of everyday life, and go through an experience deserving to be called transcendental. This was one of those moments, and it passed all too quickly. Then the spell was broken, and the sensation of earthly pleasure gone.

Three minutes later I was making myself a cup of coffee.

Frank Wightman

The laws of the sea are few, simple and austere—and take no cognizance of me and my mind.

Hilaire Belloc

And as there is a concealment of reality at sea, corresponding to the concealment of reality from our experience in human life, so also at sea there is occasionally vision, corresponding to that occasional vision that you also have in human life; but vision is much rarer than the concealment of reality.

Desmond Holdridge

A schooner, a good-sized one too, of perhaps eighty tons, rounded the cape, all her kites set, and with the breeze she fanned along the coast, bound for St. George Harbor. The setting sun shone, ruddy, on her white sails and we envied her the free wind. We thought how fine to be in a vessel that size, able to work to windward in bad weather and no toy of wind and wave as we were. We were still comparing the wretchedness of our lot with the splendor of life aboard an eighty-tonner when the day ended. We would have felt differently had we known that that same schooner was to be driven

ashore with the loss of half her crew within twenty-four hours.

Hilaire Belloc

I thought, as we stood off there on the starboard tack again losing all that we had made on the port tack just before, what men must feel when a life or a fortune depends upon the rounding of a headland.

Frank Wightman

I began to wish I could shut out the night; the solitude; the emptiness; and the soughing of the wind. All round me were the sounds that are so characteristic of nights alone on deck. The curiously dry, brushing sound that the wind makes as it streams across the surface of the sea; an ageless, eternal sound; one of the sounds heard at the Creation. The yacht's small voice as she thrusts onward: a courageous little sound. The muted "thrrapp" of a slackened rope as it hits the deck, and the creak as it rises and takes the strain.

This background of sound that comes to acquire an extraordinary significance after you have lived with it for long periods. This primitive whispering that is always ready to start immediately your companion is safely below—has a curiously diminishing effect. The scene, the sounds—especially at night—are all calculated to bring home to the man in the cockpit the sense of human littleness; to hold it before him with relentless insistence: a heavy, silent pressure of meaning.

E. A. Pye

As I sat at the tiller, saw the lights in the cabin dim, and watched the hands of the clock move slowly towards ten o'clock, I thought that the simplicity of life at sea had much to recommend it; it kept you fit, it exercised your brain and made you vigilant. There was enough danger about it to add a spice of adventure to every voyage; yet, I reflected, no one can sail all his life . . .

Joshua Slocum

I was destined to sail once more into the depths of solitude; but these experiences had no bad effect upon me; on the contrary, a spirit of charity and even benevolence grew stronger in my nature through the meditations of these supreme hours at sea.

Ernest K. Gann

When the full displeasure of the elements falls upon a man, he is temporarily overwhelmed and permanently changed within. After the trial he is either dead or forever afterward humble and discreet.

Joshua Slocum

I myself learned more seamanship, I think, on the *Spray* than on any other ship I ever sailed, and as for patience, the greatest of all the virtues, even while sailing through the reaches of the Strait of Magellan, between the bluff mainland and dismal Fuego, where through intricate sailing I was obliged to steer, I learned to sit by the wheel, content to make ten miles a day beating against the tide, and when a month at that was lost, I could find some old tune to hum while I worked the route all over again, beating as before.

Hilaire Belloc

The sea drives truth into a man like salt.

Dennis Puleston

A short train journey to London, and in a few hours I was home . . . As I went off upstairs, I knew she had been taking stock of me with the discerning eye that only mothers have. "I'm so glad," I heard her say to the others. "I was afraid he might be changed. But he isn't—not one bit!"

Departure

It's doubtful that many skippers of small sailing dinghies use the word departure to describe getting underway; they merely "shove off." Perhaps it's because there's a stateliness to the word (and to the act itself) that seemingly relates best to larger sailing vessels? Regardless of how stately the word sounds or the act is, all boats share in the symbolic significance of departure: Is it a leaving or a beginning? An escape or an anticipation? Writers reporting the finality of getting underway seem torn between what remains undone ashore and the joy of release from everything past. But if a ghost of anxiety or doubt should linger at the bittersweet moment of casting off wise skippers, to their crew's delight, can exorcise it by crying aloud, "Let the feast begin!"

Thor Heyerdahl

Now we asked the chauffeur to drive us straight to the mountains, as far in as he could get in one day. We drove up over desert roads, along old irrigation canals from Inca times, till we came to the dizzy height of 12,-000 feet above the raft's mast. Here we simply devoured rocks and mountain peaks and green grass with our eyes and tried to surfeit ourselves with the tranquil mountain mass of the Andes range that lay before us. We tried to convince ourselves that we were thoroughly tired of stone and solid earth and wanted to sail out and get to know the sea.

Francis Brenton

Now that the prospect of the sea journey was upon me I had the urge to savor the firmness of dry land, for once I sailed I would be seeing nothing but the sea for a month or more. With a small knapsack swinging by my side, I walked up the winding harbor road and turned off at a windswept rocky path toward a distant peak.

Hilaire Belloc

At sea you never can tell, and must take every inch the gods allow you. You will need that and more very often before evening. Now, as I put my head out I saw that I could not yet start, for there was a thick white mist over everything, so that I could not even see the bowsprit of my own boat. Everything was damp: the decks smelt of fog . . .

Ray Kauffman

I stood in the companionway with the warmth from the galley stove against my back and, facing the cold fresh breeze, watched the dark water slowly drown the blinking lights, and Australia was gone. The wind meaned aloft, the pipe turnbuckles whistled a high note, the stanchions a low note, and the booms, lifting and falling with each roll of the ship, creaked the sheet blocks as we sang on our way northeast.

Stanley Smith and Charles Violet

If there is ever a feeling of high endeavor in setting out to challenge an ocean in a small boat, the slightest aura of glory, courage, or heroism surrounding the members of the crew, it certainly did not attend our performance. We were depressed and overawed by the prospect before us.

Charles Landery

Dazed with activity, I scarcely noticed when *Bessie* moved out into the stream, away from the mud and the quay which she must have been considering her final resting-place. There was no chance for nostalgic farewells to England, no melancholy or happy leaning on the bulwarks, no waving to friends; instead of dropping gentle tears we sweated and hauled on ropes.

William Robinson

Venus, our old guiding star, shone out over Moorea now, and I began to wonder if it were not time for *Svaap* to be heading westward once more. The green starboard light of the schooner suddenly came into being, blocks creaked. The ship was moving, her anchor aweigh, and at last she went slowly ahead, then quicker, swung and was headed for the pass and out to sea.

I felt strange urgings in me. It is always like that when I see a ship sail—something sad, and something joyful too—but now it was more than that, for suddenly I knew that it was time for *Svaap* to leave too, and following the sun still farther to the west.

Samuel Eliot Morison

The boy and I got underway from the mooring by the usual ritual. I take in the ensign, hoist the mizzen, cast off main sheet and slack the backstays; he helps me hoist the mainsail, sway the halyards and neatly coil them. I take the wheel and the main sheet in hand, the boy casts off the mooring rode and hoists the jib, and off she goes like a lively dog let off the leash.

E. B. White

Even now, with a thousand little voyages notched in my belt, I still feel a memorial chill on casting off, as the gulls jeer and the empty mainsail claps.

Ernest K. Gann

Then we cast off all our other lines and to the pleasurable excitement of all concerned we began to make sternway and a wonderful silence prevailed. There was no traffic behind us in the stream so I refrained from blowing any whistles and because of the quiet the soft farewells from both ship and wharf seemed especially touching and personal.

Frank Wightman

. . . a sleepy murmur of waters thrust aside. She is going to sea.

Stanley Smith and Charles Violet

The surface of the harbor took on a restful, oily aspect and we were left embarrassed with sagging sails, only a few hundred yards away from our point of departure.

Hilaire Belloc

But the whole point of weighing anchor is that he has chosen his weather and his tide, and that he is setting out. The thing is done.

Woodes Rogers

October 24, 1709. Being all supply'd with Wood, Water, and Turtle, we came to sail at Eleven this Forenoon . . .

Rex Clements

. . . and we manned the windlass, tramping around the capstan to the tune of "Goodbye—fare ye well," the unforgettable homeward chanty. As we hove round, straining at the bars, the "clank-clank" of the windlass pawls was welcome music in our ears.

Our mudhook was soon awash, the cat-fall hooked on, and the anchor hoisted dripping to the cat-head.

Then up aloft to throw the gaskets off and drop the heavy folds of canvas. Tops'ls and t'gans'le were quickly sheeted home, and we began to move through the water. A cast to starboard, and the open sea lay ahead, with the lights of Pisco growing fainter astern.

One after another, all hands working with a will, our kites were spread to the gentle land breeze. A course was set, a hand sent to the lookout, and at eight bells came the familiar order: "Go below the watch," and we trooped off to our bunks, with smiling faces and contented hearts—Homeward bound!

Herman Melville

"All hands up anchor!" When that order was given, how we sprang to the bars, and heaved round that capstan; every man a Goliath, every tendon a hawser! round, round it spun like a sphere, keeping time with our feet to the time of the fife till the cable was straight up and down, and the ship with her nose in the water.

"Heave and pall! unship your bars, and make sail!" It was done: barmen, nippermen, tierres, veerers, idlers and all, scrambled up the ladder to the braces and halyards; while like monkeys in palmtrees, the sail-loosers ran out on those broad boughs, our yards; and down fell the sails like white clouds from the ether—topsails, topgallants, and royals; and away we ran with the halyards, till every sheet was distended.

"Once more to the bars! Heave, my hearties, heave hard! With a jerk and a yerk, we broke ground; and up to our bows came several thousand pounds of old iron, in the shape of our ponderous anchor.

Richard Maury

The first sailing day was a bright one. At eleven o'clock, canvas was hoisted, a conch shell sounded a farewell, and the schooner glided toward the intricate channel leading to the sea. In mid-harbor she faltered for wind, moved once again, fetched channel, slid over it, and Indian Point was seen no more.

For hours we worked seawards, and then, near sunset, the schooner felt her first ground swells. Land still guarded her, but now, over the bows, lay a line of rolling ocean, shining and cold. The running engine tried to drive the bows under, but the forward sections resisted, passing seas harmlessly over her shoulder, sending spray into our intent faces.

Herman Melville

The anchor was up, the sails were set, and off we glided. It was a short, cold Christmas; and as the short northern day merged into night, we found ourselves almost abroad upon the wintry ocean, whose freezing spray cased us in ice, as in polished armor. The long rows of teeth on the bulwarks glistened in the moonlight; and like the white ivory tusks of some huge elephant, vast curving icicles depended from the bows.

Rex Clements

Next morning was fresh and breezy, with a cold snap in the air. We singled up our moorings and rode with a slip on the buoy, till a tug came off and was made fast for'ard. At midday order was given to cast off. A few minutes later we towed past the Bluff, sail was crowded on her and almost as soon as her forefoot lifted to the first long Pacific swell the tug was let go, tops'ls and t'gallant'ls sheeted home, and we were off once more.

I never felt anything more delightful than the first gentle rise and fall of the ship to the scend of the sea. After so many weeks of lifeless equilibrium, the slanting decks and long resistless heave and roll of the hull, a-dip to the wash and tremor of ten thousand miles of ocean, gave one a sense of freedom and exhilaration impossible to describe. As sail after sail was sheeted home and the barque laid steeply over to the freshening breeze, I, for one, would not have changed places with the skipper of a battleship. Each to his taste, and mine for the open sea and a squarerigger setting sail.

Hilaire Belloc

When a man weighs anchor in a little ship or a large one he does a jolly thing! He cuts himself off and he starts for freedom and for the chance of things. He pulls the jib a-weather, he leans to her slowly pulling round, he sees the wind getting into the mainsail, and he feels that she feels the helm. He has her on a slant of wind, and he makes out between the harbor piers. I am supposing, for the sake of good luck,

that it is not blowing bang down the harbor mouth, nor, for the matter of that, bang out of it. I am supposing, for the sake of good luck to this venture, that in weighing anchor you have the wind so that you can sail with it full and by, or freer still, right past the walls until you are well into the tide outside. You may tell me that you are so rich and your boat is so big that there have been times when you have anchored in the very open, and that all this does not apply to you. Why, then, your thoughts do not apply to me nor to the little boat I have in mind.

Richard Maury

A well-wisher, one of the small group on the wharfside, went on board and knotted a streamer of green ribbon to the eye of the jib stay.

William Robinson

It was a glorious start. Our new squaresail pulled like horses with a laughing breeze on our quarter, and I learned a new thrill. Never before had I seen such a sail in operation.

A large school of dolphin escorted us out.

A squall made up. We were off for Samoa and American territory. Only the flicker of two or three fires astern betrayed the presence of a tiny lonesome world lost in a lonely ocean.

Herman Melville

Gaining the more open water, the bracing breeze waxed fresh; the little *Moss* tossed the quick foam from her bows, as a young colt his snortings. How I snuffed that

Tartar air!—as I spurned that turnpike earth!—that common highway all over dented with the marks of slavish heels and hoofs; and turned me to admire that magnanimity of the sea which will permit no records.

John MacGregor

I started for Boulogne in the dawn, when all the scene around looked like a woodcut, pale and colorless, as I cooked hot breakfast at five o'clock.

William Robinson

So we rattled in the chain and got the hook aboard and were underway along the steep black bluffs, with a cool damp land breeze laden with mysterious sensuous perfumes of exotic flowers. We moved silently, without a wave upon the purple water, and gauged our progress by the movement of a bright star along the hilltops. Soon faint and changing colors traced patterns in the east, creeping slowly through the sky like frost on windowpanes. Then suddenly, and wondrously, the golden sun leaped into sight and day was once more here.

Frank Wightman

And just after 5 a.m. on May 9th *Wylo's* heads'ls filled and she swung away from the sleeping cove. In the short dawn of the tropics I could already see the small headland gliding towards me that marked the division between the two worlds of enclosed waters and open sea; it came down to the water verdant and tautly arched, like a dancer's pointed foot in a green ballet shoe.

Desmond Holdridge

Characteristically, we did not bother to obtain clearance papers, registration, bills of health, or even evidence of ownership. We simply sailed.

K. Adlard Coles

Our voyage had commenced, and at last we were away gliding through the clean water past the reeds. Care was lifted from our shoulders, for we were free from advice, pessimism, officialism, heat and hot air.

Joshua Slocum

. . . the *Spray* . . . now filled away clear of the sea-beaten rocks . . .

Ann Davison

The tenuous thread was broken and I was on my own.

Ray Kauffman

"Tahiti for Christmas and mail from home!" was the chantey that brought the anchor on deck. . . . the day of reckoning came. We frantically felt beneath our bunks for francs and centimes, turned all our pockets inside out and soberly counted our wealth—a little less than a hundred francs remained. Tomorrow, I decided, would be sailing day. We looked over the charts and consulted the pilot book for an island where we could hole up for the hurricane season in a safe harbor until the trades set in again in April. Borabora looked the best on paper, but we planned to make all the is-lands sur le vent: Moorea, Huahine, Raiatea, and Tahaa. There was enough food aboard for many months. We needed gasoline, but it was expensive and not really necessary for downhill work. We spent the last day in Tahiti aboard, making ready for sea and watching the life of the town with a detached feeling of sadness.

The governor, Handlebar Hank, in morning coat and striped trousers, was taking his constitu-tional in the park, his flowing mustache catching the light like crossed bayonets. A bus roared down the Broom Road, crowded with singing natives and top-heavy with produce. Girls paraded the street in colorful costumes with a red hibiscus over their ears. Chinese, in black pajamas, pushed sweetmeat carts festooned with little bells. Out-is-land natives, like shrouded corpses, lay asleep in the shade of a trading company's store, waiting a passage home. A large pig broke loose and all the available male population gave chase. A big schooner came in from the Austral Islands and the deserted waterfront was immediately crowded. A German countess, with red painted toenails showing from sandals, wandered past the shipping. Two beautiful golden skinned girls, a mixture of French and Tahitian, pedaling on bicycles in long white dresses, were hailed from the ships moored to the shore. It was painful to watch the life we were leaving. That night the music from Quinn's, still playing Papio, floated down with the land wind.

In the morning, the *Director* and the *Four Winds,* and friends ashore lined the breakwater to see us off. The pilot came aboard for "zee fare-well." Our Tahitian boy and a large black dog from whom he refused to part were going with us as far as Borabora. He helped Hector take in the awning. The lines were cast off the old cannon bollards and we went to work on the windlass. The ratchet clicked and the chains groaned through the hawse pipes. A fresh breeze blowing across the lagoon shook the mizzen hard, and the sheet blocks banged on the traveler. The anchor broke out and the bow fell away. With four hands we set all sails smartly. We turned to wave farewell when a black mass of clouds hid the sun. A hard rain squall cracked down and sent us flying. Out through the pass we raced. Breakers thundered on the reef on either side. The strong squall drove us deep in the water and like a wedge we split the confused sea outside. I turned around for a last long look at Papeete but the rain, like a curtain, had shut off the land.

Joshua Slocum

On the following day, the head sea having gone down I sailed from Yarmouth, and let go my last hold on America. The log of my first day on the Atlantic in the *Spray* reads briefly: "9:30 a.m. sailed from Yarmouth. 4:30 p.m. passed Cape Sable; distance, three cables from the land. The sloop making eight knots. Fresh breeze, N.W."

Ralph Waldo Emerson

On Friday at noon, we had made only one hundred and thirty-four miles. A nimble Indian would have swum as far; but the captain affirmed that the ship would show us in time all her paces, and we crept along through the floating drift of boards, logs, and chips which the rivers of Maine and New Brunswick pour into the sea after a freshet . . . At last, on Sunday night, after doing one day's work in four, the storm came, the winds blew, and we flew before a northwester which strained every rope and sail. The good ship darts through the water all day, all night, like a fish, quivering with speed, gliding through liquid leagues, sliding from horizon to horizon. She has passed Cape Sable; she has reached the Banks; the land birds are left; gulls, haglets, ducks, petrels, swim, dive and hover around; no fishermen; she has passed the Banks; left five sail behind her, far on the edge of the west at sundown which was far east of us at morn. Our good master keeps his kites up to the last moment, studding-sails alow and aloft, and by incessant straight steering never loses a rod of way. Yet in running over these abysses, whatever dangers we are running into, we are running out of the risks of hundreds of miles every day which have their own chances of squall, collision, seastroke, piracy, cold and thunder.

Dwight Long

And so we set out.

Environment

The world as seen from the deck of a small boat under sail is often limited only by the imagination of the observer. Accordingly, a great variety of generally trenchant, useful and absorbing information about the spacious world of the sailor exists in the literature. The following selections are chosen to present a vigorous portrait of the different environments—inland, coastal, deep sea—in which man sails for work or for pleasure.

Hilaire Belloc

. . . all things are well when there is sunlight . . .

Arthur Ransome

. . . the dawn, which came up with fiery red splashes over a nickel sea.

Charles Landery

The sky was clear except for a solitary gun-puff cloud . . .

Ernle Bradford

. . . and the sea was a crinkled sheet of silver.

Ray Kauffman

. . . and the water was as unfathomable as the black holes between the stars at night.

Rex Clements

The wan and sickly daylight lasted a bare seven hours out of the twenty-four. For the rest of the time we were plunged in complete darkness, a cold, hail-smitten darkness, black as the Earl of Hell's riding boots.

Charles Landery

The wind had gone by dawn, leaving behind it a damp, sniveling day, brightening and darkening with hysterical indecision and always on the edge of tears.

Rex Clements

Beautiful as sunsets are, sunrises are even more so. To my way of thinking, sunrise over a tropic sea is the most glorious sight on God's earth. But it's too common an occurrence—that's the fault of it. It happens every day, whereas if it only occurred once in fifty years travelers would come from all over the world to marvel at it. To see in a few moments the velvety blackness of night tremble through veils of paling purple, hueless grey and all shades of azure, delicate rose and flashing gold to the imperial blaze of the risen sun is an unforgettable experience. Sunrise anywhere is a glorious sight but it puts on its most ineffable beauty, I think, at sea between Cancer and Capricorn. Looking at it one feels the same sort of illumination as the prophet of old when he exclaimed, "God is light!"

Humphrey Barton

I often sail with clever, knowledgeable folk who have one look at the sky at dawn and say: "Hmm, I don't like the look of the sky at all. We shall have more wind than we want today." The ominous signs which seem so obvious to them are usually invisible to me, so I go below and tap the glass and wonder whether they are right. But as often as not they are wrong.

Herman Melville

The clear, cold sky overhead looked like a steel-blue cymbal, that might ring, could you smite it.

Ernle Bradford

Although the sun was high overhead, there was a fresh edge to the air, a hint of approaching autumn. The sky was a hard, cloudless blue and the coast and the inland hills stood out in sharp scraped lines.

Joseph Conrad

The diffused light of the short daybreak showed the open water to the westward, sleeping, smooth and grey under a faded heaven. The straight coast threw a heavy belt of gloom along the shoals, which, in the calm of expiring light, were unmarked by the slightest ripple. In the faint dawn the low clumps of bushes on the sandbanks appeared immense.

Frank Wightman

Far away outside these gloomy regions—in some legendary clear sky—the sun was setting . . . with a wan and spectral glare in which one expected some haunted cosmic face to appear gazing sightlessly over the sea, whispering a doom through metal lips.

All we got was some thunder and a sudden gush of rain.

Charles Landery

The sky marbled with cloud . . .

Joshua Slocum

. . . and thunderbolts fell in the sea all about.

Frank Wightman

I was standing with the compass bowl between my feet when there was a blistering flash that showed me the very limpets clinging to the rocks of the northern arm of the bay . . .

Rex Clements

In an instant the lightning blazed out everywhere, zigzagging across the solid vault on every side and seemingly stabbing through and through the ship. For some minutes it was hell with the lid off. Then, with a hiss and a roar, down came the rain!

Hans De Mierre

The air was heavy with moisture and the wind had a faint iodine, kelp-like smell that promises fog.

Arthur Ransome

There was something uncanny in being unable to see in a fog so white, so luminous in itself. Yet there it was, sure enough fog, as Huck Finn would say, and we began to be worried by noises. Once or twice there were good recognizable noises made by other vessels: to these we cheerfully replied, proud of the fact that we could do as much ourselves.

Rex Clements

Far more dangerous to the mariner than gales is fog. It is the most bewildering of the many difficulties with which he has to contend. Passengers rarely seem to realize this. An estimable old gentleman once asked me, when the vessel we were in was joyously bucking into the North East Trades blowing fresh, if the weather ever got any worse. The question took me so flat aback I hadn't wits enough to tell him it couldn't get any better. The same individual slept peacefully in his bunk all the way up Channel, when we ran into a thick fog and slowed down to about eight knots. He would have been surprised to learn that he was in a hundred times more danger than ever he was before.

. . . We were creeping blindly along, feeling our way down vistas of eddying fog-smoke, when we heard a pulsing throb and the low swish of water. We looked round and the little fog horn on the foks'le head coughed violently in response to Neilsen's hurried manipulating. Suddenly a giant shape loomed up out of the mist, standing down on top of us. Neilsen worked his wheezy toy of a foghorn frantically and we jumped unbidden to the braces. There was no time to do anything, the steamer was almost into us and old Jamieson and the mate were heaving hard at the helm.

It was touch and go; only a few yards separated the two vessels, when there was a clatter of bells aboard the steamer and she swerved sharply to port. She missed our stern by only a few feet, traveling at near twenty knots . . . For a moment she towered above us like a colossal wraith of the sea, then melted rapidly into the mist.

Rudyard Kipling

There came a sound of merriment where the fog lay thicker and the schooners were ringing their bells. A big bark nosed cautiously out of the mist, and was received with shouts and cries. She was a black, buxom, eight hundred ton craft. Her mainsail was looped up, and her topsail flapped undecidedly in what little wind was moving. Now a bark is feminine beyond all daughters of the sea, and this tall, hesitating creature, with her white and gilt figurehead, looked just like a bewildered woman half lifting her skirts to cross a muddy street under the jeers of bad little boys. That was very much her situation. She knew she was somewhere in the neighborhood of the Virgin, had caught the roar of it, and was asking her way.

Sir Francis Chichester

The hailstones rattled on the skylight like piles of white peas.

Edward H. Dodd, Jr.

Overhead a gray, sloppy sky, around us a gray, sloppy sea.

Charles Landery

. . . the powerful, liverish sea . . .

Frank Wightman

All over the sky the little trade-wind clouds were scattered evenly. There was no break in the pattern; but over the island there was a mound of cumulus. It looked like a sheep in a field of lambs.

Joseph Conrad

He went on board his schooner. She lay white, and as if suspended, in the crepuscular atmosphere of sunset mingling with the ashy gleam of the vast anchorage.

Dennis Puleston

On the third day of calm a change came over the water. We noticed a line on the sea ahead of us. Was it a breeze? But no, as we drew near, we saw it was only a skim of dust. Soon it had closed around us, and on all sides, as far as we could see, stretched a level gray plain. It was dust from the distant deserts of Australia, brought over on a high stratum of wind and then dropped from the heavens like rain. So still was the sea that it did not sink, but settled gently down on the surface in a thick film.

Charles Violet

Land had disappeared, and it seemed a special display for a minute speck in the vastness of sky and water. As soon as the fiery sun dipped below the horizon the western sky turned peach-colored, then orange, and finally a deep rich red. At the same time the sky changed from duck-egg blue to indigo velvet as night came stealing across from the east. The glow in the west faded like red-hot iron cooling. It was all over by 7 o'clock, a warning that long nights were ahead.

Francis Brenton

Sunsets are often pretty in the tropics. One I particularly remember was just east of the islands. The sun had scarcely set when the western half of the sky became pink, then a rose, then a ruby red. The undersides of the few clouds radiated like fire across the sky. The topsides in contrast were a deep valley of charcoal black. It looked as though the entire sky had caught aflame. The scene lasted fully five minutes before it faded. The glow went out in the uppermost clouds, then the lower clouds and horizon dimmed as the color burned away, leaving the sky ashen grey with puffs of charcoal drifting here and there.

Alfred Loomis

. . . let me explain that in the Caribbean Sea we have seen more varieties of clouds and more combinations than the imagination can encompass. I used to cite the region of the Azores as the unrivaled cloud factory of the Western Ocean, but I shall hereafter refer budding meteorologists to the south shore of Cuba.

William Robinson

The squall clouds marched down upon us from the eastern horizon like a disorganized army fleeing the enemy, and a larger mass of them might have as many as a dozen tentacles groping toward the sea at one time, ranging from little ice-cream-cone pendants to full fledged vortices that drew up the sea to the bosum of the cloud and roared out the challenge of their short existence.

Frank Wightman

. . . the homeless clouds . . .

Ernle Bradford

I made myself a cup of tea and went back and sat out in the cockpit. Clouds were beginning to form over the island and I sat and watched the birth of a fair-weather cumulus.

A light haze began to lift out of a valley and, as it drifted, a mist which had been hanging over the nearby hillside slid towards it. An unseen dip in the hill discharged, like a minute gun, a small puff of smoke. The land was beginning to warm, and soon every bank and fold and cave was firing white shells into the air. The cloud thickened and darkened. The wind blew it sideways and, as it rose, it toppled into the shape of an old man's head. After half an hour it was full-grown, and it drifted inland to join the other morning clouds.

Hilaire Belloc

. . . I meet and am made the companion of a great wind.

It is not that this lively creature of God is indeed perfected with a soul; this it would be superstition to believe. It has no more a person than any other of its material fellows, but in its vagary of way, in the largeness of its apparent freedom, in its rush of purpose, it seems to mirror the action of mighty spirit.

Hilaire Belloc

. . . the clouds come bowling up from the horizon, messengers, outriders, or comrades of a gale.

Joshua Slocum

... the short, heaving sea, precursor of the wind which followed on the second day.

Ernle Bradford

"A breeze," she said.

"Thank God."

Between the island ahead of us and the shimmering mainland the water took on the broken silver of fish-scales.

Richard Maury

"It's coming now —the wind! Bear a hand. Light out wingsail, clew out, clew out! She's running eight, she's scudding on her rail, she's dragging her cabin tops! Here it is—the wind!"

Ray Kauffman

Tomorrow, always tomorrow, the wind would come.

Hilaire Belloc

For of all creatures the sea is most various. Though, indeed, there is truth in what a friend said to me about her (or him or it) that we should not blame the sea for moods and perils. The sea (he said) asks for nothing but to be let alone, and lies there and would be forever in peace but for sundry bullies, the moon pulling and the sun hauling and the water swung round headlands by them and over shoals and reefs and the air charging down angrily and disturbing all, till the sea cannot call its soul its own.

Herman Melville

Lord, Lord, that the winds that come from heaven should be so unmannerly! This is a nasty night, lad!

E. A. Pye

But in the end it was the howl of the wind and the snubbing of the chain at night that drove us from this lovely place.

Humphrey Barton

I took over at 0800. Conditions were absolutely shocking: the sort of thing one reads about but does not believe. A wind that has reached a state of senseless fury: a wind that soon numbs one into a dull state of hopelessness: a wind of absolute demon force that piles the sea into unstable, toppling heaps. And with the wind came at frequent intervals, the most blinding rain I have seen. It was impossible to face the wind and open one's eyes ... sea and air had become inextricably mingled.

Hilaire Belloc

Then it is that a man has most to do with the wind, plays with it, coaxes or refuses it, is wary of it all along; yields when he must yield, but comes up and pits himself again against its violence; trains it, harnesses it, calls it if it falls him, denounces it if it will try to be too strong, and in every manner conceivable handles this glorious playmate.

Edward H. Dodd, Jr.

That night the elements, racked by the storm, seemed to have lost all control. The wind sprang up from the west and, blowing a fresh breeze, darted north then south in long baleful gusts. The seas, although quieting rapidly, became more and more confused. It was impossible to do anything with the boat. She hove to first on one tack, then on another and from time to time swung about desperately in a blank calm.

John Masefield

What shocked Cruiser, though he kept his feeling to himself, was the discovery that he was now dealing with the sea. Hitherto, he realized he had dealt with the wind. In all his previous sea service the wrestle had been with the wind, to use it and master it. In all his past at sea he had been conscious of the power and fury of the wind, and had found exhilaration in the roar of a great gale ringing and shrieking in the rigging. Here, though it was blowing hard enough, there was no sense that the wind was the enemy. The real enemy was seething, leaping and appalling water so close at hand. All that waste of tumult was the enemy; and alert and on the clutch and on the pounce. Devils surged up abaft from it, and flung up fingers through the seams; and the teeth of other devils flashed out at the strakes or over the gunwale. As far as the eye could see was a dimness of tossing drab angry devil with grabbing and gleaming tusks and talons, with drift cut off sharp from the wave tops and flung flat with the scoopt scud; with strange sheers and scurries and dives and glides in the boat, which somehow seemed to find her way, guided by the hand of the savage at the helm. There was a strain on the leaning shoulder of white-darkened sail, then a pause, then an urge, then a seething of white along the gunwale and tipping over of more spray, and curses from the drenched men who were trying to sleep, and the drenched men bailing.

M. Edward Haie

. . . we met with very foule weather, and terrible seas, breaking short and high Pyramid wise. The reason whereof seemed to proceede either of hilly grounds high and low within the sea, (as we see hilles and dales upon the land) upon which the seas doe mount and fall: or else the cause proceedeth of diversitie of winds, shifting often in sundry points: al which having power to move the great ocean, which againe is not presently settled, so many seas do encounter together, as there had been diversitie of winds . . .

Psalm 48:7

Thou breakest the ships of Tarshish with an east wind.

Edward H. Dodd, Jr.

At supper time we dicussed the hurricane conditions and decided that all signs, according to Bowditch—a heavy swell, low barometer, and red heavens—were present. After supper a sou'wester, coming up strong made things still more menacing. It seemed eminently important that we do something.

William Robinson

We carried jib and mizzen and she buried her lee deck steadily and groaned and labored like a thing in agony. Hove down so far by the force of the wind she took those crushing blows on her sweetly rounded hull where they lost their destructive force.

Frank Wightman

As the sun rose clear of the horizon I waited for the breeze to come through. That moment, too, had its magic.

Hilaire Belloc

But just as dawn was beginning upon the third day, when it was already so light that the sea looked white against the black sand, and before the first touch of color had made living the edges of the inland hills, a heartening wind from those hills, cool with morning, fresh and heavy, not too strong, a friendly wind, a wind just suited to our course— for it was a point or two north of east—blew down from old Wales upon the sea.

William Robinson

At night, like a slumbering giant of mythology, the trade wind broathed more softly. But with the coming of the sun it heaved a sigh, rolled over, and soon assumed the deeper and more powerful breathing of a man at work.

Richard Baum

. . . sunshine and a sailing breeze . . .

Joseph Conrad

Then just about sunrise we got for an hour an inexplicable, steady breeze right in our teeth. There was no sense in it. It fitted neither with the season of the year, nor with the secular experience of seamen as recorded in books, nor with the aspect of the sky. Only purposeful malevolence could account for it. It sent us traveling at a great pace away from our proper course; and if we had been out on pleasure sailing bent it would have been a delightful breeze, with the awakened sparkle of the sea, with the sense of motion, and a feeling of unwonted freshness. Then all at once, as if disdaining to carry farther the sorry jest, it dropped and died out completely in less than five minutes. The ship's head swung where it listed; the stilled sea took on the polish of a steel plate in the calm.

Joshua Slocum

To know the laws that govern the winds, and to know that you know them, will give you an easy mind on your voyage round the world; otherwise you may tremble at the appearance of every cloud.

Francis Brenton

They were all fine sailing days, but unfortunately they were ideal only for sailing in the wrong direction.

Frank Wightman

. . . Far away in the gloom, pale adder's fangs stabbed viciously at the sea, and the world responded with a menacing growl.

Herman Melville

Thither and thither, on high, glided the snowwhite wings of small speckled birds; these were the gentle thoughts of the feminine air; but to and fro in the deeps, far down in the bottomless blue, rushed mighty Leviathans, swordfish, and sharks; and these were the strong, troubled, murderous thinkings of the masculine sea.

Frank Wightman

. . . small isolated wisps of cloud were scurrying, ragged and pale against the smooth and sultry sky. Beneath them, massive glacial swells were marching in serried ranks from the southern horizon like monsters fleeing before a cataclysm. A scene of violence was being enacted—without a word.

Desmond Holdridge

. . . the elemental symphony of wind and water.

Genesis

. . . and the gathering together of the waters called he seas: and God saw that it was good.

Joseph Conrad

The grayness of the whole immense surface, the wind furrows upon the faces of the waves, the great masses of foam, tossed about and waving, like matted white locks, give to the sea in a gale an appearance of hoary age, lusterless, dull, without gleam, as though it had been created before light itself.

Joseph Conrad

. . . an immensity that receives no impress, preserves no memories, and keeps no reckoning of lives.

Frank Wightman

At sunset it was calm. There was not a breath to frost the metal surface of the sea.

William Robinson

We have noticed a strange phenomenon . . . Each day for a few minutes just at sunrise, and again at sunset, there are much larger seas than during all the rest of the day. They start abruptly, last but a short time, and the sea returns to its former state.

Joshua Slocum

It was my good fortune to enter the sea on the last quarter of the moon, the advantage being that in the dark nights I witnessed the phosphorescent light effect at night in its greatest splendor. The sea, where the sloop disturbed it, seemed all ablaze, so that by its light I could see the smallest articles on deck, and her wake was a path of fire.

Ray Kauffman

The only variant was the phases of the moon, and we eagerly watched that sickle of light fill out and grow rounder each night until the dead full moon extended the horizon line miles beyond the gunwales.

Erling Tambs

Then the horrible outburst would recontinue, fiercer, apparently, and more fiendish than ever. At times the whole sky would be a dense cobweb of lightning, flooding every crack and corner with an abominable brightness, and then again, in the blackness that followed, we would be rushing through wide streaks of dully glowing water, which stood out sharply, without surroundings, without background, like a flood of luminous milk in an empty space. What it was, I cannot tell. Perhaps the phosphorescence caused by billions of microscopic beings, isolated by meeting currents—perhaps only one more among many weird electric phenomena, which added to the indescribable horror of this night. More than once I almost expected the universe to explode.

Dennis Puleston

The breaking tops of the seas glowed phosphorescently; sometimes we thought for a moment they were the lights of ships.

Richard Hughes

The schooner moved just enough for the sea to divide with a slight rustle on her stem, breaking out into a shower of sparks, which lit up also wherever the water rubbed the ship's side, as if the ocean were a tissue of sensitive nerves.

Stanley Smith and Charles Violet

On 27th May dawn crept into the sky with a pallid leer. The sea was a dismal expanse of dull grey, looking rather like an immense sheet of crumpled lead-foil.

William Robinson

. . . an undulating sea that was as smooth as patent leather.

Desmond Holdridge

. . . rolling, yeasty seas . . .

Desmond Holdridge

The winds were not strong, but they were sudden, like feints from a watchful cat. The sea was oily and overstill, as though it held itself back. "It's a weather breeder," Niels pronounced.

Frank Wightman

In the faint sad glimmerings of light the heads of the great tumbling seas were changing from black silhouettes to something that had form. They shouldered their way past like marching dinosaurs. The wind had dropped and the whole scene had lost the excitement of brisk movement. The lesser seas were tumbling about with ponderous indecision.

Rex Clements

. . . the halcyon blue and gold of the Trades and the smoking graybeards of the mighty South.

Erling Tambs

The sea was blue like a dream.

Herman Melville

. . . the watery pastures . . . the wild watery loneliness . . .

Stanley Smith and Charles Violet

. . . a dreary waste.

Hilaire Belloc

The sea in storm is the sea "all out." It is the sea with its personality at the fullest; it is Poseidon angry and shaking the world. But not even the angriest of men or gods has anger for his daily mood. The common hour is serene or dull level enough, and, though it impresses less, such routine of life forms the bulk of it; and indeed much of life is sleep. So with the sea.

Richard Maury

The *Cimba* moved restlessly; the ocean brooded on some first thought.

Frank Wightman

The sea also responds to some terrestrial pulse. At dawn and sunset a small fretful sea will run across the regular sea for about an hour and then subside. It is certainly not the product of any wind system.

Desmond Holdridge

From the spur I could see out across the Atlantic and to my amazement, its face was serene, touched only by the breath of a moderate westerly wind. The outer bay of our fiord was churned by a moderate gale. The inner bay, where we were stranded, was still being tormented by a violent storm.

Ernest K. Gann

For the wind had fallen away to nothing and we were left slopping and banging about in a convulsive, obviously embittered sea. The vast liquid which had been so enchanting only the day before now threw a continuous series of tantrums as if responding to the movements of an undersea monster taken with epilepsy.

Richard Dana

Much has been said of sunrise at sea, but it will not compare with the sunrise on shore . . . there is something in the

first gray streaks stretching along the eastern horizon, and throwing an indistinct light upon the face of the deep, which combines with the boundlessness and unknown depths of the sea around, and gives one a feeling of loneliness, of dread, and of melancholy foreboding, which nothing else in nature can. This gradually passes away as the light grows brighter, and when the sun comes up the ordinary sea day begins.

Hilaire Belloc

What I most love in the sea is its silence: a sentence that may sound strange till it is considered. For the loud noises that a man at sea remembers are not of the sea itself—no, not even in a gale of wind—but of battle between the wind and what it encounters: rigging or the ship's side, or canvas, or the play of a loose rope; the pouring of water taken in over the lee or the strain of timbers. The sea of itself is more reserved in its expression and, if it be alone in its vastness, lives in its own communion.

Because the sea lives (while the land lies inert) we cannot think of it as dumb: nor is it. But it speaks in a veiled fashion as do the oracles of the Gods, whereof it is one, the most universal and the most august of the oracles: and indeed the oracles of which we read were mostly not far from the salt and the air of the waves.

Edward H. Dodd, Jr.

The wind kept up a low hum in the rigging. Every other noise was drowned in the constant swishing of water. Out there on the seas it crashed; on deck it washed in

and out of the scuppers; in the air it slapped and thrashed; below it dripped and spattered. It was everywhere, always insistently noising its presence.

William Robinson

There are no smooth waters at sea.

Richard Maury

The sea, still up-and-down, had fallen slightly.

Stanley Smith and Charles Violet

Almost always there is a certain amount of undulating activity lifting and lowering the most glassy-looking sea.

Frank Wightman

. . . the tramping seas.

Rudyard Kipling

Harvey waked to find the foc'sle door drawn to a crack, and every square inch of the schooner singing its own tune. The black bulk of the cook balanced behind the tiny galley over the glare of the stove, and the pots and pans in the pierced wooden board before it jarred and racketed to each plunge. Up and up the foc'sle climbed, yearning and surging and quivering, and then, with a clear sickle-like swoop, came down into the seas. He could hear the flaring bows cut and squelch, and there was a pause where the divided waters came down on the deck above, like a volley of buckshot. Followed by the wooly sound of the cable in the hawse hole;

and a grunt and squeal of the windlass; a yaw, a punt, and a kick, and the *We're Here* gathered herself together to repeat the motions.

Stanley Smith and Charles Violet

. . . gray skies, dismal sea, and lurch, lurch, bang; lurch, lurch, bang.

Edward H. Dodd, Jr.

The dancing deck demanded acrobats rather than sailors . . .

Stanley Smith and Charles Violet

Only by going into the cabin and lighting the lamps could we escape the oppression of our surroundings.

Joshua Slocum

On May 10 there was a great change in the condition of the sea; there could be no doubt of my longitude now, if any had before existed in my mind. Strange and long-forgotten current ripples pattered against the sloop's sides in grateful music; the tune arrested the ear, and I sat quietly listening to it while the *Spray* kept on her course. By these current ripples I was assured that she was now off St. Roque and had struck the current which sweeps around that cape. The trade winds, we old sailors say, produce this current, which in its course from this point forward, is governed by the coastline of Brazil, Guiana, Venezuela, and, as some would say, by the Monroe Doctrine.

Erling Tambs

Strange! She would not obey the helm.

However, *Teddy* was still moving ahead; she surely had sufficient headway to respond to the rudder, and there was no sea. Here, on the western side of the point the water was almost smooth. Smooth indeed, abominably smooth! Glassy, like the polished surface of a river, where it hastens towards a precipice.

I tried again—drove the tiller hard to leeward, again and again, No response! Consternation seized me: the current had *Teddy!*

Rachel Carson

For the tides were not always as they are today, and as with all that is earthly, their days are numbered. . . . The very movement of the water over the bed of the ocean, over the shallow edges of the continents, and over the inland seas, carries within itself the power that is slowly destroying the tides, for tidal friction is gradually slowing down the rotation of the earth.

Harry Pidgeon

There is a peculiarity in the tides throughout the Society Islands that I noticed first in Papeete Harbor. High tide always occurs at about midday and again at midnight.

Edward H. Dodd, Jr.

All about us the water was behaving in a most peculiar manner, swirling about in little whirlpools, sizzling and bubbling. For a time we thought we had strayed among rocks, but, since the chart showed bold water everywhere, the nervousness was finally diagnosed as tide rips.

Joseph Conrad

"I hear it," said Lingard. "Tide rip, Shaw."

"So I presume, sir. But what a fuss it makes. Seldom heard such a . . ."

On the sea, upon the furtherest limits of vision, appeared an advancing streak of seething foam, resembling a narrow white ribbon, drawn rapidly along the level surface of the water by its two ends, which were lost in the darkness. It reached the brig, passed under, stretching out on each side; and on each side the water became noisy, breaking into numerous and tiny wavelets, a mimicry of an immense agitation. Yet the vessel in the midst of this sudden and loud disturbance remained as motionless and steady as if she had been securely moored between the stone walls of a safe dock. In a few moments the line of foam and ripple running swiftly north passed at once beyond sight and earshot, leaving no trace on the unconquerable calm.

Frank Wightman

A breathless calm and a sky like the trump of doom. Beneath what might have been a sheet of ice blue nylon, a skin of startling sheen, massive swells were crowding in from all points of a circular skyline, and where they met they humped mightily until you expected that shining skin to burst with a great tearing sound.

John Masefield

Now out of the darkness of the storm ahead, such a sea was lifting as they had never seen. The first sight of it was to them as though a low range of hills was moving bodily forward; then the effect changed in their minds to that of a line of crags. It was dark, toothy at the top with fangs, like the body of night below, and moving with a life of its own from somewhere. All there had at once the dreadful feeling that it was alive. How high it was they could not guess, but higher certainly than any wave that any of them had ever seen. It was not like a wave; it was like the Judgement Day advancing, wolfing up all the sea into its power and licking out the sky with its tongue. Cruiser could only gasp to himself, "My God, that's got us." But he had two thoughts: one for his crew, and for his boat. He cried, "Hold on, all," and contrived to get to the steering oar, and hove on it, to keep her bows onto it. It seemed to them that it crackled as it advanced as though it were breaking the air to shreds. It send out forebodings and up-bubblings that broke and wrinkled about them; all the sea seemed to know beforehand of it and to laugh and to writhe. No one of them doubted that it was the end. Perhaps it was the end of the world as well.

Frank Wightman

... Afar in the gloom astern there was a sound we knew too well: a sound somewhere between the immense whisper a big sea makes as it prepares to turn over, and the cracking roar as it does. We both groped hurriedly for something to hold on to as we jerked round to peer astern with wide and wary eyes. Against the faintest silver of the southeastern sky an Andean ridge of black water was marching hugely in the dawn. It was one of the big seas that travel alone: a rogue elephant of the ocean. Its massive head was swaying and tossing with a leisurely deliberation that spoke imperiously to some primitive center in us. And *Wylo* was already soaring up its black precipitous face. As its impending head leaned over her she increased her efforts to mount it. With a creaking groan from all her gear, she leapt again in the darkness—and reached the ridge. For a breathless moment, as we were carried fowward in a flurry of wind, we could see the black depth from which we had climbed, and, on the other side, the one to which we should presently sink. We could also look out over a boundless waste of shouldering seas; their bases as black as the night; their heads all silvered in the frigid light of the dawn. Then her stern dipped steeply; her bowsprit pointed wildly at the paling heavens; and, as she floated dizzily down to the hollow, there was a shattering roar. The mountainous sea broke ahead of her, and thundered away on its passage to the horizon, leaving behind it an acre of dully gleaming foam. Into this field of moon-flowers which had magically bloomed in the darkness *Wylo* lurched wearily—and was surrounded by a fierce hissing of millions of bursting bubbles. In the gloom a disembodied voice exclaimed: "Thank God, there was not a fifty mile an hour wind behind *that* one."

Frank Wightman

And now the day was coming. Far over the sea the shapes of the running swells were passing in slow procession across the face of the rising sun with massive deliberation and indescribable delicacy—throwing their shadows afar. A gigantic peristalsis of the sea over the burning body of the sun; a hidden function of the darkness—secret and withheld—suddenly revealed by the coming of the day. Feathered clouds seen in a long, closing perspective gathered over the sun in a marbled scene. Beneath its opulence, the sea, strangely without color, spread an endless ice-blue vista over which the swells were marching in legions, each bearing a cresset of cold fire.

Joshua Slocum

I was once more alone with myself in the realization that I was on the mighty sea and in the hands of the elements.

Richard Maury

One look at the sea and I knew that this was only the beginning ...

Thor Heyerdahl

We were still not sure of the sea; we were still uncertain whether it would show itself a friend or an enemy in the intimate proximity we ourselves had sought. When, swallowed up by the darkness, we heard the general noise from the sea around us suddenly deafened by the hiss of a roller close by and saw a white crest come groping toward us on a level with the cabin roof, we held on tight and waited uneasily to feel the masses of water smash down over us and the raft. But every time there was the same surprise and relief. The *Kon-Tiki* calmly swung up her stern and rose skyward unperturbed, while the masses of water rolled along her sides.

Joshua Slocum

To face the elements is, to be sure, no light matter when the sea is in its grandest mood. You must then know the sea, and know that you know it, and not forget that it was made to be sailed over.

Edward H. Dodd, Jr.

Although weather, a simple and unpretentious but nevertheless basic element, is, like its prototype bread, spurned by those who easily avoid it, at sea its power, and above all its omnipresence, command an awed respect. On land it must work itself into a typhoon, an earthquake, or a monstrous flood to gain duc adulation, but on the ocean its every whim is reflected by its sycophant the sea.

Samuel Eliot Morison

But nobody has found a substitute for the sweet chuckling of water like the laughter of young girls, that you hear outside the hull while lying in a small yacht's bunk.

Joshua Slocum

Waves dancing joyously across Massachusetts Bay met her coming out of the harbor to dash them into myriads of sparkling gems that hung about her at every surge. The day was perfect, the sunlight clear and strong. Every particle of water thrown into the air became a gem, and the *Spray*, pounding ahead, snatched necklace after necklace from the sea, and as often threw them away. We have all seen miniature rainbows about a ship's prow, but the *Spray* flung out a bow of her own that day, such as I had never seen before. Her good angel had embarked on the voyage; I so read it in the sea.

Ernest K. Gann

Popcorn-like frills of wavelets appeared everywhere on top of the swells.

Joshua Slocum

. . . and roaring seas had turned to gossiping waves that rippled and pattered against her sides as she rolled among them, delighted with their story.

Joshua Slocum

The waves doffed their white caps beautifully to her in the strait that day before the southeast wind.

Thor Heyerdahl

High waves and low waves, pointed waves and round waves, slanting waves and waves on top of other waves.

Hilaire Belloc

I looked to windward and saw the sea tumbling, and a great number of white waves. My heart was still so high that I gave them the names of the waves in the eighteenth Iliad: the long-haired wave, the graceful wave, the wave that breaks on an island a long way off, the sandy wave, the wave before us, the wave that brings good tidings. But they were in no mood for poetry. They began to be great, angry, roaring waves like the chiefs of charging clans . . .

Stanley Smith and Charles Violet

Smaller seas fell and climbed about the backs of their big parents.

William Robinson

And as the wind eased, some of the seas got out of control, becoming what I call "crazy seas," which tower up into a huge pyramid and break quite unpredictably.

Richard Maury

At a quarter of two, the long-awaited-for appeared. The *Cimba* climbed a wave, and looking far to windward, I saw a black shape reared from horizon to horizon.

As we dropped down a slope I knew we were fated to meet the greatest sea I had ever come upon.

We climbed again and I caught sight of its long moving body, already much nearer. This time as the schooner sank, my heart sank with her. She was too small, too thin for the purpose . . . I watched the inflexible purpose, the unfaltering purpose of the wave that now gleamed in one great moonlit plane, now darkened into heaving shadow, disappeared, lifted again, and rolled on and down toward us . . . Then, suddenly the wave was beyond and the *Cimba* was victoriously sinking to the trough. Glancing over shoulder I looked up to the receding form inclining in a tremendous slide of dragging foam to a crest, windy, shining. Already a quarter of a mile away, it made a freakish lunge toward the sky, tumbled, dropped into a smooth fall and, with infinite majesty, glided into oblivion to seaward.

Vito Dumas

. . . in the height of the waves I no longer found awe but amusement . . .

Alain Gerbault

That huge sea had proved itself a "fair weather wave," as the seamen say, for it marked the height of the storm, and forecasted the coming of less boisterous weather.

Rex Clements

The sea was a magnificent sight—an endless succession of swiftly moving hollows and ridges. The mighty, league-long greybeards, stretching out to the horizon, swept carelessly past the ship, shouldering her a point or two off her course, first on one side and then on the other, and pouring over both rails in such cataracts that from aloft the barque looked like a half-tide rock.

Joshua Slocum

I saw now only the gleaming crests of the waves. They showed white teeth while the sloop balanced over them.

Alain Gerbault

. . . here in mid-ocean the seas run shorter and choppier than any I have ever encountered. There are four or five waves to the length of my boat.

Richard Maury

It is not true that a small craft can survive any weather, nor that in storms she is always superior to a large ship. True, hers is the easier task in the average storm, for she rides atop waves the big ship labors through. Such waves, awe-inspiring as they are, have not the broken water at the apex to harm the smaller vessel; but there are others, waves an ocean cruiser may complete her life span without meeting, sufficient in broken water to confound any small craft, and in the end to overwhelm her illusive buoyancy—always her main defense. Yes, fighters though they are, there is a foundering point for all small craft.

Alfred Loomis

I believe implicitly the words of a succession of sea captains that it is only by a miracle that a small boat will live through a hurricane.

Gales, those wise old dogs tell me, are nothing to snivel over; and the smaller you are, down to a certain limit, the better your chance of coming through unharmed. Although the sea builds up into mighty mountains, the waves move in a steady procession, and you can easily live through the chop that rides them. But in a hurricane the wind not only blows with a force sufficient to rip iron hatch covers loose from their fastenings, but the sea comes in from all directions and piles up in a smother that will swamp even the tightest small boat.

Herman Melville

It was a sight full of quick wonder and awe! The vast swells of the omnipotent sea; the surging, hollow roar they made, as they rolled along the gunwales like gigantic bowls in a boundless bowling green; the brief suspended agony of the boat as it would tip for an instant on the knife-like edge of the sharper waves, that almost seemed threatening to cut it in two; the sudden profound dip into the watery glens and hollows; the keen spurrings and goadings to gain the top of the opposite hill; the headlong, sledlike slide down its other side—all these, with the cries of the headsmen and harpooners, and the shuddering gasps of the oarsmen, with the wondrous sight of the *Pequod* bearing down upon her boats with outstretched

sails, like a wild hen after her screaming brood—all this was thrilling.

Joseph Conrad

The boat soared and descended slowly; a region of foam and reefs stretched across her course slashing like a gigantic cauldron; a strong gust of wind drove her straight at it for a moment then passed on and abandoned her to the regular balancing of the swell. The struggle of the rocks forever overwhelmed and emerging, with the sea forever victorious and repulsed, fascinated the man. He watched it as he would have watched something going on within himself . . .

Charles Violet

The night was one of my worst at sea. At 10 o'clock all was quiet, no wind, flat sea. Suddenly I heard the distant roar of breaking water. It rapidly got louder and nearer; I lowered all sail and stood by waiting for the worst. Soon I could make out the phosphorescent gleam from broken wave-crests astern, and in a moment or two they were all around. The *Nova* jumped and tossed about, the waves broke aboard, and I was frightened. The roar passed away, the sea became calm, and so did I. Not a breath of wind the whole time.

Dennis Puleston

. . . Then Al shouted down to us that he saw a line of breakers far ahead. I looked over to where he pointed, but from on deck could see nothing save a rim of flat

horizon. Then, as I stared, it seemed to writhe and grow uneven. Perhaps it was my eyes—but no! All at once a distinct pillar rose up, then fell again; and then another and another, and in a moment I could see them all along the skyline ahead, plumes of dazzling white which climbed into the air and then collapsed, only to be replaced by others. As we drew nearer, they grew to be like a herd of wild horses, galloping furiously across a plain. Sometimes they tossed their heads back and reared exuberantly, then they would bend low to course at swifter pace, until once more their mad spirits sent them bounding high.

But I had to take my eyes from this strange scene, for we were drawing near. Brown patches of coral, close beneath the surface, could be seen on either hand, and there were more ahead of us. We selected a clear spot where the ship would have enough room to swing at her anchor. The lead gave us twelve fathoms, so we let go the hook.

As soon as the engine stopped, we could hear the angry mutter of the breakers.

Ernest K. Gann

The doldrums are the only place I have seen large and very sloppy waves created without a vestige of wind. The waves come from all directions, meet long enough to slap each other in the face, and run off to spread their miserable confusion elsewhere.

Frank Wightman

. . . under her slowly swaying masts, *Wylo* floated in a glittering stillness—waiting for the wind.

Hilaire Belloc

Never are we in a calm but we whine peevishly for wind. What, Dog, would you have the weather cut out for you like a suit of clothes? Is all the universe to arrange itself simply to your convenience, as it does for the very rich—so long as they keep off the sea? Will you not be content with sailing unless just that wind plays which is exactly trimmed for your miserable barque, neither too strong nor too light nor too far forward, so that you have to beat, nor so far aft that you fear a gybe, or pooping from a running sea? Will you never repose in the will of your maker and take things as they come?

Herman Melville

. . . oftentimes tumultuous and bursting sea.

Sir Alec Rose

On some occasions it was so bad I stood by the hatchway in my oilskins and wondered how much more she would take.

Joshua Slocum

In the midst of the gale I could do no more than look on, for what is a man in a storm like this?

Ernest K. Gann

Our voices were little cries against the tumult outside.

Thor Heyerdahl

For five whole days the weather varied between full storm and light gale; the sea was dug up into wide valleys filled with the smoke from foaming gray-blue seas, which seemed to have their backs pressed out long and flat under the onset of the wind. Then on the fifth day the heavens split to show a glimpse of blue, and the malignant, black cloud cover gave place to the victorious blue sky as the storm passed on.

Alec Waugh

A storm at sea is, I am sure, a noble spectacle. The beating of the sea upon one's face, the dashing of the waves across the deck, the spray turned into a rainbow by the sun, the quivering of the ship as trough after trough is breasted; it is all, I am very certain, very fine. But it is rather differently that I have seen it. Ignobly prostrate in my cabin, I have watched through half-seeing eyes my possessions heap themselves into chaos on the floor.

Rex Clements

The latter sat down on the ledge of the lamproom door, pulled off his seaboots and emptied the water out of them.

"Well," said he, "whatd'ye think of a sealife now?"

"Not too much," I replied truthfully, "if it's all like this."

Paddy chuckled. "Why," said he, "if we never

had a bit of a blow the girls would be doing us out of our jobs."

"But surely you'd call this a tempest?"

He shook his head: "There's no such thing as a tempest," said he, "except in hymns and prayer books."

"Well, what would you call it?" I asked, looking at the great foam-crested seas and the dim outline of the reeling barque.

"The hell of a dirty night," said he, and lit his pipe.

Herman Melville

Old Manx sailor: "How the three pines shake! Pines are the toughest sort of tree to live when shifted to any other soil, and here there's none but the crews' cursed clay. Steady, helmsman! steady. This is the sort of weather when brave hearts snap ashore, and keeled hulls split at sea."

William Robinson

For two hundred and fifty miles we sailed in a tremendous leftover swell, through a sea dirty with a scum of volcanic ash. Broken palm boles, coconuts, debris of all sorts, and bits of white-painted wreckage that disclosed the last grand tragedy of some unknown lives, littered the way and spoke eloquently of the recent storm's ferocity.

Edward H. Dodd, Jr.

For a seemingly interminable period we struggled with snarled lines and iron canvas.

Frank Wightman

So the sea won in the end: the sea that owes allegiance to no man: the incorruptible and faithless sea.

Erling Tambs

I can still see that weird intensified picture of the deck asplash with the downpour, which came in hissing gushes, of the shiny black rigging and of the straining gray canvas, streaming with driving rain.

Richard Baum

When the ports and the plexiglass in the scuttle turned gray with morning, the light filtering into the cabin picked out the details of that wretchedness which is a small boat's in a heavy gale. Now, as well as hearing and feeling the gale, we saw each other's dirty bearded faces, the wet and salt-caked oilskins and safety belts piled on a damp bunk aft, the sloshing pool of water on the cabin sole, dirty spoons and cups chocked in the tiny sink, damp blankets around damp men asleep.

Charles Landery

Before raising sail we checked the running rigging, set up shrouds, straightened the fo'c'sle where drawers had been wrenched open and our clothes had had a free-for-all with pots, pans, seaboots and my typewriter; even the most aristocratic of our books had joined the rioting mob.

Desmond Holdridge

Now the wind came from the south, a gentle wind. We set the spinnaker. But the sea had raised itself against us and resolved its dissonances into a consistent swell that rolled upon us from the north by east. Then it came on to blow.

The great spinnaker, bellying like an old maid's petticoat in a gale, lifted and fought, straining at its slender sheet and lashings. Its boom jaw cracked. No matter; it still held.

By ten in the morning we had stowed it.

By noon the wind had risen to half a gale; still we held on; full sail.

Edward H. Dodd, Jr.

Hove to under foresail alone, the *Chance* was in high spirits. Since she rode about four points off the wind, the seas came broad on the starboard bow—great brutes of seas forty and fifty feet high, with huge bodies and foaming crests. But she rose and fell to them with a steadiness and lack of strain that filled us with pride. Once in a great while a clump of green water accompanied by a shower of spray would jump on board. Either the wave had been deformed or a gust had sent her off too far.

From the top of the mast the sea was a glorious sight. The whole ocean seemed to have picked up its baggage and was rushing helter-skelter to the other side of the earth. The wind shrieked through the shrouds and plucked at the furled topsail. In eccentric leaps and swirls you were now almost in a wave and now in a low squall cloud.

Frank Wightman

These thrusts of wind were too short in duration to use; they were just blows from a thug's fist.

Jack London

The *Reindeer* dashed by their stern, heeling over till the cabin windows were buried, and so close that it appeared she must run them down. But a freak of the waters lurched the two crafts apart. Red Nelson, seeing that the maneuver had miscarried, instantly instituted another. Throwing the helm hard up, the *Reindeer* whirled on her heel, thus swinging her overhanging mainboom closer to the *Dazzler*. French Pete was the nearest, and the opportunity could last no longer than a second. Like a cat he sprang, catching the footrope with both hands. Then the *Reindeer* forged ahead, dipping him into the sea at every plunge. But he clung on, working inboard every time he emerged, till he dropped into the cockpit as Red squared off to run down to leeward and repeat the maneuver . . .

The *Reindeer* had jibed over and was ploughing back at breakneck speed, careening at such an angle that it seemed she must surely capsize. It was a gallant sight. Just then the storm burst in all its fury, the shouting wind flattening the ragged crests till they boiled. The *Reindeer* dipped from view behind an immense wave. The wave rolled on, but the next moment, where the sloop had been, the boys noted with startled eyes only the angry waters! Doubting they looked a second time. There was no *Reindeer*. They were alone on the torn crest of the ocean!

"Sailed her clean under, and with the ballast she carried, went straight to the bottom," Frisco gasped.

Rockwell Kent

Suddenly there's but one thing to do; and quick. We heave her to. Braced in the chains, dipped in green water to his waist, lifted all streaming out of it—to plunge again, the mate secures the jib. The mainsail fights us like a living thing gone mad; four thousand pounds of fury against thirty fingers. Inch by inch we win, and lash it tight.

Arthur Ransome

But we got little rest that night. The wind increased to a gale, and, sheltered though we were, the current kept *Racundra* across both wind and swell, with the result that she rolled me out of my bunk . . . sent things adrift that we had considered fast till doomsday . . . and used every loose thing in the ship to make a noise like a Negro band. It was impossible to sleep. All that could be done was to sit on the bunks, wedge one's knees firmly against the centerboard case, and count how many rolls *Racundra* could accomplish in a minute.

Rex Clements

"My God, she's gone!" said the bosun.

I glanced at the fore t'gallant yard, motionless against the sky. It was the last thing I ever expected to see. Nothing of the ship was visible, save the deck of the fok'sle head, like a lonely rock. Another bucket of water would have done for us.

For a few seconds we lay, as it were, stricken and aswoon. Another white-lipped monster was rolling up astern, but before it reached us the gallant old barque seemed to make a mighty effort. She quivered and labored heavily up, throwing the water from her main deck and lifting her streaming bows. As the roller swung down on us, her stern rose slowly to it, and it surged on and under, lifting the barque on its shoulders, spouting cataracts from every port.

The worst was over . . .

Herman Melville

The occasional phosphorescence of the yeasting sea cast a glare upon their uplifted faces, as a night fire in a populous city lights up the panic-stricken crowd . . . The ship's bows were now butting, battering, ramming, and thundering over and upon the head seas, and with a horrible wallowing sound our whole hull was rolling in the trough of the foam. The gale came athwart the deck, and every sail seemed bursting with its wild breath.

Hilaire Belloc

. . . and I remember thinking as I took the helm again amidst the turmoil of something I had seen written once of Portland Race: "The sea jumps up and glares at you."

Richard Maury

On the morning of the next day we again set canvas against the blow. The fisherman put her heart into the scheme, shattering a staggering, lumpy sea, wetting her sails in a blunt attempt at headway. Her gear strained as she swung up and into the drive of water, her masts over strained as she swung up and into the drive of water, her masts over to leeward, while the gentle curved bows hammered into broken, streaming waves. For an hour she plunged west with trembling luffs, biting into sea after sea in a wet, uphill tack. Then, in a rising force nine gale, for the eighth time since departure, we hove her to, bringing the total number of hours in this position to over a hundred and thirty. Through all of a day, in which ponderous ghosts of seas loomed from out of the rain-light to moan, burst, and disappear—endlessly—and through a night of flying rain the schooner lay with her head under her wing. We, her two attendants, took care of her few wants, standing vigil around the clock.

Richard Maury

Into my face drove an eighty-mile wind, freezing, and crying, and sweeping down from the far-off ice fields. The sky was naked, almost blue, and near its zenith a cold last-quarter moon shone light onto the crests of black waves, of waves traveling at high speed, now resembling tall cliffs rather than mountains; cliffs formed by cutlass-like slashes of wind, ripped into storm patterns, now of a solid un-giving black, now glowing in great fissures of infu-riated silver, and sounding iron-like above the roaring wind.

My back was to the most of the *Cimba,* to her bows that were working every moment, to her bare masts resembling stunted arms raised against the night. I saw only that small area of afterdeck, the paint work beaded with frozen water picked out by the moon, the stiff parts of ropes, wet and shining on the narrow planking.

Erling Tambs

Rain came down in torrents. Repeatedly it drowned the riding light, until I abandoned the attempt of relighting it. Only the binnacle lamp was burning, throwing its faint rays on the cockpit coaming, on a hand that was groping for a sheet or on a shining black oilskin coat.

And then the tempest broke loose. Crackling lightning bore down from out of greenish-brown poisonous-looking clouds, that crowded low above the phosphorescent masthead.

Frank Wightman

Then a black bag of rain would empty itself over us and wash off the salt.

Edward H. Dodd, Jr.

As dawn sneaked in behind a dense blanket of greasy black clouds, the water appeared in lumbering chunks. Rain fused the gray sky and leaden sea into one heaving, colorless mass, and the boat seemed to be tossing about in an aqueous element, without form or color, which had no remote resemblance to any part of the world.

Rex Clements

The Doldrums had us in their grip. We lay helpless on an oily sea, the spars sticking up idly into the still air. The heat grew terrific; bare iron was too hot to touch and the pitch bubbled out of the seams between the planking and stuck to our bare feet. From the yards the sails hung listlessly in heavy folds; we hauled the uselessly-flapping mainsail up and listened to the grind and rasp of the parrels as she rocked to some imperceptible underrunning swell.

It was exasperating. The man at the wheel leaned idly over the spokes, for she had lost steerage way; the halfdeck was like a furnace and our only amusement was scanning the face of the brazen heavens and whistling for a wind.

At times the sky would become overcast, a black thundercloud overspreading everything and then, without a moment's warning, down came the deluge! The clouds seemed to collapse, the rain fell in sheets and torrents, with such intensity that it was impossible to see more than a few yards, and the sea gave off a continual hissing roar under the violence of the downpour.

Then, as suddenly at it began, the rain stopped, the clouds rolled away and the sun shone down again with undiminished vehemence upon our drenched and steaming barque.

William Robinson

As I sat below at the table plotting my noon position, I suddenly had a feeling that something was wrong. A glance through the companionway quickly changed my uneasiness to alarm, for there, directly behind and coming rapidly up to us, still in the first throes of birth, hung the largest waterspout we had ever seen. Its long black tentacle, suspended from the lowering tumultuous mother cloud, writhed and groped half-way to the sea, like the arm of a Gargantuan octopus seeking a grip upon an enemy. Our eyes clung to it fascinated as it reached down and down, sometimes retreating but always growing again. There became audible the distant roaring or sighing sound that first warns of approach to a waterfall when traveling downstream in a canoe. Underneath, at the surface of the sea, the sympathetic disturbance suddenly became more intense as the incipient whirl revolved faster and faster, throwing off bits of foam and loose water. A distinct bulge in the surface appeared, as if sucked up by the parched column above, and rose higher every second. The spray and foam now began to be snatched upward, and before our eyes was formed a vapory connection with the descending tube, linking cloud and sea. The connection established, the base grew larger and more violent as it received the too heavy particles thrown away from the column by centrifugal force. The noise and tumult grew as the hissing of the column, the cry of the wind, and the crashing of the waters blended to form a fearsome roar. Augmented by more and more water the lower half suddenly reached maturity and groped out to clasp hands with the upper, and the sea and sky were united by a spinning weaving pillar of water.

Frank Wightman

With a spasmodic rattle of heavy drops on the deck, the rain swished away with a great sigh over the sea.

John MacGregor

A good wetting can be calmly borne if it is dashed in by a heavy sea in honest sailing, or is poured down upon you from a black cloud above . . .

Richard Maury

Although clouds were lighted by "devil's smiles" of sunlight piercing their wetness, the weather became dense, visibility was lost, a confused sea started to throw up, and before long a rainy "nose-ender" was wailing over the bows.

Unknown

When you see a squall with dark fingers, and when those fingers are working, it's time to get the canvas off.

Edward H. Dodd, Jr.

Outside, chaos had taken complete possession, a screaming, crashing chaos of which you were no longer an onlooker out an integral part of the loose elements.

Then this strange age passed slowly into another; one of weary subsidence with all life gone out of it and only a heaving exhausted sea and a stunned colorless sky. The gale faltered as the squalls became more and more disorganized. There came a final desperate thrust at noon, and suddenly the storm was gone.

Edward H. Dodd, Jr.

The squalls came almost instantaneously from nowhere, blotting out everything with their curtains of rain, and windy enough to necessitate the removal of the jib, whose physique was too worn to withstand them. One of unusual severity came across the water, beating the seas flat and hissing loudly as it swept along. Sandy and I ran to the bowsprit and had just got the jib down, still unlashed, when it struck. A blinding cascade and buffeting wind whipped Sandy's shirt over his head and tore down his slicker pants. While I was laughing gleefully at his struggles, a large wave bounced over to reinforce the rain and sent me into the scuppers. The downfall was so intense that it was difficult to tell whether we were breathing air or water . . .

Alain Gerbault

Within twenty minutes after getting under way a squall struck the cutter and tore to ribbons the staysail that I had been working on for ten solid hours. It was gone in a twinkling.

Joseph Conrad

Lingard crossed over to the port side, and looked steadily at the sooty mass of approaching vapors. After a moment he said curtly, "Brace up for the port tack, Mr. Shaw," and remained silent, with his face to the sea. A sound, sorrowful and startling like the sigh of some immense creature, traveling across the starless space, passed above the vertical and lofty spars of the motionless brig.

It grew louder, then suddenly ceased for a moment and the taut rigging of the brig was heard vibrating its answer in a singing note to this threatening murmur of the winds. A long and slow undulation lifted the level of the waters, as if the sea had drawn a deep breath of anxious suspense. The next minute an immense disturbance leaped out of the darkness upon the sea, kindling upon it a livid clearness of foam, and the first gust of the squall boarded the brig in a stinging flick of rain and spray. As if overwhelmed by the suddenness of the fierce onset, the vessel remained for a second upright where she floated, shaking with tremendous jerks from trucks to keel; while high up in the night the invisible canvas was heard rattling and beating about violently.

Then, with a quick double report, as of heavy guns, both topsails filled at once and the brig fell over swiftly on her side. Shaw was thrown headlong against the skylight, and Lingard, who had encircled the weather rail with his arm, felt the vessel under his feet dart forward smoothly, and the deck become less slanting—the speed of the brig running off a little now, easing the overturning strain of the wind upon the distended surfaces of the sails. It was only the fineness of the little vessel's lines and the perfect shape of her hull that saved the canvas, and perhaps the spars, by

enabling the ready craft to get way upon herself with such lightning-like rapidity. Lingard drew a long breath and yelled jubilantly at Shaw who was struggling up against wind and rain to his captain's side.

"She'll do. Hold on everything."

Shaw tried to speak. He swallowed great mouthfulls of tepid water which the wind drove down his throat. The brig seemed to sail through undulating waves that passed swishing between the masts and swept over the decks with the fierce rush and noise of a cataract. From every spar and every rope a ragged sheet of water streamed flicking to leeward. The overpowering deluge seemed to last for an age; became unbearable—and, all at once, stopped. In a couple of minutes the shower had run its length over the brig and now could be seen like a straight gray wall, going away into the night under the fierce whispering of dissolving clouds. The wind eased. To the northward, low down in the darkness, three stars appeared in a row, leaping in and out between the crests of waves . . .

Herman Melville

After leaving the latitude of the Cape, we had several storms of snow; one night a considerable quantity laid upon the decks, and some of the sailors enjoyed the juvenile diversion of snowballing.

Harry Pidgeon

The study of the weather, when one is depending on the wind, is a subject of never-ending interest, and one watches

the approach of the last of a thousand rain squalls with as much interest as the first.

Edward H. Dodd, Jr.

. . . the squalls as they came received all the abuse we had in us. Vile black things they were, hurling their ragged deformed shapes upon us with a vicious leer. It was inconceivable that the wind could be added to, but when a squall struck it shrieked more shrilly in the rigging and sent more stinging deluges of rain and spray.

Rex Clements

. . . a Cape Horn sea . . . the highwater mark of elemental majesty. Terrific though it is it inspires no fear. The terror and the majesty of it blot out all that . . . One merely triumphs in the exhibition of such stupendous power and sublimity. Death itself would be a small thing in such surroundings.

Desmond Holdridge

The sea was emptier of icebergs than it had been at any time since the Strait of Belle Isle. Sometimes we had been able to count sixty and seventy giants at one time; now there were a bare dozen on the solemn sea.

Frank Wightman

Then one day you will sight the top of an immense cloud that lumbers into the sky astern. Its fantastic mountain peaks, headlands, and bays, make it look like some cragged and beetling island of the skies. It will go on rising in the heavens until its base comes into view, and that base will be dark and solid-looking as rock. Into a world whose order of creation is light, graceful, and swift, those bloated things come like a winged monster of the past. By its advent you will know that the big cumuli, in whose hearts are violence and confusion, are making a raid into the territory of the Trade Wind.

Long before it reaches you, you may hear a sound like cannon balls being rolled across a ball-room floor, with hot scribbles of lightning jerking about in the body of the cloud. If it passes over you in that state your lot will be bad enough, but if, before it reaches you, it spills long skeins of gray silk that waver down to the sea, while the whole base of the cloud arches up in the middle, with a tattered black wrack hanging from it, you are for it.

Mark Twain

They sung "Jolly, jolly raftsman's the life for me," with a rousing chorus, and then they got to talking about differences betwixt hogs and their different kinds of habits; and next about women and their different ways; and next about the best ways to put out houses that was afire; and next about what ought to be done with the Injuns; and next about what a king had to do, and how much he got; and next about how to make cats fight; and next about what to do when a man has fits; and next about differences betwixt clearwater rivers and muddywater ones. The man they called Ed said the muddy Mississippi was wholesomer to

drink than the clear water of the Ohio; he said if you let a pint of this yaller Mississippi water set-tle, you would have about a half to three-quarters of an inch of mud in the bottom, according to the stage of the river, and then it warn't no better than Ohio water—what you wanted to do was to keep it stirred up—and when the river was low, keep mud on hand to put in and thicken the water up the way it ought to be.

The Child of Calamity said that was so; he said there was a nutritiousness in the mud, and a man that drunk Mississippi water could grow corn in his stomach if he wanted to. He says:

"You look at the graveyards; that tells the tale. Trees won't grow worth shucks in a Cincinnati graveyard, but in a Saint Louis graveyard they grow upwards of eight hundred foot high. It's all on account of the water the people drink before they laid up. A Cincinnati corpse don't richen the soil any."

Mark Twain

Now when I had mastered the language of this water and had come to know every trifling feature that bordered the great river as familiarly as I know the letters of the alphabet, I had made a valuable acquisition. But I had lost something, too. I had lost something which could never be restored to me while I lived. All the grace, the beauty, the poetry had gone out of the majestic river! I still keep in mind a certain wonderful sunset which I witnessed when steamboating was new to me. A broad expanse of the river was turned to blood; in the middle distance the red hue brightened into gold, through

which a solitary log came floating, black and con-spicuous; in one place a long, slanting mark lay sparkling upon the water; in another the surface was broken by boiling, tumbling rings that were as many-tinted as an opal; where the ruddy flush was faintest, was a smooth spot that was covered with graceful circles and radiating lines, ever so deli-cately traced; the shore on our left was densely wooded, and the somber shadow that fell from this forest was broken in one place by a long, ruffled trail that shone like silver; and high above the forest wall a clean-stemmed dead tree waved a single leafy bough that glowed like a flame in the unobstructed splendor that was flowing from the sun. There were graceful curves, reflected images, woody heights, soft distances; and over the whole scene, far and near, the dissolving lights drifted steadily, enriching it every passing moment with new marvels of coloring.

I stood like one bewitched. I drank it in, in a speechless rapture. The world was new to me, and I had never seen anything like this at home. But as I have said, a day came when I began to cease from noting the glories and the charms which the moon and the sun and the twilight wrought upon the river's face; another day came when I ceased altogether to note them. Then, if that sunset scene had been repeated, I should have looked upon it without rapture, and should have commented upon it, inwardly, after this fashion: This sun means that we are going to have wind tomorrow; that floating log means that the river is rising, small thanks to it; that slanting mark on the water refers to a bluff reef which is going to kill somebody's steamboat one of these nights, if it keeps on stretching out like that; those tumbling "boils" show a dissolving bar and a changing channel there; the lines and circles in the slick water over yonder are a warning that that troublesome place is shoaling up dangerously; that silver streak in the shadow of the forest is the "break" from a new snag and he has located himself in the very best place he could have found to fish for steamboats; that tall dead tree, with a single living branch, is not going to last long, and then how is a body ever going to get through this blind place at night without the friendly old landmark?

No, the romance and the beauty were all gone from the river. All the value any feature of it had for me now was the amount of usefulness it could furnish toward compassing the safe piloting of a steamboat. Since those days I have pitied doctors from my heart. What does the lovely flush in a beauty's cheek mean to a doctor but a "break" that ripples above some deadly disease? Are not all her visible charms sown thick with what are to him the signs and symbols of hidden decay? Does he ever see her beauty at all, or doesn't he simply view her professionally, and comment upon her unwholesome condition all to himself? And doesn't he sometimes wonder whether he has gained most or lost most by learning his trade?

E. A. Pye

These things interested me. I was beginning, after five months of voyaging, to look at things with a seaman's eye. I would find myself thinking, "This is a good place, sheltered from this and that direction; the bottom is clear of dangers." The land, its beauty of line and the grace of its buildings became of secondary importance.

The Sailor

To many persons the life of the sailing man appears fraught with romance and adventure. And so it is. Many sailors, however, are rather pragmatic and even conservative by nature. These traits, though necessary to ensure a happy and safe voyage, are balanced by a bigness and freshness of outlook as well as a sense of humor both ribald and puckish. The excerpts that follow are chosen to provide a balanced insight into the psyche of the generally virtuous small boat sailor.

Joshua Slocum

Then was the time to uncover my head, for I sailed alone with God.

Woodes Rogers

We allow'd Liberty of Conscience on board our floating Commonwealth to our Prisoners, for there being a Priest in each Ship, they had the great Cabbin for their Mass, whilst we us'd the Church of England Service over them on the Quarter-deck, so that the Papists here were the Low Church-men.

Alec Waugh

We picture the sailor's life in terms of adventure and romance. We think of the sailor as someone who has seen life widely; but in point of fact there is no class of person who is less familiar with what is held ordinarily to constitute life. In consequence, he retains that freshness, almost amounting to an innocence of outlook, that is his particular and peculiar charm.

William Robinson

Such is the innocence and perennial optimism of the sailor.

Charles Landery

. . . sailors were in the cafes exercising their second profession, rhetoric.

Herman Melville

Aye! Aye! we sailors sail not in vain. We expatriate ourselves to na-

tionalize with the universe; and in all our voyages round the world, we are still accompanied by those old circumnavigators, the stars, who are shipmates and fellow-sailors of ours—sailing in the ocean blue, as we on the azure main. Let genteel generations scoff at our hardened hands and fingernails tipped with tar—did they ever clasp truer palms than ours? Let them feel of our sturdy hearts, beating like sledgehammers in those hot smithies, our bosums; with their amber-headed canes, let them feel of our generous pulses, and swear that they go off like thirty-two pounders.

Oh, give me again the rover's life—the joy, the thrill, the whirl! Let me feel thee again, old sea! let me leap into thy saddle once more. I am sick of these terra firma toils and cares; sick of the dust and reek of town. Let me hear the clatter of hailstones on icebergs, and not the dull tramp of these plodders, plodding their dull way from their cradles to their graves. Let me sniff thee up, sea-breeze! and whinny in thy spray. Forbid it, sea gods! intercede for me with Neptune, O sweet Amphitrite that no dull clod may fall on my coffin! Be mine the tomb that swallowed up Pharaoh and all his hosts; let me lie down with Drake where he sleeps in the sea.

Joshua Slocum

I sat long on the starlit deck that night, thinking of ships, and watching the constellations on their voyage.

Vito Dumas

"Lord, be lavish of Thy Peace and guide to all the ports of the

world those sailors who are orphaned in the immensity of the sea."

Rex Clements

Whatever the seafarer does, he does largely. His ways are not the ways of sheltered folk ashore, nor are his morals theirs, nor his creeds. Talking of a shipmate behind his back is a far blacker vice than insobriety. And if accepted creeds sound thin at sea and catechisms of small importance, the sailor is at heart no less religious a man—and no worse a one.

Alfred Loomis

These devout Baptists, indifferent alike to the clicking cameras of the white folks and the crude oil which floats on the surface of the river, underwent their services near the mouth of a sanctimonious old sewer to westward of the *Hippocampus,* chanting continuously a stirring baptismal hymn. So captivating were both refrain and music that, waiting to cast off mooring lines, we succumbed to their lure, and now we weigh anchor and haul halyards to the newest of sea chanties:

Whosoever will, let him come,
Let him come,
And drink of the river of life.

Herman Melville

Besides these topmen, who are always made up of active sailors, there are sheet anchor men—old veterans all—whose place is on the forecastle; the foreyard, anchors, and all the sails on the bowsprit being under their care.

They are an old weather-beaten set, culled from the most experienced men on board. These are the fellows that sing you "The Bay of Biscay, Oh!" and "Here a sheer hulk lies poor Tom Bowling!" ... who, when ashore, at an eating house call for a bowl of tar and a biscuit. These are the fellows who spin interminable yarns about Decatur, Hull, and Bainbridge; and carry about on their persons bits of Old Ironsides as Catholics do the wood of the true cross. These are the fellows that some officers never pretend to damn, however much they may anathematize others. These are the fellows that it does your soul good to look at; hearty old members of the Old Guard; grim sea grenadiers, who, in tempest time, have lost many a tarpaulin overboard. These are the fellows whose society some of the youngster midshipmen much affect; from whom they learn their best seamanship; and to whom they look up as veterans; if so be, that they have any reverence in their souls, which is not the case with midshipmen.

Charles Landery

In the fo'c'sle, Peric lay beneath a patchwork quilt, his mother's parting gift, and moaned. His body flowed; it piled into a boneless mound; it subsided into a quivering slab. Occasionally, it became almost erect as he clawed his way up the ladder to the deck, his stomach and legs racing each other to see which could reach the bulwarks first.

Sir Francis Chichester

After dealing for a long time with the basic facts of life, such as survival, one's values change completely as to what should, or should not, be taken seriously. To the question, "When were your spirits at their lowest ebb?" the obvious answer seemed to be, "When the gin gave out."

Ernest K. Gann

The San Francisco waterfront abounds in salty characters many of whom have an easy command of nautical terminology, a vast knowledge of all that pertains to ships and the sea, and practically no experience beyond the end of the dock.

Stanley Smith and Charles Violet

We now come to an entry in Stanley's log of 11th July. It reads:

"We both feel we are honored with the kindliness and fatherly interest of Joshua Slocum. We draw no conclusions from this. We just feel it is so and are grateful. We do our best to act like true seamen and be efficient because there is a very definite desire to please the Old Man and to merit his interest and sympathy."

... it gave a feeling of companionship, rather like having a close friend at hand. We both sensed it independently. At the change of watch after sundown, on the day of the strange entry in the log, one said to the other: "You know, I've had a strange feeling that . . ."

"That old Slocum is with us?" interrupted the other.

"Yes."

Joshua Slocum

I was *en rapport* now with my surroundings.

Frank Wightman

The clouds; the sea; the face of the sky; the weather, were things that were rapidly taking on personality. I looked into the face of nature as the courtier looks into the face of the tyrant. I was not far from the primitive who gives names and character to these forces. Sometimes I was curiously aware of the steady pressure of something primitive—something that undermined character. Something that favored the growth of the primitive virtues; virtues that know only one duty: duty to oneself. The top of an overtaking sea licked over my hands with a black slobber. Startled, I jerked back into the cockpit.

Desmond Holdridge

There was no barometer aboard, but we had acquired a sensitivity to atmospheric pressures which told us when it had fallen. Most people feel the barometer without realizing it, for the human spirit is depressed with it. I have little doubt but that a graphic representation of suicide incidence could be related to a curve showing barometric pressure. There would, of course, be the broad relationship between suicide and economic conditions, but the variations within the economic control could, I feel sure, be shown to follow the rise and fall of the barometer. When a man who is in good digestion and without severe business and social difficulties suddenly becomes impressed with the inconstancy of his friends and the vindictiveness of his enemies, he can usually tap his barometer and discover it has fallen two tenths.

Joshua Slocum

There was no end of companionship; the very coral reefs kept me company, or gave me no time to feel lonely, which is the same thing . . .

Hilaire Belloc

. . . I soon found it useless, and pinned my soul to the tiller. Every sea following caught my helm and battered it. I hung on like a stout gentleman, and prayed to the seven gods of the land.

Joshua Slocum

. . . no man, I think, could stand or sit and steer a vessel round the world: I did better than that; for I sat and read my books, mended my clothes, or cooked my meals and ate them in peace. I had already found that it was not good to be alone, and so I made companionship with what there was around me, sometimes with the universe and sometimes with my own insignificant self; but my books were always my friends, let fail all else.

Richard Maury

. . . her crew slowly regaining a coordination with her motions, limbering backs and shoulder muscles, for no matter how long one has sailed, the first few sea days finds one imperfectly adjusted to the rhythms, the confining spaces of a ship.

E. A. Pye

It amused me to see how Bob and Anne used to come up time after time, going through the same small actions peculiar to each. Bob always looked at the compass and asked me the course. He then settled himself comfortably in the well and looked to windward. Anne's first glance would be at the hounds. Having seen that there were no ropes foul of blocks and that the gaff jaws were swinging as they should, she would look all round the horizon. Finally she would ask the course and sometimes look at the compass. As to the skipper, the crew swore that he had eyes in the back of his head and had been born saying, "You're off your course!"

John MacGregor

Vigorous health is at the bottom of the enthusiastic enjoyment of yachting; but in a common sailor's life sleep is not a regular thing as we have it on shore, and perhaps that staid glazy and sedate-looking eye, which a hard-worked seaman usually has, is really caused by broken slumber. He is never completely awake, but he is never entirely asleep.

Frank Wightman

To sit in the rain on a small deck, on a dark and squally night at sea, when one's only diversion is vomiting . . .

Joshua Slocum

He was not afraid of a capful of wind.

E. A. Pye

Anne sat behind me, wedged in a coil of rope. She said she couldn't bear being below, listening to the noise of water rushing past the coppered hull, the creaking and groaning of timbers, and the violence of the ship's motion.

Richard Maury

. . . Dombey and I separated until the time came to go on. Although we often said that only in port did we come to know one another, we needed a holiday to release us from the intimacy imposed by the cruise. Men or boys are seldom emotionally balanced to stand the strain of sharing interminable solitude. Hermits do not wander in pairs, and it is one thing to spend a week in close company with a friend, quite another, a month, a year. Emotions, temperaments, psychological balances often break cruises at an early stage. They are the forces behind the scene, forces that above all others must be mastered in voyaging.

Frank Wightman

Our bodies were tired; our bottoms were blistered; our souls were sick.

John MacGregor

At this time I felt lonely, exceedingly lonely and helpless, also sleepy, feverish, discontented, and miserable. The lonely feeling came only twice more in the voyage; the other bad feelings never again.

Herman Melville

. . . To a common sailor, the living on board . . . is like living in a market; where you can dress on the doorsteps and sleep in the cellar. No privacy can you have; hardly one moment's seclusion. It is almost a physical impossibility, that you can ever be alone. You dine at a vast table d'hote; sleep in commons, and make your toilet where and when you can. There is no calling for a mutton chop and a pint of claret by yourself; no selecting of chambers for the night; no hanging of pantaloons over the back of a chair; no ringing your bell of a rainy morning, to take your coffee in bed. It is something like life in a large manufactory. The bell strikes to dinner, and hungry or not, you must dine.

Edward H. Dodd, Jr.

Joe, after rummaging in the hold, emerges with needle, palm, and sail twine to patch a rip in the staysail. Tom, now that we are at sea, is released from the engine, and seizes the opportunity to tabulate the flowers and plants he collected at Galapagos. Alec, after vainly searching the sky for a possible landscape, decides to catch up on his diary. Skip is writing the log while Clymer with an open book on his lap strokes his elegant moustache and makes caustic remarks about the red hairs in Skip's.

John MacGregor

We know a hardy canoeist who said he would not marry unless she could "pull bow oar," and it must be a great addition to the family hearth when the help-meet can "mind her luff."

John Hersey

"Ha!" the pilot cried. "He'll find a new way for a rock to make love to a boat."

"And the children of this love will be more pilots for the New Rapids—with rock heads and cypress bottoms!"

John MacGregor

For this purpose we rowed the yawl into a quiet little river, and lashed her alongside a neat schooner, whose captain, wife and children and little dog "Lady" were soon great friends, for they were courteous people as might be expected in a respectable vessel; it is generally so.

John MacGregor

Here we found the *Onyx,* an English-built yacht, but owned by M. Charles, one of the few Frenchmen to be found who really seems to *like* yachting; plenty of them *affect* it.

Richard Maury

Dombey, Taggart, and I, despite our poor start, came to work satisfactorily together. The one solid bunk, along with a collapsible canvas one, sufficed; there was an extra hand for tight weather, and short four-hour watches for us all. But perhaps a three-man crew is not a combination. Two may side against one, destroying the delicate balance of the unit, a balance that once lost is seldom retrieved. Then, one may see a thing one way, a million men may see it exactly the same but invariably three will see it differently. And again, a vessel that may be handled by two should not have a third, for there should be nothing superfluous, left over, unused—not even manpower.

Over-manning may easily ruin a voyage. A crew, demoralized by idleness, lose the zest of the venture and often dissipate the fine sea watches with noise, lending confusion where silence is a virture.

Richard Maury

So, one day in early September, we got underway for the Kandavu Group, forty miles due south, carrying a borrowed tender over the stern, small amounts of trade tobacco, kava root, and two guests, young men of the town, to ease that inevitable strain known at close quarters . . .

Edward H. Dodd, Jr.

After five days of hilarity, we were almost ready to set out to sea again.

William Robinson

Most long voyages in small yachts seem to be continually marred by crew troubles. Extended cruising by two or more amateurs seems invariably to lead to trouble, while the same thing seems to occur when the owner sails with a paid crew of two or more . . .

Edward H. Dodd, Jr.

With head thrust forward and mouth drawn down he belligerently scans the horizon, sniffs the wind, and goes amidships for a water bucket. Wrapping the rope around one hand, he chucks the bucket over, is jerked forward, and with a mighty heave swings the bucket back on deck. With legs wide apart the water is lifted on high as a circus performer would lift a huge dumbbell. The cascade flattens out a rumpled mop of hair and crashes down to the deck. Next soap is vigorously applied, leaving a few chalky streaks on his shining skin. Three more bucketfuls complete the bath. As a cleansing process it has been a futile undertaking, but the performer now looks normal and is able to speak. Others follow until, between seven-thirty and eight, depending on the complexity of the cooking, the breakfast bell rings.

Joshua Slocum

. . . thin as a reef point.

Joshua Slocum

I once knew a writer who, after saying beautiful things about the sea, passed through a Pacific hurricane, and he became a changed man.

Stanley Smith and Charles Violet

An amusing little incident occurred one day as we were walking back to the club, and reminded us how strange we must have looked. We had stopped to admire a particularly magnificent car when a colored man came up to us and said, "Hi, you fellows, what show are you in?"

Looking nonplussed, we answered that we were not in a show.

Nothing daunted he continued, "Well, what's your religion?"

We said we didn't represent any particular religion.

"Then you must be off a ship . . ."

Francis Brenton

There was no pipe aboard, nor cigarette papers. My luggage was full of notebooks, however, which I had bought in Spain and France and the thin sheets looked as though they would make a fine substitute. I tried a Spanish notebook first, but this was made of thick paper and didn't taste too good. I switched to a French notebook. This was better, and I tore out half a dozen pages and made cigarette papers out of them. They tasted no worse than some of the French cigarettes I've smoked, but they didn't taste any better either. The paper was not very successful; it would either go out, or if a gust of wind came along it went up in flames, a classic example of feast or famine. If I happened to be puffing at the same time as the wind came it felt as though I was inhaling a solid sheet of flame. An added complication was my beard. More than once it too nearly went up in flames as I attempted to relight too small a butt. This journey was more effective than anything else I've ever tried to cure me of smoking.

John Masefield

"They're not much judges of oratory, sir. 'Do this, damn your eyes,' is the oratory they're used to."

Edward H. Dodd, Jr.

We were now all shellbacks and took great pleasure in exerting our privilege of spitting to windward. Our only disappointment came when we learned that we were not qualified to perform a certain other function to windward—an honor reserved for those who have rounded the Horn.

Herman Melville

From the wild life they lead, and various other causes . . . sailors, as a class, entertain most liberal notions concerning morality and the Decalogue; or rather, they take their own views of such matters, caring little for the theological or ethical definitions of others concerning what may be criminal, or wrong.

Their ideas are much swayed by circumstances. They will cleverly abstract a thing from one, whom they dislike; and insist that, in such a case, stealing is not robbing. Or, where the theft involves something funny . . . they only steal for the sake of the joke; but this much is to be observed nevertheless, i.e., that they never spoil the joke by returning the stolen article.

It is a good joke, for instance, and one often perpetrated on board ship, to stand talking to a man in a dark night watch, and all the while be cutting the buttons from his coat. But once off, those buttons will never grow on again. There is no spontaneous vegetation in buttons.

William Robinson

The only man I could find who was willing to leave Bali was a cross-eyed youth of perhaps twenty. He came aboard and we prepared to sail. Many a cross-eyed man have I seen—but never one like this. One pupil stared east while the other gazed to the setting sun. When he looked at me suddenly with one eye the other was apt to slide out of sight entirely. I became so dizzy and unnerved from looking at him that at the last moment I put him ashore and sailed alone.

Rex Clements

All through that shrieking afternoon, with never a jot of abatement in wind or sea, we ran blindly on our way, two men at the helm and the old man, broadshouldered and bare-headed, standing before them, conning the ship. The binnacle was useless, broken for all we knew, for the Flinders bar had gone with the skylight. Eye alone had to guide the ship now. Night came, and still the old man stood there, and next day broke and he hadn't once moved away. He rarely spoke, out with eyes ranging to port, to starboard, and aloft, directed the steering with motions of hand and arm. The navigators among us were fond of criticizing the old man, but that night he silenced criticism, as far as bad weather was concerned, once and for all. We should have been in bad plight but for his skill and endurance.

John Masefield

"My impression is, sir, that half the clipper captains are a little mad."

Alfred Loomis

. . . *Thalassa* glided past me and I noticed how much at union with his boat this sailor was—stretched at ease, one arm thrown carelessly along the tiller, head just showing above the gunwale, and face uplifted so that his eyes commanded the luff of his sail.

John Hersey

As we watched, three down-bound junks ran the rapids, and on the foredeck of each a river pilot stood like a black enormous bird on wide-planted feet, with arms raised and hands outspread, his huge sleeves and long gown flapping wildly in the turbulent air, but his head steady on his ramrod neck, transmitting signals to the frantic oarsman by the lift of a finger on one hand, the folding of two fingers on the other hand, and so by sure economical movements of tiny sinews controlling the huge, awkward vessels in the fearfully entangling waters. No wonder they were such dominant, confident men . . .

Edward H. Dodd, Jr.

There remained the five of us, crew, officers, and would-be captains. None of us could be fired, none could be compelled to do anything, each had equal authority. No arrangement on shipboard could have been more awkward, less likely to work. Yet it was working and remarkably well. Joe's word carried most weight in the sailing, but he was good-natured enough to tolerate considerable advice from Alec and myself. Clymer, controlling the purse strings, directed expenses with a fine in-herent diplomacy. Tom reigned supreme in the engine room . . . Alec occupied himself principally with photography, yachting etiquette and, by his virtue of ability to see land anywhere at any time, became the eyes of the ship. I, under the guidance of Skip and Van, specialized in navigation. We made up our minds that our equality, however dangerous, was inevitable, and after some time began to doubt that anarchy on board ship was as fatal as we had always been led to believe.

Richard Maury

Twenty-four hours later, her crew, shaved and dressed in whites, rowed the collapsible tender to the shore. The night was warm, the air still and heavy. Passing the aisles of administration buildings, silent under rows of royal palms, we crossed the American boundary, entering the native town of Colon, a haze of scarlet and orange light streaming fan-shaped from the doorways of cabarets, bars, fruit shops. Here were noise, happy confusion, wealth and dazed poverty; sought-after comforts and unsought-for dangers; here was Civilization again, out for the evening, dressed in its best and blinded by its own lights. A crowd was passing and repassing the doorways, elegant, hopeful, assured, like the blind made happy, like the old made young, searching, searching once more. A neon sign flashed "Atlantic Cabaret" over a street corner. From the silence of a back road came an exploding burst of laughter, passing off into echoes. American gobs, fruit sellers, dark, bird-like Spaniards in white pongee, dance hall girls, the firemen off some German mer-chantman, lottery sellers, and young Panamanians, arrogant and smoking marihuana. Silks and satins, gay and flowered, dungaree, linen, and khaki swung past the streaming lights. The sound of jazz came from a balcony overhead. The sharp, animated noise of castanets. The slapping of coins on wood. A loud cough from behind a closed shutter. The clatter of billiard ivories; sharp cries, and echoes of Latin laughter. And the sound rose toward the dark sky—a murmur—one moment a caress, the next, vindictive and threatening . . . "Let's have some fun!"

E. A. Pye

I thought how pleasant it was to be a crew for once and able to relax mentally, free from responsibility.

Joshua Slocum

But in order to be a successful navigator or sailor it is not necessary to hang a tar-bucket about one's neck. On the other hand, much thought concerning the brass buttons one should wear adds nothing to the safety of the ship.

Herman Melville

And let me in this place movingly admonish you, ye ship owners . . . Beware of enlisting in your vigilant fisheries any lad with lean brow and hollow eye, given to unseasonable meditativeness, and who offers to ship with the Phaedon instead of Bowditch in his head. Beware of such an one, I say: your whales must be seen before they can be killed; and this sunken-eyed young Platonist will tow you ten wakes round the world, and never make you one pint of sperm the richer. Nor are these admonitions at all unneeded. For nowadays, the whale-fishery furnishes an asylum for many romantic, melancholy and absent-minded young men, disgusted with the carking care of earth, and seeking sentiment in tar and blubber.

"Why, thou monkey," said a harpooner to one of these lads, "we've been cruising now hard upon three years, and thou has not raised a whale yet. Whales are scarce as hen's teeth whenever thou art up here." Perhaps they were; or perhaps there might have been shoals of them in the far horizon; but lulled into such an opiumlike listlessness of vacant, unconscious reverie is this absent-minded youth by the blending cadence of waves with thoughts, that at last he loses his identity; takes the mystic ocean at his feet for the visible image of that deep, blue, bottomless soul pervading mankind and nature; and every strange, half-seen, gliding, beautiful thing that eludes him; every dimly discovered, uprising fin or some undiscernible form, seems to him the embodiment of those elusive thoughts that only people the soul by continually flitting through it.

Charles Violet

I kept at the tiller all night and by morning I was subhuman, just a wet lump of humanity longing for nothing but warmth and oblivion.

Alain Gerbault

I remember that one day, after a storm, I threw overboard some books by Oscar Wilde whose lack of sincerity jarred upon a temperament rendered simple by contact with the sea.

Harry Pidgeon

From the bright lights of the beautiful yacht I returned to my scraper and paint brush.

Erling Tambs

After all, there are dangers ashore also. In fact, I had found that the dangers of the sea were mostly ashore.

Charles Violet

. . . and on long stretches between locks I amused myself by singing in harmony (?) with the single note of the engine, make chords and dischords with it . . .

Charles Violet

She had sailed for many years, usually alone except for a dog, which had become so sea-minded that if she allowed the boat to become too close to the wind it would put its shoulder to the tiller and push until the boat once more came back "on the wind."

Arthur Ransome

I think that is the secret. One could not go to sleep at the tiller with the wind aft, but, when close hauled, steering is done so much by feel, especially in the dark, that the ship takes care of the sleeping helmsman.

Rex Clements

Besides the shortage of water, tobacco was another commodity of which we were running short. Tobacco never tastes so good as in the salt air on shipboard and is almost a necessity of existence in a hard-case "lime juicer." A pipe of tobacco has often to serve in place of a meal and, rammed well down and glowing red in the bowl of a short clay, makes the cheeriest of companions in the long night watches. We felt the loss of it keenly; the last few plugs changed hands at fancy prices, and when they too were gone our search for substitutes was exhaustive. Ropeyarns, whether manila or hemp, raveled out, were tried and found very hot and heady; tea leaves had their votaries, and some hardy spirits experimented with some of the green weed that decorated our waterline, dried in the sun. But the most popular smoke was a combination of ropeyarns, coffee grounds and the bark off a pork barrel, rubbed up small and mixed in equal quantities. If it had not the flavour of best Virginia it filled a place and we were thankful.

Rex Clements

Vessels that fly the red ensign at the gaff are hardly notorious for their attention to religious observances . . . I only met one wind-jammer whose skipper conducted morning service on board every Sunday.

Her old man used to have planks placed on barrels under the poop awning for seats and just before church sent the gig away, manned by four apprentices, to pull round to other ships in search of church goers. Several skippers used to attend and the service went with a swing, a harmonium on the poop sounding very fine . . . it would need to have done a power of good to counteract its detrimental effect upon the ship's apprentices. The way those unfortunate boys used to curse as they sweated her old gig about from ship to ship, with a boatload of churchgoers in the stern sheets, would have been an education to most people. Several fellows used to go just for the fun of being pulled about gratis and listening to the oarsmen's language.

Erling Tambs

I think it pays sometimes to study the psychology of the fish.

Rex Clements

We chatted and I think I must have alluded to the awful language used by the Second Mate, for Paddy laughed.

"Oh, that's the matter, is it?" said he. "Did ever you hear of the parson who made a trip in a limejuicer, Clements?"

"No, sir."

"Well, he did; a proper sky-pilot he was, with a clawhammer coat and gafftops'l hat with backstays to it. He went out in the old *Warrego* and in the Bay they came in for a bit of a dusting. They shortened sail and, clewing up, the crew damned everything from the bilges to breakfast time. It grieved the parson to hear 'em and he spoke to the skipper.

"That's all right, sir," said the old man. "When you hear the men cursing like that there's no fear of the ship going down."

The parson went below but popped up again shortly. Pretty bad he was, and praying he'd never come. It was blowing hard—a big sea and the ship taking it green. The crowd was aloft, handing the mains'l, and the things they were laying tongue to—well, believe me, you haven't heard swearing yet. That parson he just listened, took one look around, and headed for the companionway. "Thank God, they're cursing still," says he, "oh, thank God, they're cursing still!"

Ralph Waldo Emerson

. . . the wonder is always new that any sane man can be a sailor. And here, on the second day of our voyage, stepped out a little boy in his shirtsleeves, who had hid himself, whilst the ship was in port, in the breadcloset, having no money and wishing to go to England. The sailors have dressed him in Guernsey frock, with a knife in his belt, and he is climbing nimbly about after them. The mate avers that this is the history of all sailors; nine out of ten are runaway boys, and adds that all of them are sick of the sea but stay in it out of pride. Jack has a life of risks, incessant abuse, and the worst pay. It is a little better with the mate, and not much better with the captain. A hundred dollars a month is reckoned high pay. If sailors were contented, if they had not resolved again and again not to go to sea any more, I should respect them.

John Hersey

He wanted to haul junks, drink wine, and have friends.

The Voyage

When a sailor ghosts off a charted shore or spumes past a distant cape, he is voyaging. He is no longer adrift on the transparent seas of his imagination. His dream is over. Yet all voyages, great and small, begin as dreams.

Some time ago I watched a coarsely dressed man build a very small trimaran on the shady clay slopes of a marina. Surrounded by glossy mistresses and haughty dams chattering in nearby slips, he launched his boat of interior plywood, oversized nails, and house paint. He hoisted her tiny sail and, as it filled, he smiled. In fact he smiled broadly for he was no longer dreaming. His voyage had begun.

Charles Landery   For the first time in my life I handled sail alone. True, there was little to do, and Sam had told me that little, nevertheless as I let out the slack on the sheets I had the deep thrill of having given life, or restored it, to our ship. *Bessie's* black hull made deeply contented sounds as the sail filled, the great balloon foresail curving voluptuously, a feminine sail if ever there was one. I had a sense of achievement far in excess of both cause and effect as she lunged forward heavily—she was too staid to leap. Leaning over the bow I saw a very small bone in her wide mouth. Sparkling stars of phosphorescence danced down the length of the hull until they met astern and burst together into a cloud of broken light.

I went aft and as the ship, the wheel having been lashed, was steering herself satisfactorily I was content to leave it so. The moment was too enjoyable to struggle and trim for an extra knot (besides, I did not know how!). Sitting on the gunwale, I kept an eye on the compass, which I understood, and another on the sails which I did not, only hoping the latter would behave. I was free to walk the heaving deck, happy with our engineless motion, gloating in the company of our spinning log. The whole experience was so good that it could not have been broken down into comparisons without spilling some of the happiness. Perhaps it was the nearest I have been to ecstasy. My only regret was that I could not step aside and see *Bessie* in all her newly revealed beauty. Every second alone on that wide deck (it seemed wide at the time), that living piece of wood, was of immeasurable importance.

Vito Dumas   . . . each day a little step forward, a little dot beyond the last.

Joshua Slocum   . . . I seemed always to know the position of the sloop, and I saw my vessel moving across the chart, which became a picture before me.

Ray Kauffman   We would cut a path just thirteen feet and nine inches across this ocean, like a meteor wandering through the solar system.

Ralph Stock   At the point of an indomitable lead pencil we traversed vast tracks of ocean in the winking of an eye, and explored the furthermost corners of the earth; and if there is a more fascinating evening's entertainment, I should like to hear of it.

Joshua Slocum   Slowly but surely the mark of my little ship's course on the track-chart reached out on the ocean and across it, while at her utmost speed she marked with her keel still slowly the sea that carried her.

Richard Maury   Rather hazily he considers the width of this ocean. Maps and charts make for a sort of sophisticated regard for the wide spaces of the earth, until an entire ocean may be visualized as a few inches of blue ink on the surface of a map. For the sake of argument, muses the helmsman, scale down distance from miles to feet, and on this particular passage the schooner will be seen as but a grain of dust blown slowly over a half-mile plane, a fleck of dust that can cover little more than a hundred feet from sun-up to sun-up.

Ray Kauffman   Each noon when we laid down our latitude, Lewis would ask, "How much farther to Brisbane?" And we would carefully measure from the little cross on the chart in miles, then roughly converted the miles into hours, and hours into literature, and answer: "One biography, two detective stories, four Saturday Evening Posts and two Readers Digests from Brisbane." Finally when we were only two mystery stories from the continent, we started the motor.

Edward H. Dodd, Jr.   . . . so the little dots that represented our noon positions advanced, while seas and skies remained unchanged. But as the only indications of progress, these dots, however unreal their message, always received keen attention.

Allan Villiers   It is curious how the land comes up from the sea after a passage of many days across open water, a passage the progress of which is measured until then only upon a chart with penciled lines calculated from much observation of the sun and other heavenly bodies, and the working of involved trigonometrical formulae simplified by tables. Slowly the lines across the chart head towards the darkened landmass in one corner, and for a long time there is nothing but the lengthening lines and water, water, water, which might always be the same, in the same place, only behaving differently, varying its deceits and its moods. Then one day from the whited chart and from the water the land stands up. It *was* there. It has not only its existence in dark outlines on a chart; it is a different land from that we left. It is the land to which we have been bound.

Herman Melville

While he was thus employed, the heavy pewter lamp suspended in chains over his head continually rocked with the motion of the ship, and forever threw shifting gleams and shadows of lines upon his wrinkled brow, till it almost seemed that while he himself was marking out lines and courses on the wrinkled charts, some invisible pencil was also tracing lines and courses upon the deeply marked chart of his forehead.

Rockwell Kent

I have had this instrument for years and never used it. Never known how. Its mere possession moved me. Often I have opened its case and looked at it—so beautifully contrived and made, and its bright arc so cleanly and minutely graduated. And once I found that someone had laid hands on it, for there, oxidized upon the silver, was a great thumb print. But not even to cleanse it of that would I touch it, for a stain can less obscure the graduations of that arc than the erosion of polishing.

And now at last, at noon of the 18th of June in the year nineteen twenty-nine, having for nearly forty-seven years knocked about the world East, West, North and South, in high places and in low, and been more or less finger printed and soiled but—pray God!—not too much polished off, I propose to take my sextant in hand, twist my legs around the halyards, brace my shoulders between them, and, resting one eye as it were on that fixed point of the absolute, the sun, and the other on the immutable horizon of this earth, find by triangulation where I am.

Frank Wightman

. . . anyone who can add up the household accounts can navigate.

Dwight Long

One day, according to my longitude sight, I discovered *Idle Hour* was inside the walled city of Addis Ababa, capital of Ethiopia!

Rudyard Kipling

Before long he knew where Disko kept the old green-encrusted quadrant that they called the "hog yoke"—under the bedbag in his bunk. When he took the sun, and with the help of the *Old Farmer's Almanac* found the altitude, Harvey would jump down into the cabin and scratch the reckoning and date with a nail on the rust of the stovepipe. Now, the chief engineer of the liner could have done no more, and no engineer of thirty years' service could have assumed one half of the ancient mariner air which Harvey, first careful to spit over the side, made public the schooner's position for that day, and then and not till then relieved Disko of the quadrant. There is an etiquette in all these things.

The quadrant, an Eldridge chart, the farming almanac, Blunt's *Coast Pilot,* and Bowditch were all the weapons Disko needed to guide him, except the deep sea lead that was his spare eye.

Herodotus

When you get eleven fathoms and an ooze on the lead, you are a day's journey from Alexandria.

Charles Landery

The ship was alive again, she rubbed her sides fondly against the insignificant swell.

Ray Kauffman

It was good to smell the open sea again to feel the boat heel over and smash the blue into white foam.

Erling Tambs

As usual, I endeavored to conceal my surprise under a becoming mask of indifference, implying that I had never seriously doubted the reliability of my navigation. On this occasion, however, my air of non-chalance failed to convince my wife. She laughed whenever she looked at me.

Thor Heyerdahl

We went forward yard by yard. The *Kon-Tiki* did not plow through the sea like a sharp-prowed racing craft. Blunt and broad, heavy and solid, she splashed sedately forward over the waves. She did not hurry, but when she had once got going she pushed ahead with unshakable energy.

E. A. Pye

On the fifth day out the wind veered into the northwest in a squall and we jibed over to port for the first time for nearly three thousand miles.

Edward H. Dodd, Jr.

"My God, land! Jibe her quick!" A dense black mass appeared suddenly dead ahead . . .

The sails slapped us as we scrambled down the ratlines. On deck there was a pungent smell of rotten seaweed. We could see land plainly now only about a hundred feet away.

We swung away just in time and hurried below to pore over the chart. Surely there was something very queer. Two sights that afternoon had put us far to the eastward. They had been carefully checked because of this, and there was no possibility of error. From their position we could not have been within forty miles of any land except Bird Rock. Either the lighthouse was not burning or the chronometer had suddenly changed its rate. Later at Jamaica we found that our chronometer was six minutes out . . .

Ralph Stock

"One of three things has happened," he announced: "the chronometer's got the jim-jams, the chart's wrong, or the blinking island has foundered."

Harry Pidgeon

I was unable to get a chart of the Fiji Group and Pango Pango and had to content myself with a small map, three by four inches in size, from a steamship folder.

E. A. Pye

I became really worried when my dead-reckoning put me on top of a hill a hundred feet high, and there was no land in sight!

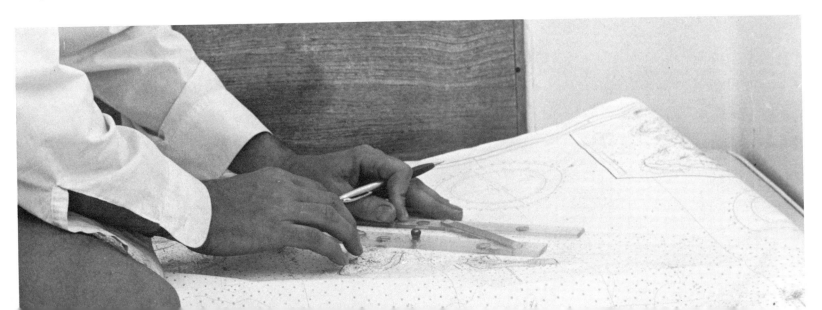

William Robinson

The sun came out and we were more at a loss than ever, for the observations put us in an impossible position, due to some strange condition of the atmosphere, probably undue refraction from the intense evaporation going on in the countless lagoons about us.

Rex Clements

. . . neat scales of miles, maps and charts have dwarfed the immensity and spoiled the mysteriousness of the world's wide spaces. What a charm there is in those old "seacards" where a well-known coast trails off into "Terra Incognita," and Australia has the hazy indefiniteness of "cold Estotiland!" On a modern atlas, wonderful record of human adventure though it be, there is no room for weirdly-shaped elephants and spouting whales. All is neatly circumscribed and labeled and even the Pacific Ocean looks no bigger than a duck-pond. Finger and thumb will span it . . .

Joshua Slocum

Being sure of the sloop's position, I lay down to rest and to think, and I felt better for it.

Francis Brenton

There was no sextant aboard. I had priced one at Tenerife and the cost appalled me. It seemed better to buy four pounds' worth of provisions and take a slightly longer time to make the journey. I had no inten- tion of paying forty-five pounds for a sextant and its related tables for the sake of saving a mere seven or eight days. After all, if Columbus could cross the Atlantic without a chart, it seemed reasonable that I could do it without a sextant. If I did not hit Canada, I'd run ashore at Argen- tina—or somewhere in between.

William Robinson

The monsoon blew fresh abaft the beam and we did the 325 miles in just 48 hours, and a quarter of this time we were under jib alone. As a matter of fact this was one time my dead reckoning was out—way out too—and was a warning that it is never safe to relax a minute from careful navigation.

Richard Maury

. . . on the entire voyage but a single star sight had been taken, the economy of sextant work being bolstered by de- veloping a skill in dead reckoning.

Joshua Slocum

But the greatest science was in reckoning the longitude. My tin clock and only timepiece had by this time lost its minute hand, but after I boiled her she told the hours, and that was near enough.

Frank Wightman

Nights in which we knelt—in a dark cabin that sometimes stag- gered and sometimes only lifted gently but was never still—before our small wireless that we could not afford to use for anything but the Greenwich time-pips, so precious to my navi- gation. Both holding watches and staring intently at the glowing dial of the instrument. Waiting . . . waiting . . . cursing the drain on our one battery. Suddenly above the swishing of waters and the moaning of the wind, "D'ye ken John Peel" would swell through the cabin, and two tense faces would smile in the darkness. The precious "pips" that we counted so carefully, followed by the voice which assured us it was "Twenty hours Greenwich Mean Time."

William Robinson

So smoothly did the days flow by that there was little to report . . . unless something out of the ordinary occurred, I wrote up the log but once a day, after plotting our noon position.

Ray Kauffman

Hector staggered forward with the running lights: his face glowed first with a warm red light as he swung into the port shrouds and then turned a ghostly green as he eased across the decks, sheltering the star- board light within his jacket. . . . Below it was comfortable and, with the companionway closed, quiet. Only a ham swinging in the galley thudded against the bulkhead and the pots and pans clink- clanked in the locker. A sea occasionally breaking under the counter yawed the ship and rumbled beneath the bilge. The water racing by the planking only a foot from my ear was the music of a fast passage that brought contented sleep.

Alfred F. Loomis

If a cruise in a yawl were all plain sailing there would be little to chronicle but the state of the sea and the color of the clouds at sunrise.

Erling Tambs

The days passed on in full contentment and tranquility. We sailed only in the daytime and hove to at night. Backing the staysail and hoisting a trysail abaft the mast, our little ship practically stayed on the same spot until we resumed our course.

Richard Maury

. . . when a vessel drops to leeward with the drift of large waves it is sometimes said she is so driven by the scend of the sea. On December 4th, upon once more getting underway, we estimated this scend to have carried us a good one hundred miles to the north and east of our course.

Edward H. Dodd, Jr.

Those days to Bermuda were all the ideal of a sailor; fair weather with the clean salt tang, taut straining sails, and clear blue water in the sunlight falling away. For most of us it was the first real taste and feel of the charm of the sea, and often someone could be seen hanging his head over the fantail to watch the water swirl by the rudder—that crystal clear, translucent water of deep sparkling blue that can be found only under the stern of a sailing ship well out at sea. Another would climb to the trestle trees where he could sit with the wind all about him, one arm around the creaking mast and feel the long jerky motion and the stiff pull of the sails when every rope and stay is alive and working. Or lying on the bowsprit one would watch the dark waves dash up to the bow and see that rounded black wedge saw its way through, tossing the water off gently. At the wheel the jerk and pull of each wave and puff of wind kept us enthralled. Always changing, always alive. The helmsman was complete monarch; he could ease her, push her, put her up for this wave and off for that one. Sailors will all talk of how they hate the wheel and we, too, later learned to count every second of time on watch; but on an ideal day with a stiff breeze and a lively sea, when you are pointing fairly close to the wind, not even the saltiest shellback could help sitting up and feeling every little kick of the wheel.

E. A. Pye

. . . the lamps and the navigation lamps were filled and lit, the dinner cooked, the helmsman relieved for his meal, the washing-up done and the precious half-hour for spinning a yarn over, it was time to write up the log and the daily journal, set up the bunkboards and turn in. I looked at the clock and found, without surprise, that I had a quarter of an hour before taking over from Anne at ten. I remembered that a cousin of mine, a mountaineer, once said to me, "What I don't understand is what do you do with yourselves all day at sea."

Humphrey Barton

We have so far remained reasonably civilized but I for one am slowly but inevitably deteriorating over small matters. I used, for instance, to fold up neatly my sleeping bag and eiderdown and stow them properly in the recess at the end of my bunk. Now I just kick them all in higgledy-piggledy down into the recess, pushing them well home with my feet, throw in a garment or two after them, stuff in my bolster (half the International Code of flags) bung up the entrance to the cavern with my pillow . . . I even use my egg spoon to stir my tea with now.

Richard Henry Dana

This day ended pleasantly; we had got into regular and comfortable weather, and into that routine of sea life which is only broken by a storm, a sail, or the sight of land.

Hilaire Belloc

. . . and the sea breeze smelt of dawn. My little boat went easy, as the sea was easy. There was just enough of a following wind dead west to keep her steady and to keep the boom square in its place right out alee, nor did she shake or swing (as boats so often will before a following wind), but went on with a purpose gently, like a young woman just grown used to her husband and her home. So she sailed, and aft we left a little, bubbling wake, which in the darkness had glimmered with evanescent and magic fires, but now, as the morning broadened could be seen to be white foam. The stars paled for an hour and then soon vanished; although the sun had not yet risen, it was day.

E. A. Pye

The days passed all too quickly; the books we had brought remained unread, although Anne would sometimes read poetry at the helm, and Christopher a thriller. I never tired of looking around at the changing sea and the sky.

Humphrey Barton

Living in a small yacht in these conditions is not very easy. A little boat does get thrown about so badly. Every movement has to be made with care. One is always holding on, or braced between two objects, or wedged in a position where it is impossible to be flung down to leeward. One can anticipate most of the movements of the yacht but not all of them. Every now and then a sea will catch her a backhanded swipe and send her staggering, or she will just fall into a part of the ocean that is missing, or she gets a sledge hammer blow that shakes her from end to end. We used to say, "Cripes! that was a bad one." Now we don't take any notice.

Edward H. Dodd, Jr.

The five of us divided the watches, moving in progression in a system so complicated that an argument invariably arose every four hours.

William Robinson

I think the gods that control the destinies of sailors were trying to make up for previous hardships. A gentle trade wind caressed our sails as we slipped mile after mile over a lazy ocean. Days were blue, intensely blue, with white fleeting clouds. But the nights were sublime, unforgettable, with a crescent moon and weird flickering phosphorescent lights on the horizon. One night, with a soft thud, *Svaap* touched some great fish—a sleeping whale perhaps.

Richard Maury

Foot by foot the crawl to windward was carried out. Afternoon passed into night and still it went on. At nine, when thirty miles off, wind and sea overpowered us until we could sail no more. After shortening down to a foresail, the helm was lashed alee, and following the customary procedure, we went below. The fuel leak had been stopped, the bilges cleaned, the cabin ventilated, and, after many attempts, a fire kindled in the stove. Beside its glowing body we had a much-neeeded meal of codfish and tea. Talk followed. Carrol, now well after facing the weather all day, told of tropical adventures, his quiet voice contrasting with the storm over the cabin top. Warren matched them with a wild, an incredible story of the wild incredible sea. The lantern swung rapid shadows across their faces as I, the quiet listener, broke silence only to urge them on.

E. A. Pye

It was cosy in *Moonraker's* cabin that night. We had eaten the last of our Flores chickens as a pilaf with rice and raisin and egg, the soft light of the cabin lamps fell on cream paint and on polished brass. Mike was asleep on a mattress on the cabin floor, Anne was writing up her diary and I the ship's daily journal. Outside, Bob was enjoying the last of his after-dinner pipe, the wind came in fitful gusts, and there was a fine drizzle of rain. Soon Anne put the books away, and I turned out the starboard lamp, trimming the one above my head, so that the helmsman could, by leaning down, see the clock and the barometer. I put up my canvas bunkboard and turned in.

Edward H. Dodd, Jr.

Of all irritating things that can happen on board ship nothing surpasses the splash of large raindrops on your face when you are immersed in the early hours of sleep. At first you pretend to yourself that you have dreamed about them; you draw the blanket over your head, and recommence sleeping with iron determination. They become more and more insistent. You curse quietly and bitterly for a moment, then you leap up tossing off your blanket. A frenzied argument follows with the approaching squall. Blankets and pillow are hurled below and after a few parting oaths you retire to sulk on the uncomfortable mess in your bunk.

A. E. Pye

In my sleep I was aware of the increasing wind and sea, so that it was difficult to know whether I was awake or not.

Edward H. Dodd, Jr.

It may seem foolishly imaginative to the landsman that one can conceive a true affection for a faraway cluster of lights and presumptuous that he can feel this loyalty reciprocated, but the seaman comes to regard his stars as very real personalities on whom he is in a way dependent and in whom he can always confide.

Richard Maury

The rain is stopping—and what is this?—the binnacle lamp is becoming dim, and a colorless light is rising all around. Slowly, out of the darkness grow the familiar outlines of cabin-tops, decks, masts—colorless, blank, grey-appearing, like the forms in a misted photograph. The clouds are parting—are gone, and loose, undeveloped waves also take on grey as a gloomy bar of light comes to float on the eastern skyline. The watch looks on dispassionately. He is thankful for the dawn, but its arrival does not move him as did the twilight; in fact, in contrast to that hour, this is the time he becomes most careless, the hour he is most likely to take an unnecessary chance. The light increases, and wet through, he locks the idle helm, stands up, yawns, stretches himself, stamps his bare feet. His throat, his nostrils, feel stiff with salt. Walking aft he pulls at the trolling line, sees the empty lure skip water far astern, then turns and with hands on hip regards the schooner. She is still working on the beam airs, still pressing the issue. Why doesn't she stop, for once! With a yellow haze brightening to the east, the man ends his reverie, looks at the time, goes below. The other is sleeping soundly, oblivious of all that has happened since midnight, for on this passage the off man is never roused to handle sail. Taking a match from a waterproof tin the watchman starts the stove, fills the kettle and sets it to boil. The noise he makes does not disturb the other. Going on deck . . . the sea has become almost blue, the sky cloudless, slick, the schooner white, while the sun, just cutting the horizon, is shining on the wet uppers of the sails. Remembering the binnacle light, he dowses it, takes off sou'wester and coat, and steers ship until, ten minutes later, on looking at the pocket watch, he goes below, shakes the other and says, "Time's up!" Reaching deck he hurriedly strips to the waist, throws the clothes down the hatch, pulls a mop out of the lazarette and begins splashing bucketful after bucketful of sea water onto trunking and decks, leaving the schooner which is still talking to the sea, to move for herself. Several flying fish lured by lighted port holes lie on deck amidst a school of minnows shipped in one of the heeling squalls. When the mop has made the white and yellow paintwork shine in the sun, he lays it on the gallows frame to dry, and sets about coiling down lines of all description. Presently there is a sound from the hatch and he sees the relief coming up bearing tea and biscuits and heading for the steering well. He joins him.

"How was it?" the newcomer asks, staring at the horizon. He seems profoundly amazed, incredulous at something out there. He is sleepy.

"Broken up. She's lucky if she ran three and a half. But see—there's a nice little wind making in the south."

At this the relief wakes up: "Good! There's some herring below for you."

"All right. West by south."

"West by south; all mine."

And the watch—after welcoming the new wind slanting over a fresh sea—disappears down the companion.

William Robinson

The night was beautiful beyond description and I ached to prolong the moment into eternity as we ghosted out of the grand bay and found the pass in the starlight by the break in the white of the surf. It is always a thrill to sail through a pass, but doubly so at night.

Alfred F. Loomis

The first appearance on deck of a morning is generally an occasion of some repressed grumpiness mitigated by a keen interest in our surroundings and the things which concern the boat's sailing. A glance around and aloft to determine the present and future condition of the sea; a question of the helmsman concerning the course and log reading; a cigarette rolled in the lee of the dinghy and smoked with deep inhalations; a perfunctory application of fresh water to the face and teeth: all these things are necessary before we feel ourselves to be the equal of the one of us who has watched while we have slept. His inevitable superiority is the more keenly felt when, as on this morning, we look over the side and see the jagged bottom a few fathoms beneath us.

Yes, he's known about it all the time; has taken soundings, consulted the chart, and decided that we can hold the course without lessening the depth. And so we can, but at the expense of our aplomb.

Richard Maury

Left alone, the man holds the tiller in one hand, the teacup in the other. He is not fully awake and sniffs deeply of the pungent salt, always strongest at this hour; sniffs also of other odors, of damp paint wetted by night dew, of saturated cordage and sail cloth. But the fragrance of the tea is supreme and he holds it near while his eyes leave the compass, take in the schooner, then wander over the ocean that is gleaming, sharp-cut, a blue glow lifting with the light, and so fresh that it is as though creation had taken place a moment before. Over shoulder, the sun that had been red and heavy expands and begins circling the sea. Grey horizon clouds break up, turn white and start across the sky. The day is well underway.

Rex Clements

One morning at daybreak, we sighted a small barque, out-wardbound, and were able to thank our lucky stars we weren't aboard her. She was plunging close-hauled into the fierce squalls, with only her lower tops'ls set. Her crowd must have been having a lively time, for she was digging into the seas as though she were trying to scoop the South Atlantic up and throw it over her shoulder. We ran past her very quickly. She was port-painted, and, I should think, by the cut of her, British. The weather was too bad for us to speak, and she was soon swallowed up in the mist and spray astern.

Frank Wightman

. . . alternately scudded and wallowed . . .

. . . monotonously pickled and rinsed.

Richard Maury

The sun grew hot, the sea resembled blueing water, and we decided to hold a sailor's holiday. After ripping up the floorboards to air the bilges, we carried every scrap of clothing on deck, laid on the lifelines mattresses, old sail, spare canvas, hoisted a string of clothes to the signal halyards, and stopped shirts, blankets and dungarees to the stays with sail twine. The schooner resembled an old clothes shop rolling over the Pacific.

Vito Dumas

. . . I decided to inspect the damage to the hull, hoping that it was only a graze; but I found a plank cracked. I repaired it with a strip of inner tube, stuck on with paint and held in place by a plank which I screwed on.

Stanley Smith and Charles Violet

We noticed an odd thing in the afternoon; some bubbles coming from the bow as the *Nova* glided through the water reflected a distorted view of us sailing; each looked like a miniature ship in a dome-shaped bottle, complete in every detail.

Vito Dumas

For in my navigation it was no question of a storm here and there, but of an endless succession of dirty weather.

Richard Maury

All through the day the *Cimba* raced before a West Indian chocolate gale, baring her red and black boot topping, climbing and planing with intense effort, her sails curved and gripping the wind as the cotton raked stiff-bunted under the glowing sky. Sunset, and she continued to sweep down miles, lurching into the night of an old moon, which made the swing of the sea appear as a rush of green and bronze, with scattered crests, rolling brass-headed, flaming in hazy light. Her bows gashed the living sea, her entire underbody thundered. And in the morning she was still storming onwards, straining, overeager, a flash of wake screwing astern in the early sunshine, her mainsail skintight and biting at the backstays. Noon found Dombey, sextant in hand, taking last sights before landfall. She was still moving and I held her with a stiff helm.

Joshua Slocum

. . . and putting my great lantern in the rigging I lay down, to the first time at sea alone, not to sleep, but to doze and to dream.

Vito Dumas

The roving eye looks out for something new; everything is interesting. Among the clouds of all shapes and colors I picked out two that seemed to give the figure 99. What did it mean? Perhaps the duration of my second leg, to New Zealand. It turned out to be very near the truth (104 days).

Joshua Slocum

One could not be lonely in a sea like this.

Edward H. Dodd, Jr.

That night, while we were sailing free before a fairly strong northwester, the wind suddenly shifted northward jibing the main. The boom tackle held until everyone got on deck, and then the eyebolt suddenly tore out. The big boom shot over, fetching up on the forestay. Fortunately there was not wind enough to snap it and the stay held. At the time Tom alone was awake at the wheel; Alec his watchmate slept peacefully on the fantail. The rest of us, feeling the jerk, had scrambled on deck and, still half asleep, started crawling toward the halyards. Before anything could be done, however, she came across. Sandy prostrated himself on his face, acquiring a black eye, and the boom tackle, whipping across the deckhouse, wrecked havoc on the paint that had been applied to it that afternoon. Everything was straightened out with no resultant damage, except to the paint, which everyone managed to wipe at one time or another. Well awakened by now, the pajama-clad, paint-bespattered members of the crew bestowed quiet abuse on the watch and retired.

William Robinson

There followed days of supreme sailing. The seas piled up on our quarter and we slithered from one white-topped sapphire ridge to the next, driving her to the limit under mainsail and a small spinnaker. I would turn in at seven o'clock in the evening . . . Absorbed in trying to identify the various creakings and galley noises that blended with the rushing sound of the sea on the other side of the $1^1{}_8$ inch planking next to my ear, I would fall asleep . . . At 1 a.m. I would take the wheel, turn out the compass light, and steer by Orion . . .

Richard Maury

We worked amid the hot calms of the Spanish Main, came to know its windless nights, its nights of mysterious squalls; pushed the schooner against head currents, maneuvered her into shoal water, beached her for painting, and lost every plate aboard and the only pair of binoculars in what came to be known as the "ninety-dollar squall." We deviated up rivers, along silent banks of damp jungle, and by the time *Cimba* picked up old moorings, had learned rudiments in trading for pineapples, pigs, and yams.

Ernest K. Gann

The wind held fair and as a consequence our return to the perculiar tranquility of the marine world was accomplished to the melody of many low key noises.

Francis Brenton

This is as close to nature as I'll ever be, and I began to rely on instinct to gauge what the day had in store. I noted the shapes and directions of clouds and connected them with weather conditions. The yacht was always creaking and groaning, and I soon knew all the different sounds: the slapping as a halyard slackened, the knock as the tiller rope worked loose, the grinding of the whisker pole as it slipped from its proper position on the mast, the knocking of something adrift in the cabin. Even as I changed course, the noise of the sea changed. Sometimes I heard squeals and squeaks from the sea, but I never did find out what these were.

Frank Wightman

I could always tell when she was coming about by the creaking of her steering tackles, followed by a grunting and grinding as the rudder swung hugely through the dark water beneath her counter. Then I would see the shape of those great dark sails dissolve in soft confusion, and steeved bowsprit that seemed far off in the night obediently ruled a line across the island heights.

Charles Landery

Rudyard Kipling wrote of "that packet of assorted miseries which we call a ship" and nothing could have been truer

of *Bessie* at this time. Wiping off the water that was dripping through the deck head on to my book, I found sour, unfriendly consolation in the knowledge that Sam's bunk was twice as wet. At such moments, *Bessie* herself was the only contented thing in the horizon's unsteady circle; her self-satisfaction was annoying as she squatted confidently on the sea, like a sentimental hen brooding over a dummy egg, unaware of everything and everyone in her absorption.

Frank Wightman

. . . a passage small in mileage and great in experience.

Vito Dumas

Storms helped me along, fine weather held me back.

Charles Landery

. . . sea, ship, and stomach.

Leonard Wibberley

Navigation then is not merely fixing one's position, but an extension of being—an extension of our minds into the heavens, an extension of our minds into the past, so that for a while we are contemporaries of the long dead.

Herman Melville

The long night watches of the sailor are eminently adapted to draw out the reflective faculties of any serious minded man, however humble or uneducated.

William Robinson

I looked over my charts and began to feel horribly microscopic and unimportant and exceedingly far from home. It seemed quite impossible that we had come so far. The thousands of miles that lie far ahead often appear insuperable. Distance lends them an aura of awe. But as one progresses, each step is studied and accomplished as an independent chore. Before one realizes, one has succeeded in completing what seemed originally a colossal undertaking— not by one long-sustained strenuous effort but rather by a connected series of short efforts, each one a complete whole.

Richard Maury

What would be the perfect cruise? . . . a cargo-carrying one, for the romance of yachts is not as potent as the romance of working ships.

John MacGregor

. . . with only some dot of a sail, hull down, far far off on the horizon, a little lonely speck fixed in hard exile; but very probably the crew in that vessel too were happy in the breezy morn, and felt themselves and their craft to be the very "hub of the universe."

William Robinson

Suddenly, for the first time, I awoke to a full realization of the enormity of the task ahead of us. Infinity, the old familiar term of geometry days, took on a concrete meaning. It was the distance to Tahiti.

John MacGregor

It was a strange and pleasant life for me all the summer, sailing entirely alone by sea and river fifteen hundred miles, and with its toils, perils, and adventures heartily enjoyed.

Joshua Slocum

. . . and the world changed . . . to the light of a homeward-bound voyage.

Joseph Conrad

"The traveler knows the time of his setting out, but not the time of his return," observed the man, calmly.

Charles Landery

Progress was slow but without pause. The unhurrying barnacles, blindly fulfilling their obscure purposes, steadfastly built up their crusty shells; our ship lagged in relation to their industry. The weather was freakish and seasonal, sometimes warm enough for shorts, just as often consisting of cold rains and depressed gatherings in the fo'c'sle.

John Masefield

She was making probably twelve knots an hour in what seemed a succession of staggering pauses followed by lifting thrusts forward. She seemed to bow down till her

bowsprit was deep in smother and her eyes submerged, then after a check amid the bubble she would rise and rise and clear what seemed like half her length all shading with running water and surge herself forward still rising and rolling . . .

Rex Clements
Most log-lines are only marked to record twelve knots. When the ship is doing more than that the man at the reel gets a jerk calculated to dislocate his shoulder . . . A yarn is told of one of the famous flyers of the 'sixties which once had the man holding the reel— a Chinaman—jerked clean overboard and lost in consequence of the terrific speed the ship was traveling through the water. I don't vouch for the truth of the story; but when a windjammer is logging something above the ordinary she is always said to be doing "twelve and a Chinaman."

E. A. Pye
Drive, drive, watch after watch; down topsail, in reefs; out reefs, up topsail; spinnaker for genoa, genoa for spinnaker; nothing must be left undone to keep the log spinning as fast as the ship could turn it.

Richard Maury
And so into another night, the wind stiff, the sea piling, the schooner trooping, trying hard, pounding, working with her back through every hour.

Herman Melville
. . . as the wind howled on, and the sea leaped, and the ship

groaned, and dived, and yet steadfastly shot . . . further and further into the blackness of the sea and the night, and scornfully champed the white bone in her mouth, and viciously spat round her on all sides.

Richard Maury
. . . I came on deck early the next morning to find the seas a great confusion of blue, exploding, white capped; the sun lighting the sweep out to the horizons, and the wind, blowing under an immense light of turquoise, driving us south over broken sea. The northeast trades were here! They were too far aft to wing us at our best, but even so, as I took the tiller from Dombey the *Cimba* smoked, holding a flashing bone in her teeth. Now, on the horizon to windward, clouds, small and distant like the studding sails of a *Flying Dutchman*, hove in sight, sailed down, scudded overhead, huge, sun-drenched, rushing to leeward faster than the white-wooded schooner over the rich, windy ocean. The masts glistened, the backstays tautened, and sails and clouds moved bunted against a bright sky. The *Cimba* was fetching flying-fish weather, to run with a long loping rhythm for the West Indies.

Joshua Slocum
Her mast now bent under a strong, steady pressure, and her bellying sail swept the sea as she rolled scuppers under, curtseying to the waves. These rolling waves thrilled me as they tossed my ship, passing quickly under her keel. This was grand sailing.

Herman Melville
Hurrah! This is the way to sail now. Every keel a sunbeam! Hurrah!

Frank Wightman
A big island sloop, deeply laden, was running through from the east. She was surrounded by an acre of foam as her blunt bows exploded the seas like a broaching whale.

Herman Melville
The ship tore on; leaving such a furrow in the sea as when a cannon-ball, missent, becomes a ploughshare and turns up the level field.

Frank Wightman
She was heeled down perhaps three planks and the wind was one point free.

Herman Melville
The ship was sailing plungingly; astern the billows rolled in riots.

John Masefield
The ship was running on, with the same desperate haste . . . It was now in the wildness of an angry morning, with a low, hurrying heaven and leaping sea, that showed green under the gray, and rose and slipped away with a roar. The ship was careering with an aching

straining crying from every inch of her, aloft and below. Her shrouds strained and whined and sang, the wind boomed in her sail, the sheet blocks beat, the chain of their pendants whacked the masts. All the mighty weight of the ship and cargo heaved itself aloft, and surged and descended and swayed, smashing the seas white, boring into and up and out of the hills and hollows of the water, and singing as she did it, and making all hands, as they toiled, to sing.

Frank Wightman

Then she threw up her bows to the first of the seas driven in by northeast trade wind ... At that moment—with thrusting urgency—the ocean wind streamed into her sails. They filled with a great smoothing-out of wrinkled canvas, and *Wylo* put her cheek down to the waters and started to smash her way to the freedom of the seas.

Richard Maury

The two craft came together, lunging over a skeleton-work of spume, diving, swinging in the trade wind chop, rolling their cloth over vast shadowless space, tense with movement, restrained, dancing rather than racing, leaving their crews to the calculation of results.

Rex Clements

... a large barque spooming along under full sail and homeward bound.

E. A. Pye

The wind was free. *Moonraker* smoked along. From astern came a sloop, a rakish vessel with her great flowing mainsail and long boom, the water foaming at her pretty bow. As she romped past us, her crew lined the bulwarks, holding aloft a rope's end mocking our puny speed.

Herman Melville

Now it is not with ships as with horses; for though, if a horse walk well and fast, it generally furnishes good token that he is not bad at a gallop, yet the ship that in a light breeze is outstripped, may sweep the stakes, so soon as a t'gallant breeze enables her to strike into a canter. Thus fared it with us. First, the Englishman glided ahead and bluffly passed on; then the Frenchman politely bade us adieu, while the old *Neversink* lingered behind, railing at the effeminate breeze. At one time, all three frigates were irregularly abreast, forming a diagonal line; and so near were all three, that the stately officers on the poops stiffly saluted by touching their caps though refraining from any further civilities. At this juncture, it was a noble sight to behold those fine frigates, with dripping breasthooks, all rearing and nodding in concert, and to look through their tall spars and wilderness of rigging, that seemed inextricably entangled, gigantic cobwebs against the sky.

Toward sundown the ocean pawed its white hoofs to the spur of its helter-skelter rider, a strong blast from the eastward, and, giving three cheers from decks, yards, and tops, we crowded all sail on St. George and St. Denis.

Frank Wightman

Wylo was executing a slow, stately dance ...

William Robinson

The Pilot Book for this region is less than useless. Time and again it refers to "a conspicuous bush" as a landmark by which to locate an island or a harbor. When it is necessary to use bushes as outstanding landmarks it speaks poorly for the landscape.

Thor Heyerdahl

But over the whole horizon to the east a ruddy glow had begun to spread, and far down to the southeast it gradually formed a blood-red background for a faint shadow, like a blue pencil line, drawn for a short way along the edge of the sea. Land! An island!

Ralph Stock

This, then, was the navigation that master mariners made such song and dance about! Well, we must be master mariners, that was all we had to say! We had summoned Madeira, and Madeira had appeared! We were not at all sure that we had not discovered Madeira!

Alain Gerbault

There were more signs of the nearness of land ... dead butterflies on the water.

Herman Melville

Slowly wading the meadows of brit, the *Pequod* still held on her way northeastward toward the island of Java; a gentle air impelling her keel, so that in the surrounding serenity her three tall tapering masts mildly waves to that languid breeze as three mild palms on a plain.

Richard Maury

We sailed west seventy miles, eased sheets in the moonlight and stood on under western Albemarle, under steep and black cliffs charged by breakers leaping with a roar a hundred feet up the rock. In looming shadow, great upright washes of sea, phosphorus filled and whitened by the moon, mounted, glowed brightly, and in thunderous explosion upon explosion collapsed into darkness. The *Cimba*, following some two hundred miles of coast, moved quietly all the next day, the sleeping sea under her, the massive form of Albemarle Island high above, grey, uninhabited, of sulphur, alkali, of great ranges of basalt, dropping so steeply at sea edge that we, hugging the shore, sailed with a thousand fathoms beneath keel. All day long sea mews planed mast-high over the water, with stiff-winged albatross scouting far above them, occasionally diving to a green sea broken by porpoise and the wake of sluggish sharks.

William Robinson

Ran over shoals not on chart—about five fathoms minimum. One learns what it felt like in the early days, days of

Cook and Tasman and all the rest, for navigation here is practically a case of feeling your way, unaided by accurate charts . . . Woodlark, for instance, is only dotted in roughly.

Frank Wightman

She had been surging along smoothly and lazily. Now she developed an odd trip in her stride . . . Then it broke on my city-dulled senses. This was the first of the coast's backwash thrown out to sea by that still far-off outline. It would have been too slight to be perceptible to the eye; even if it were day the eye could have detected nothing odd in the run of the seas—but *Wylo* was registering it. She was running from the rhythm of the open sea into the restless heave round the island.

William Robinson

The night dragged on, every hour an eternity. A gulp of burning raw whiskey now and then kept us going. Sometimes an instinct would suddenly grip me and without knowing why or how, I would sense that we were close to the land and so we would pick our wave, taking the time from the clock below, and get on the other tack. It may be that the abrupt bluffs of Bauro affected the sound waves in some manner, thus explaining the seemingly inexplicable instinct.

Charles Violet

Quite suddenly it was all over, and the *Nova* was riding up and

down over more rhythmic waves. While getting the water out of the cabin, as the *Nova* jogged along quietly under jib and mizen, I realized the possible reason for the nasty patch of sea. Getting out the chart I looked carefully along the track course and spotted a dotted line encircling a small area of water 240 feet down, but immediately around it the sea-bottom was nearly 6,000 feet down. It must have been that undersea hill that caused all the commotion.

Edward H. Dodd, Jr.

Christmas Eve, recalling as it did the civilization of the North, found all hands removing the luxuriant growths on their faces. Once young again, hanging stockings was a logical step. An assortment of dirty socks that had been neither worn nor washed since Panama were pinned on the rail of the galley stove. Although Sandy expressed grave doubts that Santa could crawl through a Liverpool head, during the night, chips of wood, rope ends, and bits of dried fish found their way into the socks. Tom and Alec secretly decorated the forecastle with green sprigs and red beans. A tree was represented by a celery stalk sprinkled with salt. Even the mistletoe branch, with tapioca sewed among the leaves, hung in the galley doorway.

Toward noon the thermometer climbed to 122° on deck, but the *Nautical Almanac* assured us that it was the 25th of December.

Woodes Rogers

January 1. 1708. Fresh Gales of Wind from the WNW. to the

WSW. with Fogs, but indifferent smooth Water. This being New-Year's Day, every Officer was wish'd a merry New-Year by our Musick; and I had a large Tub of Punch hot upon the Quarter-Deck, where every Man in the Ship had above a Pint to his share, and drank our Owners and Friends Healths in Great Britain, to a happy New-Year, a good Voyage, and a safe Return.

Woodes Rogers

February 14, 1709. That same day, in Commemoration of the antient Custom in England of chusing Valentines, I drew up a List of the fair Ladies in Bristol, that were any ways related to or concern'd in the Ships, and sent for my Officers into the Cabbin, where every one drew, and drank the Lady's Health in a Cup of Punch, and to a happy Sight of 'em all; this I did to put 'em in mind of Home.

Rex Clements

Obviously the Scylla of classical mythology was an octopus. The rocks she was supposed to haunt on the Italian side of the Straits of Messina is just such a place as a rock-dweller like the octopus would choose. Charybdis on the other hand is nothing but a tide-rip, and well I know it . . . Between them—the octopus and the whirlpool—the mariners of old must have had a strenuous time in making the passage of the Straits.

Samuel Eliot Morison

The winds were more prosperous than they had been to Ulysses, and we romped safely under sail between Scylla and Charybdis. Scylla, incidentally, is now a struggling town, which according to our cook contained not one honest man; and Charybdis is a very feeble whirlpool, a mere whiffle on the water. Something must have happened since Ulysses' day to reduce it; or Ulysses, like so many sailors, was a liar.

Herman Melville

Cut off from all those outward passing things which ashore employ the eyes, tongues, and thoughts of landsmen, the inmates of a frigate are thrown upon themselves and each other, and all their ponderings are introspective. A morbidness of mind is often the consequence, especially upon long voyages, accompanied by foul weather, calms, or head winds. Nor does this exempt from its evil influence any rank on board. Indeed, high station only ministers to it the more, since the higher the rank . . . the less companionship.

Edward H. Dodd, Jr.

On the third day we suddenly discovered that the sea was covered with bits of floating pumice. At first only sparse, it soon grew very thick. From the masthead it stretched out like a long curved road across the sea. It was soon left behind, but presently we noticed a queer activity in the water. In areas so large that the movement was scarcely perceptible, it swirled about gently in different directions. For a while we were exceedingly puzzled, but later, when we again encountered a band of pumice, we realized that we had probably been sailing over a volcano that was merrily rumbling away several miles below us!

William Robinson

That evening . . . I think we sailed directly over an uncharted shoal, although even today I am uncertain about it. We were under full sail with a fresh breeze, doing about seven knots. I was at the wheel when I suddenly noticed discolored water around the ship. Leaping to my feet I saw what looked exactly like bottom, not more than six or eight fathoms down, extending unbroken as far as I could see in all directions. Mottled yellowish brown and light green in color, it raced past beneath our keel, threatening full disaster . . .

If it was not a shoal, it must have been some kind of marine organism. It could not have been a reflection of clouds because by chance the sky was clear at that time—so rare a condition that I noted the fact in the log. This was in 46° South Latitude and 128° West Longitude. The nearest sounding on the chart, just one, showed 2,440 fathoms about thirty miles to the west-northwest. There were no other soundings recorded within about two hundred miles.

Desmond Holdridge

When morning came we were plunging through the sunlit sea under winged-out fore and main, the *Dolphin* careering along joyously like a hobbyhorse on the dewy green of an unmowed lawn.

Hilaire Belloc

The wind rose, and for half an hour I kept her to it. She had no more sail than she needed; she heeled beautifully and strongly to the wind; she took the seas, as they ran more regular, with motion of mastery. It was like the gesture of a horse when he bends his head back to his chest, arching his neck with pride as he springs upon our Downs at morning. So set had the surging of the sea become that she rose and fell to it with rhythm, and the helm could be kept quite steady, and the regular splash of the rising bows and the little wisps of foam came in ceaseless exactitude like the marching of men, and in all this one mixed with the life of the sea.

Desmond Holdridge

. . . the spray-cursed cockpit . . .

Harry Pidgeon

. . . the gorgeous cloudland that always lay ahead.

Ernest K. Gann

. . . the wind held fair and as a consequence our return to the peculiar tranquility of the marine world was accomplished to the melody of many low-key noises. Our senses were lulled by the consistent soft whirring of the wind about our ears, the liquid thumps of the water as our bow plunged into backs of countless waves, the almost inaudible hiss of the sea creaming along the hull plates, and before mealtimes the incongruous rattling of pots from the galley. For our eyes there were the garish dawnings and all through the day the wild monuments of cloud to be admired, and beneath them a sparkling carpet of blue marble, perpetually dancing and veined with white. At night there were the stars to reach out for; and it seemed they could be fondled with the hand as well as admired with the brain . . .

Frank Wightman

Again *Wylo* was chasing the far horizon. The horizon that always escapes the ship and leaves her alone in the center of an enchanted circle.

Ernest K. Gann

. . . 31 degrees and 18 minutes at an instant in Greenwich time when the people of that rather dull London suburb are drinking breakfast tea.

William Robinson

. . . low islands . . . infinitely small fragments of beauty thrust up from precipitous ocean depths.

William Robinson

Varua recovered her balance, gathered steerageway, and rushed off nakedly into the night without a scrap of canvas.

Hilaire Belloc

When you are in a crowded fairway at night, always give way; it is the only rule. And have the sense to behave as the lawyers do: forget that there is such a thing as justice, let alone honor or pride.

Hilaire Belloc

"Let us play the fool, and see if there are no adventures left."

So I put my little boat about until the wind took her from forward, such as it was, and she crawled out to sea.

It was a dull, uneasy morning, hot and silent, and the wind, I say, was hardly a wind, and most of the time the sails flapped uselessly.

But after eleven o'clock the wind first rose, and then shifted a little, and then blew light but steady; and then at last she heeled and the water spoke under her bows, and still she heeled and ran, until in the haze I could see no more land; but even so far out there were no seas, for the light full breeze was with the tide, the tide ebbing out as strong and silent as a man in anger, down the hidden parallel valleys of the narrow sea. And I held this little wind till about two o'clock, when I drank wine and ate bread and meat at the tiller, for I had them by me, and just afterwards, still through a thick haze of heat, I saw Grisnez, a huge ghost, right up against and above me; and I wondered, for I had crossed the Channel, now for the first time and knew now what it felt like to see new land.

Frank Wightman

"Seems to be a life of greetings and farewells."

"I'll say."

Life and Death

Occasionally one finds passages in the yachting literature that provide thoughtful comments on, or that evoke thoughts about, life and death. Such passages, whether direct, oblique, or symbolic, provide a necessary balance to the generally ebullient, light-hearted writings of sailing men and women.

Alan Villiers

It blew one day off Recife. And, it was sad to see the land birds driven out, fighting to stay above the sea but always going down—and once down, never coming up again.

Herman Melville

So near the hull did they come, that the bony creak of their gaunt double-jointed pinions was audible. As the ship under light airs passed on, leaving the burial spot astern, they still kept circling it low down with the moving shadow of their outstretched wings and the cracked requiem of their cries.

Carleton Mitchell

Perhaps a tree standing almost at the tip of Punta Espinosa came closest to symbolizing for me the wonder and mystery of the archipelago. Equatorial sun burned my bare shoulders as I looked upon swimming penguins. Sea lions by the hundreds ranged between the fingers of the outermost ledges, the bulls roaring ceaselessly at invaders real or imaginary, while mothers nursed pups in the coves. Scarlet crabs, bright as painted tin, darted in and out of surf creaming onto coal-black lava. Frigate birds wheeled and bobbies plummeted from a blue sky into green shallows. And there before me were the stark skeleton branches of a tree which somehow had managed to ahieve maturity in sand laved by salt water. As I came closer, sea lions sleeping at the base lifted their heads, and marine iguanas, which had climbed into the branches to come closer to the warming sun, spat at me through their nostrils. The tree and its denizens vividly recalled that I was an intruder.

Herman Melville

Soon the ships diverged their wakes; and long as the strange vessel was in view, she was seen to yaw, hither and thither at every dark spot, however small, on the sea. This way and that her yards were swung around; starboard and larboard, she continued to tack; now she beat against a head sea; and again it pushed her before it; while all the while, her masts and yards were thickly clustered with man, as three tall cherry trees, when the boys are cherrying among the boughs.

But by her still halting course and winding, woeful way, you plainly saw that this ship that so wept with spray, still remained without comfort. She was Rachel, weeping for her children, because they were not.

Samuel Eliot Morison

Just as farmers regulated plowing and sowing by the phases of the moon so sailors and fishermen believed that flood tide meant strength, and ebb tide, weakness. If he survived an ebb he would improve with the flood, but he would always die on the ebb. It was a pretty conception that the sailor's spirit would wish to float out of the harbor with the ebb and once more survey familiar scenes—kelp-marked ledges, foaming tidal rips, circling sea birds, friendly lighthouses, before it left for another world.

Erling Tames

My condition began to trouble me. It struck me that the Almighty Owner of the *Teddy* might have it in his mind to discharge the skipper. Therefore I tried to teach Julie to work out a noon latitude, giving her at the same time hints from my rudimentary store of nautical knowledge, pertaining to courses, winds, steamship lines and so forth.

No less important, it seemed to me, though much more unpleasant, was the task of instructing my wife how to dispose of "the body." It was evident that if I should die, Julie would not have the strength to lift my heavy carcass out of its bunk and carry it on deck. Yet, if this should happen, she would presently be faced with the immediate necessity of committing it to the waves. It must be remembered that we were in the tropics. But whenever I broached the subject, my wife would ram her fingers into her ears and flee.

Alan Villiers

There is something strangely attractive, some glimmer, maybe of the elusive and indefinable thing called romance, something of adventure and of life as all men would have it lived—if they knew how—about the setting out of a big sailing ship for the sea.

E. B. White

And with the tiller in my hand, I'll feel again the wind imparting life to a boat, will smell again the old menace, the one that imparts life to me: the cruel beauty of the

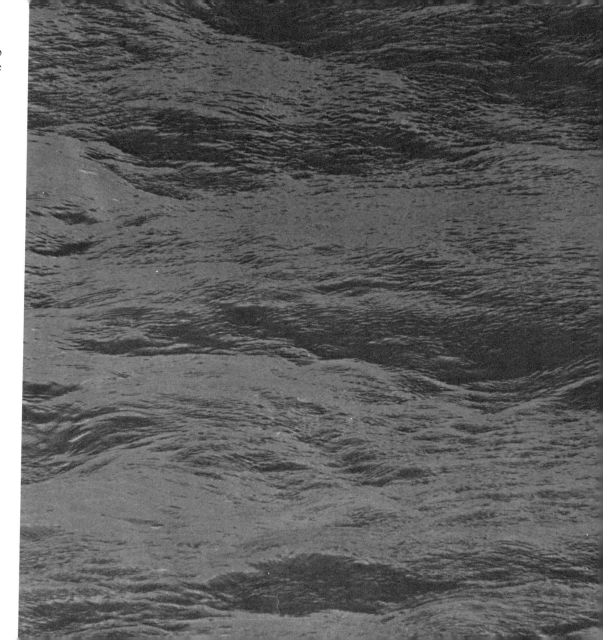

salt world, the barnacle's tiny knives, the sharp spine of the urchin, the stinger of the sun jelly, the claw of the crab.

Thor Heyerdahl

Sometimes, too, we went out in the rubber boat to look at ourselves by night. Coal-black seas towered up on all sides, and a glittering myriad of tropical stars drew a faint reflection from plankton in the water. The world was simple—stars in the darkness. We lived, and that we felt with alert intensity. We realized that life had been full for men before the technical age also—in fact, fuller and richer in many ways than the life of modern man. Time and evolution somehow ceased to exist; all that was real and that mattered were the same today as they had always been and would always be. We were swallowed up in the absolute common measure of history—endless unbroken darkness under a swarm of stars.

Alan Villiers

A little before two we backed the main yard. The Finnish ensign was flying aft, at half mast. The helmsman slowly tolled the wheel bell—melancholy, moving sound. We moved for'ard to where the body lay in state, quite close to the mast where he was killed; Captain Svensson took the lead, and we bore the funeral stage slowly along the wet main deck and on to the poop, all hands carrying it. We would have buried him, in the ordinary course of events, from the quarter deck, just by the break of the poop—traditional place for sea-burials. But there came too many and too heavy seas there and we had to go on the poop. Here, in the open space between the poop capstan and the bole of the mizzen mast a rough flag-draped stand had been made, and here we laid the stage with his remains. The ship lurched heavily and pitched and fell uncomfortably in the seas; we laid the stage 'thwartships that it might keep its place. The water washed sorrowfully around the low main deck, and lapped gently at the rusted old grey sides; here and there it broke into a little fitful spray; the wind had dropped a little, and moaned now softly and dismally in the rigging; the ship was stopped, with the main yards backed, and had no steerage way; aft the log hung over the rail lifelessly, where the mate had forgotten to haul it in. Bareheaded, deeply moved, the crew gathered around, rolling slightly with the motion of the ship, finding some difficulty at times in keeping their feet. Everybody was there, the two mates in their Sunday best, with white collars on—how strange they looked!—the sailmaker, who had shaved, the cook with whitened face and black-rimmed eyes, the eighteen-year-old A.B.'s and the sixteen-year-old ordinary seaman, Swedish Finn, Frenchman, Londoner, Australians, West Indian negro.

The captain began to read the service. There was a Swedish prayer book in the ship, that had belonged to one of the boys, and an English New Testament. These were used. The canvas shroud was draped with the Finnish flag—white and pale blue—because there was neither English nor Australian in the ship. There was no flag, except the Finnish. But the colours of that—purity and loyalty—were appropriate ... Sometimes we could not hear what the Captain said when the ship lurched to meet a sea as she wallowed there and the wind momentarily moaned louder in the rigging. A great white albatross swooped by; there came nothing else to join us in our lonely service.

It was the first sea burial I had seen. I never want to be present at another. The deep solemnity of it, the lasting penetration into the very roots of one's being, the awful impressiveness of this last earthly ritual that marks an end and a beginning, leave a scar on one, witnessed as a member of a sailing ship's crew at sea, that never can be forgotten. Ashore it is different. You go away. You see other people afterwards, other scenes. You do other things. You *have* to go on, and think of other things. But at sea the scene remains unchanged, and nothing ever happens, until the voyage ends, to soften poignant, tragic memories. You cannot forget! Nor think of other things; there is always too much to remind you ...

The Captain read a Swedish prayer, and one of the Australians who had once done a little lay preaching in a tiny South Australian church, said an English prayer. We sang a hymn—"Nearer My God to Thee"—in Swedish and in English, those who were Swedish in the language, and those who were English in theirs, together. It made no difference. We sang another Swedish hymn, an old, old chant of infinite sadness. And then the Captain gave a short address, in his own language, addressing the dead by name, as is the Swedish custom, as if he still lived and were there, as if the spirit were there listening to the last oration the body would receive ...

There followed prayer, and a long service. I saw the cook's white face gleaming wet; the voices of the sailors singing the hymns rose fitfully above the sighing of the wind; they were grown older by years, these boys, in one night; boyhood was gone from them utterly ... The darkness came down, imperceptibly. We carried him to the side. The hatch was tilted slightly; there was a dull splash as the weighted shroud entered the water ... And so it was all over.

Rachel Carson

For all at last return to the sea—to Oceanus, the ocean river, like the everflowing river of time, the beginning and the end.

Sea Life

When he is offshore, particularly when far offshore in the seemingly lifeless wastes of water and air, any encounter with life is
exciting to the sailor. Closer to the land and its complexities, however, his feelings are as varied as are the varieties of life he finds.

Edward H. Dodd, Jr.

"These god damn cockroaches think they own the ship."

William Robinson

I wonder if you have ever seen a tropical cockroach. They are more than two inches long, fly like birds, and become so voracious that they start in on sleeping humans. I have seen men with the soles of their feet eaten off in the night by these brown pests. Ours had not reached that stage yet but had been increasing rapidly. We had already rid the ship of them more than once but it is impossible to keep them off, for as soon as one lot was exterminated, a new batch would fly aboard, or come in with supplies. A rat came aboard for the first time when we were in Madang and we set a trap for him. During the night the trap went off with a bang, and I rejoiced. In the morning I found a large cockroach in the trap. He, and not the rat, had sprung it and got caught. This should give some idea as to the size of these insects.

E. A. Pye

We made a determined war on cockroaches. The first had come aboard at King's Bay, Tobago, on a leg of lamb. It raced for the shelter of the engine room and reached it half an inch ahead of the hammer with which Christopher had tried to kill it. It looked a huge beast, nearly three inches long and full of babies. It was disconcerting to know that a female could have thirty thousand babies in its normal sex life.

Charles Landery

Thirty minutes later I was introduced to my first ship's worm. I made no attempt to hide my distaste and the worms in their unperturbed thousands looked at me in the eye with equal loathing, aware that their position in the double planking was stronger than mine.

"Worm!" said the surveyor quite unnecessarily, "No teredo! Wouldn't expect it of course! Still, thought I'd say so . . ." he added cheerfully and I tried to feel optimistic, gathering that this teredo must be even more repulsive than the squiggles of white slime now glowering at me.

Amos A. Evans

August 11th, Tuesday, 1812. Caught a red headed Woodpecker aboard this morning in 60 fathoms water, distant from land 150 miles.

Ernest K. Gann

Gridley brought with him a parrot called Rebecca, after a notorious Mexican whore. She was a crotchety bird so continuously at odds with captivity that she bit anyone who ventured near her cage, including her master. Rebecca was foul-mouthed, and except when her cage was covered she kept up a continuous insulting commentary on her shipmates and, if ignored, angrily kicked seeds and general parrot debris all over her area of the saloon.

Frank Wightman

For the next few miles on our way out to sea, we should be surrounded by the seabirds of the coast; birds that never go far from the land. A very vocal throng; full of cries and complaints. For to them the sailor is a "client"; these beggars of the sea are full of cries for alms. Soon they will turn back to the island, and their place will be taken by the ocean birds, an aloof and reticent company; these patricians of the ocean go about their affairs with a remoteness that never acknowledges the existence of man. And even they will leave us eventually, for the depths of the ocean sea is a region that is unpeopled by anything that flies.

Dennis Puleston

Daily we watched the sky and the barometer for signs of trouble. John told us to watch the sea birds. Before a storm, he said, they would be heard wailing distressfully.

William Robinson

A tiny canary fluttered out of the sky exhausted, made a try for our jibstay but missed, falling into the sea. Without clothes as usual, I dove in, swam under him and took him in my hand. On board he took a few drops of water and perched on the hatch. A few moments later he feebly took off again—circled the masthead like a tiny Lindbergh—and headed for South America, 75 miles away.

Frank Wightman

A flock of sea birds high up. So unbelievably white their plumage, that the light seemed to shine through them. Gleaming and remote, they seemed to sleep against the dazzling sky on wings that never moved until at some mysterious signal, they started to drift and winnow amongst themselves—weaving lazy arabesques among the clouds. No call. No sound. No movement of the sleeping wings.

William Robinson

At 6:45 p.m. I caught another bird out of the air, this time a pretty little grey tern who made quite a disturbance for a few minutes. When I put him on deck he could not take off by himself but had to be tossed into the air before he could leave. This is the way with sea birds—put them on a ship's deck and they cannot fly off.

Rex Clements

Preeminent amongst them were wandering albatross, the very queen of sea birds, with a wingspread averaging from ten to fifteen feet. Glorious birds these are, with snow white breasts, black markings on their long narrow wings and powerful hooked beaks. They live entirely at sea and must even sleep in the air, for they only go ashore, on one or other of the rocky desolate islands scattered about these high latitudes, during the breeding season. They seem fond of a ship's company, or perhaps experience has taught them that such intruders usually leave a trail of scraps in their wake, for two or three are nearly always in sight from a sailing ship's deck. When they alight on the surface of the sea in search of food they splay out their broad webbed feet, pushing the water before them, and so deaden their way.

Their powers of flight are wonderful and most fascinating to watch. They fly for hours without a movement of their wings more than an occasional, almost imperceptible tilt that changes their elevation. They seem to have the faculty of remaining almost stationary in the air, but when they decide to go ahead, they can pass a running clipper as though she were standing still. And the harder the gale blows, the more calm and serene is the albatross. With the wind howling across the ocean, with never a thing to break its force between New Zealand and the Horn, and the ship under a goosewinged maintop's'l, the albatross floats in the air with never a flicker of its wings, unconcerned that the wind is rising 80 miles an hour. Head on, running, or even athwart the wind, they plane or hang motionless with never an effort. The albatross' consummate mastery of the air has never been satisfactorily explained and must give aviation experts food for thought.

Edward H. Dodd, Jr.

Now a man may be well educated in science. He may be superbly indifferent to horseshoes and broken mirrors. He may not believe in God. But let him watch the mocking eyes of an albatross when he has seen this bird only twice before in his life, and on both occasions just before the only two gales he has experienced, and, for all his past credos, I maintain that he cannot prevent his heart from beating faster.

And these two birds had no sooner settled close by on the water, than Alec, who had not yet seen them, stuck his head out of the after cabin and said he thought the barometer was going down much too fast.

Harry Pidgeon

In many places I have seen brilliant phosphorescent displays at night. In Meli Bay, for the first time, I noticed a marine creature swimming that leaves a phosphorescent streak behind, and when one of them stops for a time, the water all around becomes phosphorescent. On one occasion the surface of the bay was a multitude of phosphorescent streaks ten to fifteen feet in length.

Harry Pidgeon

In these latitudes the phosphorescent sea sometimes takes on a very strange appearance at night. Once when the water was quite smooth, the whole expanse resembled a plain of snow . . .

Harry Pidgeon

One day, when the *Islander* was moving along at a good clip before a fresh breeze, a school of small squid came on board from aft. They passed my head as if shot out of a gun, striking sails and rigging with such force as to knock off the heads of some.

Thor Heyerdahl

We had several times observed the large white shells of cuttlefish eggs, lying floating like ostrich eggs or white skulls on the blue swell. On one solitary occasion we saw a squid lying wriggling underneath.

William Robinson

We are getting quite foul along the after part of the bottom, deadwood, bilges and rudder. The trouble seems to be a strange species of barnacle, soft, almost transparent, jelly-like and shaped exactly like the black cloves one finds in pickled things.

Rex Clements

The easy way we were making through the water gave us an opportunity to rig the grating the carpenter had made, and try to scrape some of the barnacles off our bottom. Lines were passed under the ship and bent on to each side of the grating, which was then hauled slowly back and forth under the hull, beginning for'ard and working aft. It was slow work, but successful in removing a great quantity of barnacles, even if the resultant increase in speed was scarcely appreciable.

William Robinson

It was remarkable to see queer rubbery barnacles, and grass, growing and spreading while we were making good progress through the water all the time. They seemed to flourish better during the voyage than they did later while *Svaap* was anchored for weeks at a time in lagoons in the islands.

Rex Clements

On one occasion we sailed over to San Lorenzo, the island that shelters Callao Bay to seaward, and made a landing on its shores. We picked up a few shells there and saw a number of large crabs. The old man said they were deepsea crabs and often met with hundreds of miles from land. They were big, vicious creatures, a dull mottled green in color, with most business-like pincers. They scuttled about rapidly and differed from our English crabs in that their shells and claws were flattened, with sharp serrated edges. Their shape enabled them to swim very quickly and it is surprising with what speed they can move along just under the surface of the water, working their legs as though they were walking on land.

Ray Kauffman

That night, as we were watching a friendly lighthouse on Miarang reefs, one of the very few atolls in Netherlands India, I noticed, although the night was moonless, that the water gradually changed from the India ink, spark-flected sea of off-soundings to the pale whitish color of moonlight over a shoal, white sand bottom. The line of the horizon disappeared in a pale reflected light. We sounded. There was no bottom at twenty fathoms. With a bearing on the lighthouse, we checked an accurate position well offshore in six hundred fathoms. The sounding lead and line failed to leave the usual trail of phosphorescent sparks, but it was clearly visible in the peculiarly lighted water. A school of porpoises, invisible off the beam but breathing audibly, rushed across the bow; and their markings, even the blowhole in the tops of their heads, were as plainly discernible as if seen in broad daylight. The seams in the black hull stood out and the sails were ghostly white. It was lighter than a full moon night, yet there was no moon and the light came not from above but from the water. Shadows were inverted.

Vito Dumas

. . . I thought I heard breakers; I was practically becalmed—it would be . . . No. The noise came from an enormous school of porpoises approaching ahead.

Francis Brenton

It was still nightime, and the rest of the school of dolphins were fat, ghost-like apparitions, the phosphorus so thickly plastered on their bodies that when they leap out of the water, fragments shot from their fins and tails like a hail of shooting stars.

Frank Wightman

. . . the little puffing breaths of the porpoises curving lazily round us sounded like someone sneezing in church.

Rex Clements

Sharks put in an appearance and we caught several. The first one we hauled aboard was a female, for it had eight young ones inside it. These youngsters were perfectly formed and exactly like their parent, but on a smaller scale. When we cut the mother open they slithered out on deck, all very much alive and each about two feet long.

A great difference of opinion arose concerning the young sharks. Some of the crew said they were unborn and had never yet left their mother. Others said they had been duly born, but had swum back down the maternal throat at the sign of approaching danger. I was never able to discover the truth of the matter, but, of the two hypotheses inclined to the latter. For sharks in embryo they were too much alive, too exact replicas of the big one. There was no indication of "growing to the head" as children and most animals seem to do, and besides I always thought sharks spawned like other fish, and did not bring their offspring into the world like mammals. But, on the other hand, to swim down a shark's throat and be cast up again sounded a bit far-fetched and savored too much of Jonah and the whale. Anyhow, the men cut them up and cooked them for supper, but in view of the doubts as to their nativity, I gave them a wide berth.

Rex Clements

The Mate cut some strips of the (shark) skin, which is exceedingly rough and dries as hard as a board, for cleaning purposes in place of sandpaper.

Rex Clements

. . . an absurd-looking creature called a sunfish. It was about 20 inches across, with a skin as prickly as a hedgehog's. As it lay on the deck, breathing heavily, it had a fussy important look, like a city alderman after a good dinner.

Edward H. Dodd, Jr.

. . . Alec spied a large sea bat alongside. Aches and blisters were forgotten in the rush for the dinghy. With Tom and Alec rowing and me poised in the bow, harpoon in hand, we set chase. About eight feet by six, more or less diamond-shaped, he was a huge beast who seemed to propel himself by shooting wrinkles across his body.

Dennis Puleston

One authority, having studied many of the logbooks of the whaling captains of 50 years ago, has estimated that an average of 122 tortoises was taken away by every ship. Without food or water they would be kept in the hold until the cook's axe decapitated them and they were made into stew. In one case, 18 months after a whaler had called at the Galapagos, the sailors were clearing out the hold when they found, wedged behind some barrels of oil, a tortoise, still alive!

Herman Melville

Ropes were dropped over, and presently three huge antedilu-vian-looking tortoises, after much straining, were landed on deck. They seemed hardly of the seed of earth. We had been abroad upon the waters for five long months, a period amply sufficient to make all things of the land wear a fabulous hue to the dreamy mind. Had three Spanish custom house officers boarded us then, it is not unlikely that I should have curiously stared at them, felt of them, and stroked them much as savages observe civilized guests. But instead of three custom house officers, behold these really wondrous tortoises—none of your schoolboy mud turtles—but black as widower's weeds, heavy as chests of plate, with vast shells medalioned and orbed like shields that have breasted a battle—shaggy too, here and there, with dark green moss, and slimy with the spray of the sea. These mystic creatures, suddenly translated by night from unutterable solitudes to our peopled deck, affected me in a manner not easy to unfold. They seemed newly crawled forth from beneath the foundations of the world. Yea, they seemed the identical tortoises whereon the Hindu plants this total sphere. With a lantern I inspected them more closely. Such worshipful venerableness of aspect! Such furry greenness mantling the rude peelings and healing the fissures of their shattered shells. I no more saw three tortoises. They expanded—became transfigured—I seemed to see three Roman coliseums in magnificent decay.

Rex Clements

All that night we heard a curious scratching noise coming from the rocks to the south'ard of us; it sounded very weird and suggested the scraping of multitudes of tin pans. The old man said it was the calling of penguins.

Frank Wightman

. . . and after anchoring her I had stood listening to the thousands of penguins giving that mysterious tribal chant with which they greet the setting sun. Each bird's contribution is something like a musical snore, but the massed effect is evocative and compelling. Heard from a distance at which *Wylo* was lying, individual voices were merged in the great mosaic of sound, and suddenly I realized that this was the sound effect that should accompany a Breughel painting of a country fair. These birds were medieval peasants. There are forest laughs, bursts of drunken song, squeals from wenches, sudden upsurges of mass laughter, old men droning a bar or two on the rebeck—and behind it all, the sound of thousands of earthy folk well-dined.

Rex Clements

While passing Mas a Tierra, but some miles distant, the last of the little penguins we had caught in Independencia Bay disappeared overboard. The little chap had been all alone for several days, his companions having one by one disappeared. He used to waddle disconsolately about the decks, or stand with his head poked out of a scupper-hole for hours at a time watching the distant horizon. Apparently the sight of land proved too much for him and, "Hell or Melbourne," thought he, "here goes," for he squeezed through and dropped into the sea. We watched him striking out for the land and I make no doubt he reached it with ease, for penguins are marvellous swimmers.

Sir Francis Chichester

I collected some weird creatures in the sargasso weed. One horrible thing looked like a miniature dinosaur with six stumpy legs, each of which had a big sucker instead of a foot.

Rex Clements

Crossing the Sargasso Sea we ran into huge fields of the strange weed that . . . drifts about in long wavy lines, or thick sluggish meadows, hither and thither before the wind.

The Sargasso Sea is a wide expanse lying in the heart of the North Atlantic, somewhat nearer to the West Indies than to Africa. Untroubled by ocean currents, it is bounded on all sides by the Gulf Stream and the North Equatorial Current. It is a weird expanse of water, colder than the neighboring seas, covering the profundities of the Bahama deep. With depths untroubled by moving currents, it resembles a cold silent vortex in the midst of warm, encircling, swiftly running streams.

Weird stories are told of the Sargasso Sea—of monstrous shapes that float occasionally to its surface, and of derelicts—antique worm-eaten old craft—encountered after drifting for ages on its stagnant waters. The floating meadows of weed are big and strange enough to give rise to God knows what fancies; perhaps in bygone days they were larger still; in any case they were considerable enough to cause much apprehension to mariners in 50-foot caravels.

The *Arethusa* ploughed her way through several fields of many acres in extent. For two or three days, the surface of the sea was never free from long, fringing lines and isolated clumps of weed . . . we fished for specimens, dragging them on board and preserving pieces in bottles of salt water. We caught great clumps by means of a grapnel . . . The weed is a yellowish brown color with large blob-like berries. These were yellow but at some seasons of the year assume a pink tinge.

The weed harbors a multitude of minute forms of animal life—tiny crabs as big as one's fingernail, seahorses, delicately-tinted jellyfish . . . In one lump we found the most curious fish mortal eyes ever looked upon. It was about four inches long, dull yellow in color, with black blotches all over it. Its eyes were expressionless and protruding, with two horns sticking out above, and its body covered with sharp thorny prickles. But the unique feature was its legs—four stumpy, web-footed and distinct legs.

Rex Clements

"What are ye?" said he, "divil or man or baste?"

The uncanny object swept down on us, grazed our shoulder and went swirling and gleaming by. As it did so the mystery was explained. It was a dead whale. Stripped of every scrap of skin, with its blubber exposed to the salt water, it glowed and sparkled all over with a shimmering phosphorescent light. The processes of decomposition had swelled it to a monstrous size, and its bulk lay on the water like a great bladder . . . The grotesque apparition was gone in a few minutes, swallowed in the gloom astern, with its luminous halo and noisy following (of birds). It made a very weird and not easily forgotten sight. What a ghost story it would have given rise to, I thought, if seen from a little distance by the daring but credulous mariners of old!

Rex Clements

These latter (humpback whales) are amusing creatures to watch. They have a trick of rolling over and with their flippers waving in the air as though they were immensely tickled at something . . . .

Sir Francis Chichester

Sensitive animals like whales, I thought, must know that the boat is there, but, as they came on unswerving, my confidence vanished. I believe that many small boat disappearances have been due to whales. Those charging *Gipsy Moth* were only small ones; 15 to 25 feet long, but they were big enough, and I picked up my horn and blew the hardest blast I could. Twenty feet off they dived under the stern and came up 50 feet away on the other side. There was a lot—I thought about 100—milling round at speed. Suddenly they all dashed off towards the west at full speed, leaving a seething white wake. Then I noticed an equally big school coming at full speed from the west. They met head on, and there seemed to be about an acre of seething boiling white water where they milled round madly. Then, as one, they all dived, the surface became smooth again, and I saw them no more. Were they meeting for love or for war. I wondered.

Rex Clements

We also captured several pretty little nautilus—Portugee men-o'-war, is their sea name. They are met with cruising about the Equatorial regions in whole fleets. Nothing can be prettier than to see thousands upon thousands of these adventurous little mariners driving over summer seas before a gentle breeze. They look like a fleet of fairies—as though King Oberon had put to sea with all his court.

Frank Wightman

. . . the sea was covered with a great fleet of frail pink Portuguese men-o'-war. Delicate, fan-shaped things, blowing along before the wind. They were clustered so thickly on the sea's face, it was impossible to avoid them, and in our wake they bobbed and eddied. As *Wylo* glided through this flower garden which had suddenly bloomed on the face of the sea, the downdraught from her sails capsized the fragile things.

Alain Gerbault

I sighted some Portuguese men-of-war, a sort of flat jellyfish showing a long blue fan as a sail. There have been many discussions by mariners about them. Some say they can only drift to leeward, while others have maintained they can actually work to windward like a vessel. From my own observations of the shape and angles of their sail-like fans I conclude they are hove to and drift slowly to leeward.

Seafood

The modern sailor can be fastidious, even elegant, in his eating habits and choice of food and drink aboard ship. Creativity in culinary matters is another thing. Independent of time, money, refrigeration, or locker space, creativity is a quality unique to the man and the making-do with what is at hand.

Rex Clements

Stedman used grimly to tell us that the regulation breakfast in a lime-juicer was two draws at one's pipe and reefing another hole in one's belt.

Dennis Puleston

A yachtsman sails on his stomach . . .

John MacGregor

Now, as I had often to begin work by first frying food at one or two o'clock in the moonlight, and as it would have a greedy sound if the next attack on eatables were to be called "second breakfast," the only true way of settling this point was to consider the first meal to be in fact a late supper of yesterday, or at any rate to regard it as belonging to the day bygone, and therefore beyond inquiry, and so to ignore this first breakfast altogether in one's arrangements. The stomach quite approved of this decision, and was always ready for the usual breakfast at six or seven o'clock, whatever had been discussed a few hours before.

Samuel Eliot Morison

But for me, the odor of smoke from the Charley Noble when you start a fire in the shipmate stove with bits of driftwood. Neither spruce bough nor birch twig has the delicious, spicy odor of smoke from a fire made of fragments of an old, brine-soaked lobster trap found cast up on the shore, mixed with hardwood chunks from a carpenter shop.

Harry Pidgeon

It was now raining and blowing hard, so we dived below, built a roaring fire, and were soon eating fried penguin eggs and hot cakes.

Frank Wightman

And then our water went bad. We had filled our tanks at the island and had wondered at the queer taste of it when we first drew from the tanks. Now it was a dark-brown color and smelled of dead rats. I was for drinking it as it was. The smell was no proof that it was bad; look at the smell of some dishes man eats for pleasure.

Joe Richards

There was a shed on the wharf and a big pile of black chunks that looked like coal clinkers covered with mud, retrieved for some strange reason from a sunken barge. "What's that stuff?" I asked a fellow on the wharf. He reached over, lifted a clump, twisted his knife into it and popped an oyster into my mouth. It was the first raw shell food I had ever eaten.

I have devoured steamed clams till they came out of my ears. I was gone on oyster stew, but for the life of me I couldn't abide raw shell food till that day. It was unbelievably delicious, sweet and slightly salty with a fragrance of the sea as subtle as the faint perfume of a modest woman. It braced me like a shot. I sat on the great heap of oysters with my pocketknife and glutted myself till it was too dark to see. Then I kindled a fire in the stove and slept like the just.

Hilaire Belloc

. . . still watching them, I say, I groped round with my hand behind the cabin door and pulled out brandy and bread, and drank brandy and ate bread, still watching the seas.

Herman Melville

One clear, cold morning, while we were yet running away from the Cape, a rawboned, crack-pated Down Easter, belonging to the *waist*, made his appearance at the mast, dolefully exhibiting a blackened tin pan, bearing a few crusty traces of some sort of a sea-pie, which had been cooked in it.

"Well, sir, what now?" said the Lieutenant of the Deck, advancing.

"They stole it, sir; all my nice *dunderfunk*, sir; they did, sir," whined the Down Easter, ruefully holding up his pan.

"Stole your *dunderfunk:* What's that?"

"*Dunderfunk*, sir, dunderfunk; a cruel nice dish as ever man put into him."

"Speak out, sir; what's the matter?"

"My *dunderfunk*, sir—as elegant a dish of *dunderfunk* as you ever see, sir—they stole it, sir!"

"Go forward, you rascal!" cried the Lieutenant, in a towering rage, "or else stop your whining. Tell me, what's the matter?"

"Why, sir, them 'ere two fellows, Dobs and Hodnose, stole my *dunderfunk*."

"Once more, sir, I ask what that *dunderfunk* is? Speak!"

"As cruel a nice—"

"Be off, sir, sheer!" and muttering about non compos mentis, the Lieutenant stalked away; while the Down Easter beat a melancholy retreat, holding up his pan like a tambourine, and making dolorous music on it as he went.

(*Dunderfunk* is made of hard biscuit, hashed and pounded, mixed with beef fat, molasses, and water and baked brown in a pan. And to those who are beyond all reach of shore delicacies, this *dunderfunk* in the feeling language of the Down Easter, is certainly a "cruel nice dish")

Rex Clements

We soon grew to like the food, rough though it was, and eked out our scanty fare by concocting various dishes beloved of apprentices. The chief constituent of all of them was sea-biscuit broken into pieces and baked with small morsels of beef or pork and called "cracker-hash"; sea-biscuits soaked into a pulp with water and sugar, and known as "dogsbody"; or—most delectable of all—sea-biscuits pounded up fine in a canvas bag, by the simple process of hammering it on the forebitts with an iron belaying pin, and then mixed into a thick stodgy cake with fat, sugar or molasses, and baked in a bullybeef tin. This was "dandyfunk" and the most esteemed delicacy on our bill of fare.

Ray Kauffman

"The day after the day after tomorrow," he said, "I'll take you to a hotel and we'll all have a hot bath and a drink and then I'll buy you the best dinner you have ever eaten. We'll start with oysters, brown bread and stout. The oysters are better in Australia than anywhere in the world. Then we'll have prawns or lobster; a mixed grill with steak, chops and kidneys; crisp lettuce; and fresh strawberries in cream!"

"Hush!" we shouted as we soaked a stringy piece of pickled New Hebridean cow and boiled up two cups of rice.

Arthur Ransome

The recipe for marmalade on *Racundra:* First buy your oranges; then eat your oranges, but do not throw the peel into the sea. Then boil the peel. Then—but here I must revert to our actual discovery, which was made on *Kittiwake* and not on *Racundra,* which is a far steadier boat. Then make an inadvertent movement from one side of the boat to the other and upset the whole boiling into the bilge. Collect the orange peel from the bottom boards and stew once more with plenty of sugar, when the result will be indistinguishable from the best English marmalade. The important discovery, apart from the fact that by this process you can both eat your oranges and have your marmalade, was the upsetting. Until that event we had not known that the water of the first boiling should be poured off, and the final stewing down with fresh water, and this last is the whole secret of marmalade.

Edward H. Dodd, Jr.

Naturally the talk of the morning centered on waterspouts and Sandy gave us a "waterspout souffle" for luncheon.

E. A. Pye

. . . and we sat down to a supper of oysters, wine and the most delicious peaches that I can remember.

Francis Brenton

. . . turtle steaks soaked with rum and lemon.

Edward H. Dodd, Jr.

That night one of the steaks was broiled for supper. Several authorities were quoted to prove that porpoise had to be soaked in vinegar for several days before eating, but our fresh steak was wholly delicious and even the liver and heart tasted quite normal.

Arthur Ransome

So we lived on cold bacon, tinned herrings and beer, and relieved our feelings by punching the barometer.

Edward H. Dodd, Jr.

Skip complacently pronounced it iguana, a beast which in spite of its formidable appearance is quite harmless and is eaten with great gusto by the natives. Whereupon we presented it to Sandy for our main supper course. Having prepared the animal, Sandy refused to eat, and the rest of us, even though it was well disguised in a cream stew, had seen enough to make our appetites a bit more meager than usual. It was, nevertheless, quite palatable, the taste, like that of all other strange beasts, closely resembling chicken.

Dwight Long

. . . Timi caught a kingfish weighing 20 pounds. He fixed a portion of it up raw with vinegar and lime juice, and I enjoyed it, for I had not eaten that way since we left the islands.

Ray Kauffman

Bonito, cooked, is dry; but eaten raw it is the prize seafood of Polynesia. The dark red meat is cut in cubes, then soaked in lime juice, salt water and sliced onion for a few minutes until the outside of the meat is bleached white. The fish is then drained and a sauce of coconut milk and salt water is added. It is really delicious, does not smell fishy and tends to satisfy the craving for fresh beef.

E. F. Knight

The old-fashioned seafood is the best after all. Salt beef and salt pork, even after it has traveled a few times around the world, and is consequently somewhat malodorous, forms a far more sustaining diet than the very best of tinned meats. The instinct of the sailor teaches him this; as a rule he detests the flabby, overcooked stuff out of the cans, and, even if he tolerates it, will always prefer to it the commonest mess beef, which in odor, taste, and appearance would be horrible to a fastidious person. But let this same person have been at sea for a few months and the chances are that he will look forward with pleasure to the days on which the salt junk appears on the ship's bill of fare.

William Robinson

There is constant tribal warfare and cannibalism. The following description, which I quote from Erskine, held true in full until very recently, and in part today:

"The people are inveterate cannibals. Enemies slain in war are eaten by them. They will go to other villages and exhume bodies that have been buried two, three, or more days, bring them home, cook and eat them . . .

They have found human flesh preferable to pork, and strangely enough the connoisseurs claim the flesh of the native to be superior to that of a white man which they say has a salty taste.

Woodes Rogers

He came at last to relish his Meat well enough without Salt or Bread, and in the Season had plenty of good Turnips, which had been sow'd there by Capt. Dampier's Men, and have now overspread some Acres of Ground. He had enough of good Cabbage from the Cabbage-Trees, and season'd his Meat with the Fruit of the Pimento Trees, which is the same as the Jamaica Pepper, and smells deliciously. He found there also a black Pepper call'd Malagita, which was very good to expel Wind, and against Griping of the Guts.

Woodes Rogers

. . . There are abundance of petty Kings, who live upon their particular Rivers, on which they decide their Quarrels with Canoes, and the Conqueror eats up the Conquer'd; so that one King's Belly proves another's Sepulcher . . .

Francis Brenton

Her [the boat's] anti-fouling paint was red and was favorite food for the goose-necked barnacles which thrived on its spicy flavor all the way over.

Erling Tambs

Those weather-bound fishermen in Cedeira taught us to eat barnacles and octopus, which, after overcoming our first foolish aversion, we found delicious fare. The barnacles grew in big clusters along the rocky shores and were gathered at low tide. They were easy to clean, and when boiled in salt water, their long necks tasted very much like shrimp.

Sir Francis Chichester

I found a handsome six-inch squid on deck . . . It seemed just the thing for a good bouillabaisse, but I couldn't face eating it.

Rex Clements

To human taste it (octopus) is quite flavorless and I have seen sailors chew it when tobacco is scarce.

Francis Brenton

Between meals I had been eating barnacles for the past few weeks.

I ate them in Arab fashion: pull the barnacle, bite the end, and the meat inside the stem comes free . . . a better fare was the green eelgrass growing on the waterline. I couldn't get enough of this, for it had a pleasant taste. It looked like spinach, and when squeezed dry between finger and thumb, tasted like salted spinach, and it was no doubt jammed with vitamins. Even the mushrooms . . . had long since proved to be nonpoisonous. At first I had just nibbled on them. Then I had found that they were firm and sweet and quite up to commercial standards. As it was, I soon ate the (log canoe) hulls bare . . .

And this was no time to dwell on looks or fancy preparations or so I rationalized. Surely small crustaceans cannot be any worse than such large crustaceans as shrimp, crab or lobster. Small fish or eggs are no worse than large fish or caviar. Minute jellyfish . . . can be compared to octopus or squid, which are delicacies of many people's choice. Plankton then, if just a large meal on a small scale . . . Instead of thinking of my meal as barnacles, eelgrass, jellyfish eggs and plankton, I thought of it as oysters, spinach, squid and shrimp.

Thor Heyerdahl

In good plankton waters there are thousands in a glassful. More than once persons have starved to death at sea because they did not find fish large enough to be spitted, netted, or hooked. In such cases it has often happened that they have literally been sailing about in a strongly diluted, raw fish soup.

And, bad as it smelled, it tasted good if one just plucked up courage and put a spoonful of it into one's mouth. If this consisted of many dwarf shrimps, it tasted like shrimp paste, lobster, or crab. If it was mostly deep sea fish ova, it tasted like caviar and now and then oysters.

Ray Kauffman

. . . . he slowly plucked the feathers and Gerry made a stuffing from broken sea biscuit, chopped onion, sage, seafowl eggs and diced bacon.

Jack London

The aroma of coffee arose to Joe's nose, and from a light iron pot came the unmistakable smell of beans nearly done. The cook placed a frying pan on the stove, wiped it around with a piece of suet when it had heated, and tossed in a thick chunk of beefsteak. While he worked he talked with a companion on deck, who was busily engaged in filling a bucket overside and flinging the salt water over heaps of oysters that lay on the deck. This completed, he covered the oysters with wet sacks, and went into the cabin, where a place was set for him on a tiny table, and where the cook served the dinner and joined him in eating it.

Rex Clements

Another species of ocean bird of which we caught several was the "mutton bird." At least, that is the name given it by sailors; I believe its more correct name is a shearwater. It is called a mutton bird because the

two fillets of flesh cut from either side of the breast, when steeped in vinegar and grilled, are reputed to taste exactly like a cut from a shoulder of mutton.

Dwight Long

After finishing our meal we would always wash up immediately, and if there were any leftovers, Hugo would have a meal. Timi would let my dog lick the plates clean before washing them in boiling sea water and putting them away.

Hans De Mierre

Sea pie, alternate layers of salt beef, corned beef, flapjacks, sliced onions and potatoes in individual layers.

E. A. Pye

We sounded the water tanks and found we had at least twenty-five gallons left; all the fruit, except a melon, two oranges and a few moldy lemons had gone and we started on vitamin tablets to keep off scurvy. We had finished the last of an enormous pumpkin the previous day and the potatoes were growing long shoots, but were still good to eat. We had finished the bacon and were sick of the sight of biscuits. Anne made drop scones and scone-bread on alternate days, which we regarded as a great treat. Of the tins, corned beef was the favorite meat, with tongue a close second, grapes and peaches the nicest fruits.

Joshua Slocum

. . . so I made a fire and very cautiously stewed a dish of pears and set them carefully aside till I had made a pot of delicious coffee, for both of which I could afford sugar and cream.

Charles Violet

First of all bottles of wine were placed on the table, and we had a long drink; then the "mouse" (ship's boy) brought in a large crusty loaf, about a couple of pounds of butter, a bucket of oysters, a pot of lobsters and a dish of radishes. A man next to me opened up the oysters with his sheaf-knife, and handed them to me, but a dozen were all I could manage; then the skipper picked a fine lobster, broke it in two, and passed me the flaky tail part. I helped this down with radishes and strong Algerian wine, throwing the debris into a tin on the cabin floor.

· In the middle of this orgy two yachtsmen cautiously descended the ladder. They had come to pay a courtesy call on me, found no one in the *Nova,* and guessed that I might be aboard the fishing boat. One was M. Herve, secretary of the Societe des Regates Rochelaise, and the other a well-known yachtsman from Bordeaux. Although refusing to eat they joined us in wine. It was a jolly party, and did not break up until 4 p.m. By this time the skipper was very drunk, and I, alas, was sick.

Samuel Eliot Morison

The prize dish in Greece is a Turkish heritage called *Iman biali,* meaning "the Iman fainted" (presumably from joy). It is eggplant cooked up with tomatoes, onions, almonds, half a dozen herbs, served cold with olive oil.

Richard Maury

Supper: hot tongue, potatoes, biscuit, China tea.

Joshua Slocum

The bill of fare that evening was turtle steak, tea and toast, fried potatoes, stewed onions; with dessert of stewed pears and cream.

E. F. Knight

. . . stewed shark and onions is not a dish to be despised.

Frank Wightman

To save baking bread at sea (a trapeze act when there is any sea running), we had bought an ancient tin of army biscuits. These were like firebricks when fresh, and like crepe rubber when the humidity of the tropics worked on them for twenty-four hours. We tried heating them. They turned into bathroom tiles. Soon the monotony of the wake was relieved with a sprinkling of biscuits.

Desmond Holdridge

. . . I cooked a kind of oatmeal pancake . . .

Edward H. Dodd, Jr.

From the very first luncheon, the cooking of meals had been a controversial element. With the aid of, or perhaps in spite of, his cook book, Sandy had improved beyond all expectation, but bread making was the great stumbling block. Various formulas having failed, experiments started. A famous one was conducted by Tom. After considerable literary search he prepared a yeast culture on a potato. The dough was carefully mixed with this invigorated yeast, and set behind the stove to rise. Many blessings fell upon that large grey lump that evening. It was to sit all night and be baked the next morning. Along toward midnight, while Tom was at the wheel still preoccupied with the chemical composition of the staff of life, Sandy appeared from the galley.

"Hey, Tom, the gottam dough was rising so fast I had to put a brick on it."

E. A. Pye

Christopher got breakfast, conjuring up toast to enliven the moldy bread.

Edward H. Dodd, Jr.

. . . Sandy had contracted to make doughnuts. With the eager assistance of two men, the batter was completed. Little bubbles in the deep grease showed that the pan was ready. He fashioned an experimental one and let it carefully into the pan. A mass of bubbles arose; there was a soft hiss, and the doughnut disappeared. A wave of superstitious terror passed through our hearts and another was quickly tried. Only a few crumbling cinders resulted. A third was dipped in and swiftly whipped out. It was very emaciated but still present. Sandy chewed it speculatively, spat out of the hatch, and compared it to various unprintable stuffs. A careful check-up followed which finally discovered that baking soda, instead of baking powder, had been used.

Joshua Slocum

When the savory chowder was done, chocking the pot securely between two boxes on the cabin floor, so that it could not roll over, we helped ourselves and swapped yarns over it while the *Spray* made her own way through the darkness on the river.

Vito Dumas

. . . I made myself a large cup of chocolate, accompanied by dates and sea biscuit well buttered.

E. A. Pye

We were thankful to get out of the heat and we sat down to a lunch of cheese and bread, grapefruit, and the juice of two oranges laced with rum.

Sir Francis Chichester

. . . I thought that here was the occasion to change for dinner, to put on my green velvet smoking jacket . . . and to sit down to a royal feast of grapefruit; cold salmon, with fresh potatoes and onions; ginger nuts and

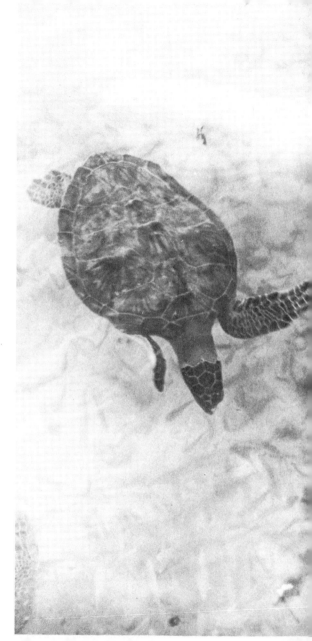

Danish blue cheese; almonds and raisins; coffee. But it was not to be; when the time came for dinner, I was too tired.

Ernest K. Gann

It is the last of twilight before we are finished. We turn for port and make a bowl of soup, gnaw on some bread and salami, and warm our guts with heavy red wine.

Richard Maury

. . . A stout meal: limed papaya, Vienna schnitzel and rice, blocks of gravied carrot, French bread, tinned New Zealand butter, native beer, cake and Chinese ice cream; black scented coffee. And mail . . .

Joshua Slocum

. . . the bill of fare consisted mostly of flying fish, hot biscuits and butter, potatoes, coffee and cream—dishes readily prepared.

E. A. Pye

. . . "tiller soup," the standard dinner on *Moonraker* in winds of force six and over. Two tins of meat soup, slices of cold ham and potatoes, either cooked in the pressure cooker or used up from a previous meal. The whole panful is heated until the ham is hot and served in the largest bowls we have.

Richard Maury

The helmsman stays at his post unrelieved, the man below handing up the lunch before disappearing for the afternoon. There are several tough planks of the eternal ship biscuit, a little salmon, but today instead of tea or cocoa there is only the daily ration of lime juice and water, somewhat sugared, a sea tonic of old with a citric tang giving the illusion of a cool drink. The meal over, he dowses the tinware in the wake, then puts it by until going off watch.

John MacGregor

The healthful relish with which a plain hot breakfast of this sort is consumed with the fresh air all round, and the sun athwart the east, and the waves dancing while the boat sails merrily all the time, is enhanced by the pleasure of steering and buttering bread, and holding a hot egg and a tea cup, all at once.

Charles Violet

. . . keeping up my strength with bread, cheese and bananas, washed down with a rather sour wine.

Erling Tambs

There were twenty bunches—half a ton—of bananas, which it seemed impossible to place until at last I hung them, ten each, on two solid poles lashed securely to the shrouds, one on either side.

Afterwards, at sea, these bananas proved a permanent danger, chafing against each other with the motion of the ship and dropping all over the deck to make traps for the big feet of a sailor hurrying forward at night to attend to some necessary detail of navigation.

E. A. Pye

The wind remained light, and on the fourth day a hot wind from Africa ripened every banana in the ship. We held a banana-eating competition, which Christopher won with seventeen at a sitting; Anne was next with seven; and I was out of sight astern with four.

Harry Pidgeon

A long-continued diet of prunes had given me a wonderful appetite for oranges.

E. A. Pye

. . . and a bumboat rowed off with a side of bacon, three hands of bananas, baskets of peaches, passion fruit, melons, lemons and oranges, one hundred and fifty eggs, potatoes, onions, beans, and fresh and salted butter, which we kept in tins surrounded by fresh water.

Ray Kauffman

Green bananas lashed to the rigging, strips of drying fish hanging like pendants from the shrouds, the cockpit filled with oranges and lemons, and two cooked hams swinging easily from the carlings in the galley contributed to a feeling of prosperity.

John MacGregor

I had in this case a serious disturbance within, yet not mental. Strawberries and cream imprisoned with mushrooms did not agree.

Sir Francis Chichester

I made up my salad beds that day. These "beds" were most valuable in giving me fresh greenstuff, but I had to resow them often. I began by sowing on flannel, but I found that soft paper did very well, and this was a good discovery, because combing out the old roots from the flannel to reuse it was quite a chore.

Warwick Charlton

. . . some mustard and cress seeds . . . planted three days ago on wet cotton wool in a cut-down biscuit tin were ready to be eaten.

William Robinson

Our daily ration was cut to six very small potatoes, half a tin of sardines, half a tin of soup, and a tin of evaporated milk. Oh, yes, and one onion. I have never been without the latter and believe that it had a great deal to do with our health.

Edward H. Dodd, Jr.

. . . the remainder, two packages, were placed in a tin lashed to the truck of the mainmast. Thus any extra smokes could be had only by climbing the mast and one cigarette only was allowed per trip up.

K. Adlard Coles

We made some toffee, partly to kill time, and partly because of its value as food in bad weather that might come.

Edward H. Dodd, Jr.

The foremost question was, of course, ice.

Auxiliary Motors

He had sailed for years and had owned a variety of small boats but he had never owned an engine, not even a kicker. Instead, he studied the sky from his kitchen window, looked at the wind direction finder (a gift from his wife) mounted atop the dormered attic, listened to local weather reports, considered whether the winds were right in force and direction, and then decided if he would sail that day.

Whenever I kicked the starter on my boat I'd look over to where his sloop was kept. As I watched, he masterfully pushed his sloop from its slip. As I motored into the wind to hoist the main, he was leisurely placating an ebbing tide or accomodating a following breeze.

Dennis Puleston

The only reason that *Uldra's* engine never failed was because she did not have one.

Frank Wightman

My experience with engines is that if you depend on them they fail you, but if it just doesn't matter, they serve you.

Farley Mowat

. . . There remained only one area of real uncertainty—the engine. . . . She was a seven-horsepower, single-cylinder, make-and-break, gasoline-fueled monster, built in the 1920s from an original design conceived somewhere near the end of the last century. She was massive beyond belief, and intractable beyond bearing. In order to start her it was first necessary to open a priming cock on the cylinder head and introduce half a cup of raw gasoline. Then you had to spin her flywheel which was as big as the wheel of a freight car and weighed about the same.

There was no clutch and no gear box. When, and if, the engine started, the boat immediately began to move. She did not necessarily move forward. It is an idiosyncrasy of the make-and-breaks that when they start they may choose to turn over either to left or to right (which is to say either forward or astern), and there is no way known to man of predicting which direction it is going to be.

Once started, the direction can be reversed only by snatching off the spark wire and letting the en-

gine almost die. On its next-to-final kick it will usually backfire and in the process reverse itself, at which instant one must push the spark wire back in place and hope the beast will continue turning over. It seldom does. At least it seldom did for Jack and me. To properly dominate a make-and-break engine one must have grown up with it from childhood.

According to mythology the virtue of these engines lies in the fact that they are simple and reliable. Although this myth is widely believed I am able to report that it is completely untrue. These engines are, in fact, vindictive, debased, black-minded ladies of no virtue and any non-Newfoundlander who goes shipmate with one is either a fool or a masochist, and is likely both.

Charles Landery

Their engine started with a superior chuckle . . .

Frank Wightman

. . . that tin Judas down below . . .

K. Adlard Coles

The smelly monster rose to the occasion, backfiring with incredible fury; bang! tut-tut, bang, bang, bang—BANG! The crowd started shouting but I, busy with the carburetor, could not hear. Bang, bang, bang! the British yacht was going . . . Bang, Bang, Bang, Bang!

Ray Kauffman

Gerry said that he was now convinced that the most valuable sail on board was the Diesel.

William Snaith

. . . the gasoline breeze.

Rex Clements

. . . a perennial fair wind under her counter . . .

William Snaith

At last, the god-damned engine is silent.

William Robinson

An odd quirk existed in the mechanical department. When the little ship was fighting strong winds or current, the chief engineer would spray sea water all over his steaming engine with a sort of oversized Flit gun—a supplementary cooling system the engine had apparently survived for years.

Charles Landery

On the eighth day, Sam . . . tinkered with the engine in a forlorn way, passing the time, really, while I, being of little faith, loafed and mocked. Perhaps it was the mockery and perhaps it was the ability of the others: but probably it was just cussedness that brought the engine to life with a roar. It was not a man-eating, red-blooded roar however, just the cry of a lion turned vegetarian and very uncertain of himself.

Dennis Puleston

Although even on the rare occasions when it was on its good behavior, it was only able to push us along at a speed of four knots in calm water, it acted with all the pomposity of an elderly and choleric Anglo-Indian colonel. There was something singularly futile about its noisy fumings, clankings, and squeakings. It imperiously demanded many careful attentions and, when it was given them, would, as likely as not, subside into ineffectual mumblings. The truth was, it was old and worn out. Like the Indian colonel, whose liver has been wrecked by too many years of self-indulgence, it was ready to be pensioned off.

Ernest F. Gann

We have an iron wind.

Richard Baum

I used my engine for two years, and then, taking arms against a sea of troubles, cut my troubles in half by pitching *Little Dipper's* engine overside . . . Life afloat was vastly simplified. No more worry about fouling lobster pots. No more anxieties about cigarettes, drip pans, backfire baffles. No more work on spark plugs, coil, or stuffing box. A welcome reduction in yard bills. Guests forebore to make schedules, and so proved better company. When the engine went overside I began really to enjoy what I had bought a boat to get: the freedom and zest of sail.

Frank Wightman

There was a certain charm in the experience, too, though this may have been nothing but its novelty. Without the steadying effect of sail, every sea did what it would with her, and I could imagine this mode of "sailing" could become monotonous—it was too like motoring: more throttle, less throttle, steer here, steer there. It called for nothing in the man on board; what accomplishment there might be in arriving was the engine's. Here there was none of the lure of playing off against each other irreconcilable forces to achieve your purpose. With this method of progression I was sure I should soon miss that balancing of the planes of the cunningly wrought sails against the winds to gain an end that demanded imagination and skill. Here the end was too easy, undemanding and inevitable.

Alfred Loomis

. . . we had already discovered that without a motor or a husky pair of sweeps a sailboat is 25 percent helpless.

Francis Brenton

Even the harshness of the motor . . . had reminded me too vividly of scheduled routes and stops.

Frank Wightman

. . . the blessed honesty of the sails.

Frank Wightman

Presently they shut down the engine and there was tranquility again. The lovely sounds of the night and the sea came back, the more by their contrast to enchant. Now, too, I could hear the sounds of a big schooner under sail; all those softly creaking and stressed sounds of a big, full-bodied vessel responded to their urge; the breathy, swelling note as she dragged herself heavily free of the swell that climbed her sides; a huge and rumbling sigh as bluff bows spread a sea.

Desmond Holdridge

In a vessel whose sailing qualities were so unsensational as the *Dolphin's,* a motor was a boon . . .

Alfred Loomis

On a breathless night there is something in the lazy drone of the motor and the undeviating wake of phosphorescent water stretching out astern that gets me almost as much as the keener joys of sailing. Every resolution of the propeller means something, and every mile puts us in a more favorable position to employ the wind when it comes in again.

William Robinson

As a matter of fact we found the weather strangely upset and had to run the engine for two or three hundred miles to get out of a region of doldrums half-way across, in what should have been the heart of the trade winds.

Edward H. Dodd, Jr.

Entering and leaving ports it was a necessity, but on the ocean it was a nuisance. The noise, smell and heat were enough to keep it quiet . . .

Frank Wightman

The silent "machinery" of sail may be outdated, but its every working part is visible, and quickly reparable when it goes wrong.

Hilaire Belloc

I would rather die of thirst, ten miles off the headlands in a brazen calm, having lost my dinghy in the previous storm, than have on board what is monstrously called today an "auxiliary." The name is worthy of the thing. By auxiliaries the Roman army perished. Further, it is a nasty foreign sort of term. Call it the machine and tell the truth. I am told by those who use the abomination that it is ashamed of itself, and often will not start, as though to say, "You came out to sail the seas, and I am reluctant to cheat wind, weather, and tide in your favor."

Charles Landery

Whenever the swell eased, so did his illness, and Peric went back to the engineroom, staying below for as long as his stomach could bear it. Despite his determination and courage, however, he never stayed there long. Soon he would reappear on deck, his face gangrenous with green skin and black oil as he ran for'ard to recuperate, stopping on the way for an unphilosophic glance at the sea, doing his best to relinquish a dinner he had been too sick to eat. Eventually the auxiliary was repaired, although it only ran so long as someone oiled it every twenty minutes and it amused itself by spitting the oil right back at the donor. Finally, when it had deluded us into thinking it would run forever, it stopped, leaving us, by mistake, with a soft, ambitionless wind, the kind you might expect to find on Sunday loafing at the corner of Main Street.

Samuel Eliot Morison

What makes this day so memorable is its freedom from the mutter of motors. The lobstermen have finished hauling their traps and are home eating supper. There is no sound but the lapping of the waves on the shore, the lazy clanging of Spurlings Ledge bell buoy, and the distant barking of a dog.

William Robinson

The trade wind blew straight out of Mopelia pass, so only power would get us in. We tried it, doing six knots through the water. We gained inch by inch, creeping almost imperceptibly between the sharp jutting ledges of coral. Halfway in, the channel shoaled and the current boiled still faster under us. Our forward motion ceased. We tried for back-eddies so close to both edges that we could have jumped on the reef. The waters, seeming to resent this invasion, gathered power and slowly we lost ground. There was no room to turn.

It is a great game this. No place for a man with too many nerves or one who won't take a chance once in a while. We had taken one here—the longest one—and it seemed we had lost. But there was a possible way out: retard the motor a trifle, keep bucking the stream at four or five knots to retain control, actually going astern slowly with the current which was now doing better than six. Slowly we retreated in this manner, and after what seemed hours our stern poked its way out into free water and we breathed again.

Edward H. Dodd, Jr.

The galvanized gasoline tanks, aged two years, had begun to flake. Moreover, the gasoline sold to us in New London had obviously been liberally watered. The poor motor was in consequence running on a gritty solution one quarter of which was water.

Arthur Ransome

. . . an obstreperous motor, tucked away in the stern, makes up for the want of the love and thought that went into the lines of the older vessels.

Leonard Wibberly

This petulant servant . . . is useful as a mooring . . . take it out, attach a length of stout chain to it . . . useful for holding off lee shores.

Ernest K. Gann

. . . he reached resolutely for the large wheel which when turned would release air to the *African Queen* and by a dependent alternation of sucking and blowing, start the reaction he so much desired.

Now he boldly turned the great wheel. The *Queen* hissed, farted obscenely, and returned to death with a sigh of finality.

Ernest K. Gann

The exhaust of *Don Quixote's* engine was short, so it would not interfere with passage of the sail across deck and it was aimed straight up in the air. As a consequence it blew the most perfect smoke rings I have ever seen and sometimes I would start the engine in port just so visitors could admire the display.

E. A. Pye

We were so hemmed in by vessels the evening we left that I wasn't sure we could get out, but I wasn't going to use my engine in this stronghold of sail. It was blowing hard. We put a couple of reefs in the mainsail, hove up the anchor, missed the bowsprit of *Fair Toil* by inches, slipped under the stern of the *Sunbeam R.,* tacked by the jetty where the Lakes had come to see us off, and made for the open sea. At least that is what I wrote in my Daily Journal. But it was really more like this: "Back the jib, Bob. My God, she's not coming round! Yes, she is . . . Anne, pull in the lee sheet . . . Stand by to go about . . . Lee . . . Oh . . . Stand by to fend off that chap's stern . . . Hell, that was a close shave . . ."

Landfall!

The nearness of land!

At the impending making of a landfall all of a sailor's senses are aroused. As the drama of a landfall begins, his emotions become as varied as are his senses for he knows that a voyage, which now rewards perserverance as it had demanded skill, is ending. As the sailor makes his landfall, in home waters or closing a foreign coast, he is aware also of strong but opposing thoughts: a lusty approval of a job well done, a wistful note that a sea-journey is ended.

Charles Landery

Steering into a rising, benevolent moon, our sails curving generously, Cyprus was 300 miles away. We were no longer going there; we were arriving.

Ray Kauffman

The fresh trades singing in the rigging and the ship tugging at the helm brought Gerry and me out of our lethargy. Hector was dragged out of his bunk to polish what brass there was. We painted the dinghy and scrubbed the topsides while the ocean flew beneath us. We dug out shoes, fuzzy with mold, but found we could no longer force them on our feet. Carefully, clean white ducks were folded by the bunks. I issued a round of fresh water and all hands tortured their faces, shaving off salt crusted whiskers two months old. Land became an obsession and we tossed restlessly in our bunks at night. The quiet existence of the previous week was gone. The complexities of life came back with the proximity of land. Before, we had peacefully submitted to the unconquerable sea; but now we chafed at every hole in the breeze, swore at poor Hector if he was half a point off the course, and trimmed the sails to even the slightest imaginary change of wind. We hated our conqueror with its monotonous procession of waves that tossed our stern a thousand times a day.

Frank Wightman

We had twelve hours of daylight, and if we did not sight the coast, I should conclude that Brazil was merely a geographical expression.

Joshua Slocum

A thousand emotions thrilled me when I saw the island, and I bowed my head to the deck.

Hilaire Belloc

So sharply divided are the sea and the land in the memories and instincts of our race that coming thus into port, even into a port of one's own country, has about it something of discovery and change.

William Robinson

The best time to make a new harbor is just at dark. One can thus run the whole gamut of sensations twice. There is the first entrancing impressions of the new haven by the last failing rays of light; and there is a night of anticipation with the promise of a complete revelation at dawn.

Frank Wightman

We both had good eyes and ears, that by now could interpret quickly and accurately those almost imperceptible signs that the sea gives you of the approach of land when it is invisible to the eyes. If there was nothing to see or hear, we should feel that unmistakable hesitation in the rhythm of the sea that is caused by a steep coast sending out its backwash from a distance.

Dennis Puleston

I was at the tiller, when suddenly I shouted: "Look! There's New York!"

Geoff and Nicky bobbed up out of the hatch and vainly searched the skyline ahead.

"I don't see a damned thing except mist," grumbled Geoff.

"I don't mean over there," I replied. "This is our landfall on New York right here!"

They turned and saw I was pointing down into the waters around us. We were sailing through a sea of milk-bottle tops, cardboard cups, orange peel, broken crates and other strange marine life, which told us, as surely as though we had seen the distant towers of Manhattan, that we were drawing near port.

Hilaire Belloc

But of all those sacramental sights the chief is the landfall from very far away. When a man after days at sea first hesitates whether some tenuous outline or level patch barely perceived, a vast way off, is land or cloud and then comes to the moment of certitude and knows it for land, all his mind changes; the ship becomes a different thing; the world, which has been formless and simple, takes on at once name and character. He is back among human beings.

Richard Maury

The way in which land is picked up from the deck or rigging of a small craft is always a fascinating one. The land does not slowly appear out of mist, nor does it come suddenly to stand boldly on the horizon. Rather, it first appears as a vision, as a happy portent arriving out of thin air, out of a vastness of space, to lie with utter humility upon the curved lip of the sea. First, it is not there, then, at the flick of an eyelash, there it is, a flimsy mirage that may or may not be more than a low and wandering cloud.

Dwight Long

It was almost sundown when I saw what looked like two small molehills straight off our bowsprit.

Frank Wightman

Then suddenly the whole of that lovely land stepped out to meet us.

Ray Kauffman

Even the beaches were in shadow from the overhanging dense growth, and in the lowlands the bowlegged mangroves stepped out into the sea.

Charles Landery

Over the bows, I saw trees like pepper-trees, their narrow leaves trembling and fussing. This, I was finally certain, was the way to travel, quietly letting places introduce themselves, and not spiraling earnestly to catch up with the past, with local color, or with whatever it is one simply must take home from a "cruise."

Dennis Puleston

Toward midnight we began straining our eyes, searching the blackness for that one tiny wink of yellow that would mean safety.

But the light was out.

All at once we saw the velvety silhouette that was land . . .

Joseph Conrad

"Here she is!" said Shaw, who, clad in a spotless white suit, came just then from forward where he had been busy with the anchors. "She is well on, sir, isn't she? Looks like a mudflat to me from here."

"Yes. It is a mudflat," said Lingard, slowly, raising the long glass to his eye. "Haul the mainsail up, Mr. Shaw," he went on while he took a steady look at the yacht. "We will have to work in short tacks here." He put the glass down and moved away from the rail. For the next hour he handled his little vessel in the intricate and narrow channel with careless certitude, as if every stone, every grain of sand upon the treacherous bottom had been plainly disclosed to his sight. He handled her in the fitful and unsteady breeze with a matter-of-fact audacity that made Shaw, forward at his station, gasp in sheer alarm. When heading toward the inshore shoals the brig was never put round till the quick, loud cries of the leadsmen announced that there were no more than three feet of water under her keel; and when standing toward the steep inner edge of the long reef, where the lead was of no use, the helm would be put down only when the cutwater touched the faint line of the bordering foam.

Hilaire Belloc

Of the many things which the modern world has lost, one which

it should deeply regret is the coming into a foreign harbor under sail. The gradual approach, the uncertainty and skill of entry, the uncertainty of hour, the human and as it were domestic craft of the thing, especially in a vessel of no great size, make it an adventure compared with which our mechanical repeated precision may rather be called a doom.

Hilaire Belloc

The gliding stopped; there was a slight thrill. She had hit Wales: an underwater, advance guard of Wales. The man at the helm was not apologetic, he was not humble, but he was at least subdued; and he said, "Her will float soon, so her will!" . . .

The flood lifted her foot, she swung off, and we went off again up the darkness, with the least of little airs to give steering-way.

Alan Villiers

It was night by the time we had closed with the approaches to the harbor (Rio). It was my first visit to those waters and I did not go in. A quiet landbreeze blew in the shrouds and we hove-to under easy canvas to await the sea breeze of the morning. I might have gone in for the breeze at first would have led us in. But, I could not distinguish the buoys from the neon lights round the waterfront and on the hills. (The chart was not very helpful.) I would not go in by night. The way in was clear enough. It is finding the anchorage in a strange place by night, that is difficult. In the morning I saw that we could very well have gone. The harbor was open, safe, commodious. And now there was no breeze.

Thor Heyerdahl

When the raft was on the inward tack, we swung after her on the rope and came so close to the thundering reef that we caught a glimpse of the glass-green wall of water that was rolling away from us and saw how, when the seas sucked themselves back, the naked reef exposed itself, resembling a torn-up barricade of rusty iron ore.

Richard Maury

Twenty yards off the entrance a languid swell moved in, glided for the stern, elevated us, paused. The inclining top of glass moved slowly, curved, mounted, acquired an edge, a thin line of agitated water that arose, trembled, grew higher, whiter, broke—exploded, and flung us headlong at a narrow coral mouth. Down into a mill stream, green and foaming, barred with eddies and wild currents, we ran, at ten–eleven knots. The bows swerved, uncontrolled, the engine coughed, missed a stroke, continued. A woman screamed; then the noise of the pass drowned out all sound. A triangular wave caught us, half submerged us, ricocheted us into the coral to starboard; the helm was jammed over, the masts jumped, the entire rigging quivered. The bow cut past the coral, missing it by yards, angled down water, headed for mid-channel, into an island of bright submerged coral, then, forced over by propeller, by rudder, drew away just in time . . .

Hilaire Belloc

Lord, what a tangle of dangers are here for the wretched mariner! Rocks and eddies and overfalls and shooting tides; currents and horrible great mists, fogs, vapors, malignant humors of the deep, mirages, false ground, where the anchor will not hold, and foul ground, where the anchor holds forever, spills of wind off the irregular coast and monstrous gales coming out of the main west sea; and, most terrible of all, Wild Goose Race . . .

It seems that in Wild Goose Race a boat is taken up and pitched to heaven and let drop again, twirled round like a teetotum, thrown over on her side, banged off sideways with great stunning blows upon the cheekbone and blinded all the time with cataracts of spray, the while the air is filled with a huge mocking laughter.

Ray Kauffman

The dinghy was tossed over the side and we rowed across the shallow water to the little islet. But, before the boat had scraped on the sand, our landing was protested by the raucous screaming of thousands of birds, and the top of the islet rose in the air and wheeled overhead. White gulls and sooty terns nested there, huge gannets bravely guarded their downy young; and the warm musty smell from the birds mingled with the fishy smell of the reef. The islet was only six feet above high tide and less than two hundred feet long. To the south and east where the sea thundered on the reef were the remains of old sailing ships. A huge iron-studded timber was imbedded in the sand, bits of copper were strewn around the islet and, on the outer reef, the stocks of two large anchors marked the spot like beacons. A chain, overgrown with coral, twisted through a shallow pool like a dead sea serpent. There was nothing else but the sea and the reef and this little dot of dry sand under a cloud of birds. I looked back over the lagoon and was reassured by the sight of the *Hurricane*.

E. F. Knight

We soon found that it was necessary to exercise caution while approaching this island. Nearly two miles away from it there was a shoal over which the sea was breaking heavily; we passed between this and the island as directed by the chart, and kept close under the shore, where the dark violet of the deep sea was changed for the transparent green of comparatively shallow water. Here again we had to pick our way through outlying rocks and shoals. One of these shoals is particularly dangerous, for, as there is some depth of water over it, the sea only occasionally breaks, and for a quarter of an hour there is nothing to indicate the danger, so that a vessel might be taken right on to it.

When we were close to it the sea happened to break, and the sight was a lovely yet a terrible one. A huge green roller, very high and steep, suddenly rose as if by magic from the deep; then swept over the shoal, and, when it reached the shallowest part, its crest hung over, forming a cavern beneath, through whose transparent roof the sun

shone with a beautiful green light; and lastly, the mass overtopping itself fell with a great hollow sound, and was dashed to pieces in a whirl of hissing foam. Had the old *Alerte* been there at that moment her end would have come swiftly, and perhaps ours too.

Rex Clements
For a few minutes we seemed lost and swallowed up among the roots of the mountains, gliding ghost-like past echoing walls of polished rock, with no sound save the lapping of the water and the faint reverberations of our voices. For a few minutes we slipped silent along, then, turning slightly to port, emerged suddenly into the sleeping waters of Pisco Bay. We stood in to the shore as near as was prudent, then let go our anchor, splitting the still night with the roar of twenty fathoms of cable. Sail was made fast, and, setting an anchor watch, we went below for the night.

Hilaire Belloc
. . . just as it grew quite dark, the sound of the slight surge to leeward receded and disappeared so that we knew we had turned the headland and opened the first bay of that long island arm of the sea. Our chart showed us good berth and good holding ground, and a good berth for the night granted that there should be no other craft about. We heard none such through the fog; no voice, no swinging spars, no movement at all. So when we had got well into the bight, we dropped anchor; trusting to luck that, as she swung to her chain, she would not strike shoal ground nor anything near. Had we still had the dinghy I would have gone out and explored, and made certain and risked my chance of getting back aboard through the mist, but, having no dinghy, we had to take things as they were, and these seemed secure enough, for we were well out of the fairway. The first of the night was interrupted by the perpetual call of the great horn upon the headland, but before midnight the fog lifted, the sound ceased, and a profound silence fell upon the sea and the land. We had also the comfort of seeing that we had plenty of room to swing, with the shore perhaps a quarter of a mile away.

Jack London
When to leeward, the splendid craft rounded to the wind, rolling once till her brown bottom showed to the centerboard and they thought she was over, then righting and dashing ahead again like a thing possessed. She passed abreast of them on the starboard side. They saw the jib run down with a rush and an anchor go overboard as she shot into the wind; and as she fell off and back and off with a spilling mainsail, they saw a second anchor go overboard, wide apart from the first. Then the mainsail came down on the run, and was furled and fastened by the time she tightened to her double hawsers.

Ray Kauffman
I shouted above the crash of the surf on the shingle, "Get the headsails off."

The iron jib shanks rattled against the stays as the canvas fluttered down. We had plenty of way and coasted toward the head of the bay.

"Take down the mainsail."

Gerry cast the halyards off the belaying pins forward and Hector clawed the heavy canvas down on the boom. Bottom was clearly visible. The ship slowly rose and fell in a long swell. I rounded up as a strong gust of wind rushed out of the valley; shaking the mizzen and stopping our headway.

"Let her go!"

The anchor went over with a splash and the chain rumbled out of the hawse pipe and stopped with a jerk at the windlass. The ship fetched up hard on the chain and came to rest, just thirty days from the Galapagos. I called Hector aft to help take off the mizzen. Quickly we furled the sails, breathed a sigh of relief and looked around. A Melville picture had come to life!

Here was a deep valley like Typee, its floor a forest of tall coconut palms and breadfruit trees, backed by sheer mountains, lush green to their very summits. The chart gave the name of the bay, Hanai Nai. The beach was crowded with natives. A tall gaunt figure in white clothes under a huge pandanus hat walked through the crowd, stepped on a ledge of rock and hailed us in English. We spilled the dinghy overside. After a month of sun, water poured in the open seams. Hector bailed us ashore and we landed in the surf behind the rocky ledge, getting wet to our waists.

Uncertain of our balance, we staggered across the narrow beach.

Frank Wightman

... the island with its broad swathes of volcanic colors; sulphur; cobalt; strident metallic green; and one complete hill on which the bouldered summit protruded from a cone of deep crimson.

Dennis Puleston

I found myself on a beach of sand, wet and firm from the sea. But after I had taken a few steps, it became dry and soft, with here and there a tuft of wire grass. It was thus, in a howling squall at midnight, from a wrecked ship on a desolate coast, that I landed in America.

Becalmed

When the face of the sea is completely fair or its mien is placid, it is most treacherous. But in these unnerving calms there is an element of awe that suggests the spirits of wind and water, tiring, have departed for a while, perhaps to enjoy a siesta. In time the winds blow, the sails fill, the boat moves from its bewitched quarter and the sailor looks out on a sea that is moving in its beauty.

Joe Richards

Now and again when we rose on the inflated crest of a glassy swell I could see the protruding end of a buoy stuck like a splinter in the flat hand of the sea.

Ray Kauffman

But in the morning our exuberance had died with the wind until we lay writhing on the uneven surface of a glassy sea like a drunken porpoise.

Charles Landery

The pleasures of being becalmed had been worn threadbare; there is a limit to untutored star-gazing . . .

Joseph Conrad

When about a mile off the bank and nearly in with the stern of the yacht the brig's topsails fluttered and the yards came slowly on the caps; the fore and aft canvas ran down; and for some time she floated quietly with folded wings upon the transparent sheet of water, under the radient silence of the sky. Then her anchor went to the bottom with a rumbling noise resembling the roll of distant thunder. In a moment her head tended to the last puffs of the northerly airs and the ensign at the peak stirred, unfurled itself slowly, collapsed, flew out again, and finally hung down straight and still, as if weighted with lead.

Ernle Bradford

Now the mainsail hung empty as a sailor's pockets . . .

Joseph Conrad

There was no wind, and a small brig that had lain all the afternoon a few miles to the northward and westward and westward of Carimata had hardly altered its position half a mile during all these hours. The calm was absolute, a dead, flat calm, the stillness of a dead sea and of a dead atmosphere. As far as the eye could reach there was nothing but an impressive immobility. Nothing moved on earth, on the waters, and above them in the unbroken luster of the sky. On the unruffled surface of the straits the brig floated tranquil and upright as if bolted solidly keel to keel, with its own image reflected in the unframed immense mirror of the sea. To the south and east the double islands watched silently the double ship that seemed fixed amongst them forever, a hopeless captive of the calm, a helpless prisoner of the shallow sea.

Edward H. Dodd, Jr.

All night we slashed about without enough wind to blow out a match. Morning arrived with a red swollen sun that crawled wearily up through the dank and heavy air. The sea, although now almost flat, panted feebly with just enough motion to keep the boat swaying so that the gaff of the mainsail lunged from side to side viciously shaking the loose canvas. We ought to have taken in all sail and waited patiently, but we could now see the blue ragged shape of the Point in the distance. Out at sea, on a long leg, calm was a matter of course; but so near shore, even though the noise of the sails nearly drove us insane, we felt compelled to take advantage of every gasp of wind.

In almost no time one became very tired. The complete stillness everywhere was more exhausting than heavy work in a storm. Sleep was a hot sticky business interrupted by nightmares and food was dry and tasteless.

There we sat on the very doorstep of the port to which we had been looking forward all along, as the final jumping off place to the South Seas, and nothing to do about it. According to the Pilot Book, calms were frequent north of Panama at this time of year, and had been known to last four or five weeks. Tom proposed towing the *Chance* with the dory. Joe declared that he would row the twenty odd miles to shore and fetch a launch.

Another stifling sleepless night.

In the morning Manzarillo Point had disappeared. A two-knot current was slowly taking us out to sea.

Ray Kauffman

For five days we lay becalmed and all the swell was gone from the sea. It was literally a sheet of glass, a great deep blue mirror on which the ship hung motionless over her reflection two miles off the bottom, the only spot around three hundred and sixty degrees of horizon excepting the garbage and waste that had been tossed over the stern. After three days, we started the engine to move away from the potato peels and onion skins.

Richard Maury

There was not a sound from sea or sky for two days. The schooner swayed only when we moved within her; her sails were dropped; an awning was spread over deck, and we waited for wind on the cabin tops. The calm stretched wearily into distance. We thought we saw mirages upon the horizons, and all day long the sun fell from hot, vacant skies, brutally blue. Sharks swarmed around the hull, threw their heads into the glare and rubbed them against the stern—a splash, a cushioned blow against the hull, a momentary glimpse of a grey, vicious-eyed head. It was incredible! The cabins echoed as they rammed us. We hit them with wind booms, and when that had no effect we left them to their weird sport until they drew off, and Good Hope, itself a mirage, floated into the west, somewhere between sky and sea, and held there.

Finally, like a living breath, a northwest wind began to blow. The awning was housed, the sails were swung up the naked masts—and the white schooner plunged again, shook us, and ripped a thin wake with her narrow sides.

Frank Wightman

An island schooner, bleached white as a bone by the sprays of the sea, lies motionless in the glare. In the shadow cast by her lifeless sails dark bodies lie in the abandoned postures of sleep. Her helmsman—the only man on board awake—droops over her useless wheel. His jaws are moving with the unhurried and faultless precision of a machine, a rhythm broken only when he sends a smooth parabola of saliva arching over the side.

On her deck a tiny brown pup glares truculently at us as we glide past. A little graven image

with one ear cocked up, it suddenly jerks convulsively and a jagged splinter of sounds zips across the stillness. The sound an angry cockroach might make. Turning its back, it sits down and with imbecile gravity goes through some incomprehensible routine of cleansing or exploring.

Ralph Stock

But stark calms are a wearisome business. Every function of a ship has ceased. It is as though she lay dead in a stagnant pool, and any movement of spars or canvas were the rattling of her bones. Also, it is an aggravation to the restless insect called man, adrift in a breathless waste of waters, to know that leagues lie ahead of which he is incapable of covering a yard.

John MacGregor

Some feelings that came up then from deep recesses in the mind were new, but too new and unnamed to put in words.

Joshua Slocum

Evening after evening during this time I read by the light of a candle on deck. There was no wind at all, and the sea became smooth and monotonous. For three days I saw a full-rigged ship on the horizon, also becalmed.

Ray Kauffman

It was a comfortable calm and we quieted our restlessness with

the *Hurricane* philosophy: "What's a day or a month or a year?"; or sometimes more briefly stated when everything is done that can be done: "To hell with it"; and we dragged the mattresses out on deck and dug deep in the ship's library for books we had not read. And then there was always the vague undercurrent of hope that perhaps in a few hours the wind would come, and with plenty of food and water aboard there was a snug feeling of content. It is almost impossible to be completely unhappy when you are surrounded by groceries and books and the sea and the sky in weather so beautiful that it would even be beyond the most imaginative dreams of a California-conscious citizen.

Desmond Holdridge

We besought Providence to let us trade in our windless swell for a used hurricane.

Dwight Long

. . . and all things come to an end . . . even calms . . .

Ernest K. Gann

But there was no wind at all and vulgar things were written in the logbook about doldrums . . . someone wrote in the logbook, "There is not a breath of air . . . so it is possible to piss over either side—straight down."

Ernest K. Gann

Sailors who have

greatly sinned may expect to mildew permanently in the doldrums . . .

Ernest K. Gann

There are numerous tortures designed especially for sailing men—perhaps to keep them humble. One is the pure physical torture of being becalmed in a rolling sea . . . It is worse than being in a storm and even more exhausting. And while his body cries in protest, the ship cries with him for a sailing ship becalmed is a world of tortured noises.

We were not in any danger except . . . cannabilism if the calm continued.

Arrival and the Harbor

Philosophy wisely instructs that life's joy is found in the pursuit of a goal, not in its achievement. How this applies to certain aspects of seafaring such as arrival in harbor, I am not sure. I do know that the finality of arrival, the ending of a cruise, is sweetened by the delights, often in abundance, that a harbor offers.

Charles Landery

Seamen have difficulty in knowing the citizens of the countries they visit, and seldom have interests beyond the waterfront, which is not surprising. Yet they probably get a more genuine sense of a port, if only of its honky-tonks, than is discovered by a tourist in a week's visit. The sailor's straightforward demands are easily dealt with, if not always satisfied, and while these may be crude they are alive and give contact with humans, something the guided visitor usually misses. The seaman seldom wants to explore, to memorize date-burdened facts in the hope of being word-perfect by the time the cruise is over, his snapshots printed, and his neighbor's peace already undermined. The tourist sees only a little more since he is blinkered by his determination to see "everything." What is wrong is not touring but the tourist attitude, that slavish dependence on the beaten path . . .

K. Adlard Coles

. . . and the waves broke aboard in flying spray as *Annette* lay close hauled to the wind. Lee-o-o!—and she came up with sails thrashing and blocks clattering their protest, as the ropes whipped the deck in rage. Helm over; and *Annette* slipped astern, fell off on the other tack; and, gathering speed, ran like a harried hare into the shelter of the harbor.

Charles Violet

Night fell when I was within half a mile of the coast. The lights of a fair-sized town led me to believe there must be a harbor attached to it, and after several unsuccessful attempts to find it, but only hearing heavy surf, I had to spend the rest of the night tacking slowly back and forth in front of the lights.

Frank Wightmann

For us, coming in from the sea, the sound of surf was curiously evocative and comforting, although to seamen there are times when it can be the most dreaded of sounds. After the limited and inhuman vocabulary of the sea, it is the voice of the earth that is friendly to man.

Thor Heyerdahl

I was completely overwhelmed. I sank down on my knees and thrust my fingers deep into the dry warm sand.

The voyage was over. We were all alive.

Charles Landery

At sundown we were abeam the light on the bay's western arm. The wind had scarcely the breath to mist a glass. Gradually we neared shore; the town became a line of lights with long squiggling reflections, crawling out to meet us, invitingly cheerful and making both sea and night doubly black. There was no moon. Iorgos, leaving the wheel, came up into the bows, shivering and hugging himself tightly as if he were snuggling down into his skin in search of warmth. Identifying a row of evenly-placed lamps as the main jetty shown on the chart, we ignored Iorgos' protests and left them well to port, our pilot moaning that we were heading away from the caique berth. Soon we were taking soundings just as quickly as we could make up the line and heave the lead again; our leadline, of rough sisal slipped harshly through my numbed hands, the saltwater being warm at the first touch, then harsh.

We found a three fathom bottom sufficiently consistent to be more than a bank and at last the anchor was let go. The harsh grinding of the links as they rushed through the hawse pipe was a quick chant of thanksgiving. The running chain slammed once against the deck, then lay taut and still. The hull trembled and *Bessie* settled to anchor, cable, wind, and what little tide there was. Shore sounds were faint and broken. Peric could scarcely be persuaded to come below for cocoa; he leaned on the gunwale, staring at the land, promising us the freedom of the town, and behaving as though he had anchored after having been away on a hazardous voyage of years. From Famagusta to Limassol was less than a hundred miles by land, yet I too felt that a long voyage had just been completed. Actually, we had been two weeks at sea.

In the too critical light of day, Limassol shrank; last night it had spread sparkling along the black coast in a great curving welcome; today, two miles away, it huddled in on its own center and did not even ask us our business. We neither met nor looked for an official, no policeman wanted our passports, and we were content that things should be so casual.

Charles Violet

. . . I was jerked back to the worries of the world when the *Nova* grounded to a sudden standstill on a gravel bank. I tried the depth of water all round and found several inches less than the draft of the *Nova.* It was a difficult job to get going again, but sustained effort of oar and outboard, coupled with rocking the boat to grind a channel for the keel, got us free.

Desmond Holdridge

And this awful channel, which should have had a name with such a roll of thunder as Gotterdammerung . . . was called Mugford Tickle.

William Robinson

Tine and Zizi were up forward performing the sailor's favorite chore, passing the chain on deck and shackling it onto the anchor.

Humphrey Barton

Entering port is, I think, the cream of the sport. A strange port, a yacht with no engine, a quiet summer's night and there one has all the makings of a pleasant and most interesting little bit of seamanship.

Richard Maury

The land seemed to reach out, to gauntlet the schooner, to strip her of her freedom, of her illusions as well as her sails, of her slight but immaculate power.

Ray Kauffman

When entering a port by day, you watch it grow out of the sea; and, before the anchor is on the bottom, you are already familiar with the town, its streets and warehouses, the customs and the post office, but, at night, only the lights. . . .

Frank Wightman

Always, the distant island grew. Its smooth, puppy-fat outline was now developing quirks and crotchets of character. Craggy upheavals of rock; spiky mountain peaks; a scrabble of headlands; indulgent beaches . . .

William Robinson

To sail into Pago Pago Bay is one of the achievements of a lifetime. Great mountains hem you in. You enter deeper and deeper and think you have reached the end, wondering that there is no sign of habitation. Suddenly you round an unnoticed point and discover the real harbor—completely hidden from the sea.

William Robinson

Seafaring might be compared with a drug habit which obliges one to suffer at intervals in order to experience peaks of elation. One of these peaks is the delicious sense of anticipation when making port for the first time in a new land with its unknown people. Everything is still fresh, untasted, mysterious, and desirable . . .

Francis Brenton

What had looked like a cosy little town from far out to sea proved to be rows of shacks . . .

Ray Kauffman

I looked out at the streets and the excitement of the town slowly permeated every fiber and I was eager to take part in the life. . . .

Ernle Bradford

As we came through the narrow neck of the bay the town sculled itself up a low breast of hill in front of us. The houses were white as icing sugar and the narrow streets mounted on uneven steps past doorways where garlics and salted fish swayed in the sun.

Charles Landery

We entered the poorly-marked channel, passing the points where once, supposedly, the massive feet of the Colossus had stood, and then we were in Mandoracchie Harbor, the "Harbor of the Galleys," face to face with a magnificent finale. We had arrived on the day of a fantastic wash, a grotesque Monday. The port was crowded with sailing ships lying three deep and stern-to the quay; the "galleys" were showing their dirty linen to the world for all had raised their sails to dry them in the sun. The wrinkled canvas was in every shade of white and tan, the ships' hulls were bright contrasts in blues, whites, greens, and yellows. The light-colored buildings of the modern city, the elaborate mosaics and patterns on certain walls, the rich but sober tones of the old city's thick and once protecting fortifications, all joined in the gaiety. There was a light-blue sky with cherubim clouds; behind us, ten miles to the north, the Turkish mountains on Cape Alypo were touched with purple, capped with snow. It was, after all my depression, an exhilerating morning, an excellent morning on which to enter a new port.

Allan Villiers

The seabreeze was late that day. It was afternoon before we came bowling into the harbor. The wind—when it came—was fresh and fair and we ran splendidly, turning the bay waves to white and carrying a full press of canvas right to the anchorage. This was the way to do it! (I forgot that I should have been willing to hire a tug.) We dip to the forts, heel a little to the freshening breeze. I straighten up for the anchorage. We see the big Brazilian schoolship alongside in there. They will be watching us. We are close up now off the navy yard. The port officials' launch comes out, following us, wondering perhaps what we are going to do. What, run right through the harbor? But the boys have been well schooled. A whistle blows; in come the royals and the t'gallants after them, the courses are hauled in a brace of shanks, and the fore and mizzen tops'ls follow. Down helm! Spanker to windward! Haul down the headsails! She flies into the wind. Back the mainyard! With the main tops'l full aback, she comes to a full stop. Let go! The anchor is down, the backed

tops'l pulls out the chain. Then, it is up and furl everything with a harbor stow.

The officials come on board complaining that we have a rope ladder instead of a gangway.

Hilaire Belloc

We cast anchor in the very midst of that solemn bay with its half-circle of huge mountains looking down upon an empty sea. The giants were dim in the haze, but the more enormous, and I revered and worshiped them.

We so cast anchor because I had to wait for the tide. I could not run up the long, winding channel through the sands of Port Madoc until the flood should be with me, and that would not be until the gloaming, between eight and nine o'clock that night.

Therefore did we lie thus in Harlech Bay, gazing at the great hills of Wales.

Ernest K. Gann

A day or so before reaching port there would be a great primping and grooming of shore clothes and the body lavished with attention. A very few minutes after the vessel was secured to the wharf an assembly of total strangers appeared momentarily on deck and then disappeared in the direction of the local settlement as fast as they could go.

Edward H. Dodd, Jr.

We were met at the pier by the Commodore, who very kindly asked us to dinner. He then established himself as

a true yachtsman by passing the supreme test, the sine qua non of intelligent yachting hospitality, when he asked us immediately to have a bath.

Ray Kauffman

At five o'clock in the morning, all hands shivered on deck. A cold damp fog had settled down, the wind was gone, the rigging dripped and the spars were shiny in the gray morning light. The shipping around us had come to life and the deafening blasts of their fog whistles reverberated over the water. A huge, rusty red cargo ship steamed across our bow as we were struggling with the anchor, and the officers on the bridge looked disdainfully down from their great height. The hook came on deck, gray with mud; we washed it off with the deck brush, started the motor and steered after the rusty red cargo ship. The lighthouse keeper gave a friendly wave. Two steamers whistled rudely behind us and we moved over to the side of the channel to give them plenty of room to pass. The tide was running in and we made good time. The sun streamed down, melting the haze, and the sea breeze came in and blew the low mist off the river. A square block of concrete with a huge mouth smelled of sewage. Jellyfish like huge multi-stemmed mushrooms floated by the ship. Houses raised on pilings lined the river; and ferryboats, launches, skiffs and tugs plied up and down and across. A passenger ship from China with a tug shoving at her bow was docking. . . .

Hilaire Belloc

Men need harbors almost as much as they need the gods.

Edward H. Dodd, Jr.

Upon landing, our first consideration was of course a bath; the second a glass of beer.

Herman Melville

Still another way of killing time in harbor, is to lean over the bulwarks, and speculate upon where, under the sun, you are going to be that day next year, which is a subject full of interest to every living soul so much so, that there is a particular day of a particular month of the year, which, from my earliest recollections, I have always kept the run of, so that I can even now tell just where I was on that identical day of every year past since I was twelve years old. And, when I am all alone, to run over this almanac in my mind is almost as entertaining as to read your own diary, and far more entertaining than to peruse a table of logarithms on a rainy afternoon. I always keep the anniversary of that day with lamb and peas, and a pint of sherry for it comes in the Spring. But when it came round in the *Neversink,* I could get neither lamb, peas, nor sherry.

Richard Henry Dana

On the following night, I stood my first watch. I remained awake nearly all the first part of the night from fear that I might not hear when I was called; and when I went out on deck, so great were my ideas of the importance of my trust, that I walked regularly fore and aft the whole length of the vessel, looking out over the bows and taffrail at each turn, and

was not a little surprised at the coolness of the old seaman whom I called to take my place, in stowing himself snugly away under the longboat for a nap. That was a sufficient lookout, he thought, for a fine night, at anchor in a safe harbor.

Humphrey Barton

There is usually an anti-climax to a long voyage. Ours is bucketing rain and a great element of doubt as to where we are.

E. A. Pye

I realized that the balance between sailing and sightseeing must be carefully watched; while we still had the urge to stay, that was the time to go.

Dwight Long

No sooner has one become acquainted with the peculiar perils of one port of call than one leaves to encounter an entirely new set of perils at the next.

Stanley Smith and Charles Violet

. . . and a few stunted wind-drunk trees stood silhouetted against the sky.

Frank Wightman

Islands with names like battle-cries; like hunting songs. Islands' names like curses; like prayers.

William Robinson

. . . Cannac, a little abrupt guano-covered rock, surrounded by thousands of sea birds and a terrible stench.

Frank Wightman

After the impersonal voice of the sea, *Wylo* lay in a sheltered bay with the voices of frogs coming over the still water. In the evening we rowed over in the dinghy and stepped ashore on our first island of the Caribbean.

In the failing light the beach curved like a golden sickle to the far promontory, which was a pattern in jet against the evening sky. From about our threshing feet as we dragged the dinghy through the shallow water to the beach, strange fish, with the protruding eyes of frogs, wriggled along the surface of the water, only half submerged. Large moths and bats flitted silently among the bushes. The gentle brushing sound of the dinghy's keel plowing through the sand sounded unnaturally loud in a silence broken only by the breathless lapping of waves hardly more than ripples turning over on the sand. Tiny frogs were making a sound like someone tapping a wineglass. We saw several of these. One was sitting in a patch of damp sand under a rotted coconut. When he sounded his note he developed, for a moment, an enormous double chin. A little fat Buddha, about the size of a pea, with a musical voice. A pelican sat on a rock with his head drawn back and that goitered look all pelicans have when they sit down. He looked like a bad case of indigestion. Hawks hung stationary against the burning sky. Far out beyond the spit of sand that sheltered *Wylo,* the Equatorial Current was flowing past like a mighty river. In the indulgent hush of the evening the palms whispered their endless legends. And the dear ship lay on the glowing water, inside a spit of sand on which pirates could have been carousing.

When the light failed, a host of tiny flies came out of the bushes and settled on us with a whoop. They were no larger than midges but they bit like tigers. We tried walking in the water up to our knees. Then we had to fight for our arms and necks. We turned and ran for the little gray hull that was waiting for us behind that sand spit. By the time we had rowed 20 yards from the beach they left us.

After supper we sat in the cockpit listening to the voice of this new land, and savoring the feeling of security and the prospect of a whole night in our bunks.

Richard Maury

In the clear sunrise we waded to an island off the mainshore, and on the way, each of us, unassisted, speared a shark with a shaft of limewood. We returned with eggs, sea shells, a pair of small tropic birds, and scantily clothed against the noon sun, paused a moment in the cool of Mopihaa's graveyard—a little group of rotted stones and ancient boards marking the graves of eight or ten natives, an unknown sea captain, and a mysterious Swiss baroness, who it is said still haunts the shore on moonlight nights. We opened coconuts and drank deeply while looking down the white coast. The *Cimba* was resting. Young palms, vivid and green, swept in one line almost to the horizon, rolling and flashing in a wind that was gone with dramatic suddenness, to leave them hushed, hanging green over the old graves. A fine undulating rain of sunlight fell through the shadows massed about the trunks. And then once more the wind stirred in the south. The fragile silence was over. Booming—brushing tree-top to tree-top—the gust staggered up the beach before an advancing wave of moving sunlight and shadow, tossing leaves that ripped like silk, sweeping by, salty, flecking the sand, hard running for the misty sea. Again, a hollow silence, the coconut leaves strung like colored glass against the sky . . .

Frank Wightman

This island was the most lush and fertile we had seen. It had a quilted opulence of appeal that was a little overpowering.

Carleton Mitchell

It was probably just as well we did not know the complications awaiting us in Wreck Bay as we stood on the beach of Isla Genovesa, called Quito Sueno, Nightmare Island, on some early Spanish charts. To be confronted by nature Galapagos-style was enough as a starter. But again the birds came out to meet us, to guide us, to make clear that the island was not a desolate waste, but a veritable Garden of Eden for those who belonged. And we were welcome. The first greeters were a pair of swallow tail gulls, noisy little fellow with big bright eyes rimmed with orange. They are night feeders, and might have considered our pre-dawn meeting offshore sufficient introduction. They advanced to our feet and retreated, leading us up the beach, to proudly present a ball of fluff in a nest under a thorn bush where the beach ended. While we admired, they stood on tiptoes and bragged loudly.

Next came the mockers, which we were soon to think of as dead end kids, precocious but naughty urchins, at once amusing and infuriating. The advance guard deployed in the dinghy as we alighted, peeking into camera cases and trying to sip from the water bottle; others scurried away from under each footfall, darting back to investigate a shoelace or discarded matchstick. Meanwhile the main body marched along as a flanking escort, chattering among themselves, obviously discussing what the strange bipeds who walked instead of flew away from the sea would do next.

Frank Wightman

In the evening when the air was full of flickering bats, we went for a walk on our new island. On a lonely savannah a wooden house leaned crookedly, its windows smashed, its doors gone, its life over. Round it the bats whirled. It sagged amongst trees which had once been its owner's pride, and the eternal trade wind had streamed all their gnarled branches in one direction. On this breathless evening they streamed still, as though—like the house—they lived in the past . . .

We walked to a place where the sea came

darkly into an invisible beach. And there we turned back—to find we had lost our way. Well, it was a small island, *Wylo* was sleeping beneath her riding light somewhere on its other side, we were on holiday—if we had to walk right round the island we should find her.

Ray Kauffman

Although we lived with a Polynesian family, danced with and made love to the girls, and fished with the men, I never knew whether we were accepted because of ourselves or our tinned beef.

E. A. Pye

I remember the long trumpet-like note of the conch shell which the fishermen blew as they tacked towards the land in the early morning.

Frank Wightman

To the visitor whose approach is from the sea . . . it is first startling, then depressing; but after the island has worked its magic on you, these seedy, shop-soiled towns are accepted. Soon you find yourself regarding them with a rueful affection—like being under the spell of a beautiful woman with flat feet.

Dennis Puleston

As far back as 1565 a customs report describes it as "a very proper town, well furnished with good mariners, where commonly tall ships do ride . . .

Rex Clements

Every sort of rig and nationality was represented. There were tall and stately British clippers, four and five-masted American schooners, white-painted South Sea traders from the islands, huge port-painted Frenchmen, sharp black-hulled Germans, hard-case Nova Scotiamen, Italians, Norwegians and Danes—graceful clippers and lumbering sea-wagons, barques, barquentines and schooners, lofty or squat, smart or lubberly, with a sprinkling of steamers and coasting vessels and a whole medley of smaller craft.

Frank Wightman

The tiny harbor (the crater of an extinct volcano) was nearly circular in form, and round the circle the old quays curved—with island schooners tied up to them unloading their cargos with the old-fashioned block and tackle of the leisured age of sail. The air throbbed with a deep-throated chorus of hauling chanties—and over everything was the smell of spice.

William Robinson

The air was heavy with the scent of lovely flowers, and there were strange land noises. We could hear a milkman making his way about town, and soon all the sounds of a community awakening. Birds, dogs, cattle, it was all so strange to us. I put up the quarantine flag and gave myself over to the ecstasy of it all—the glorious feeling that comes only at the end of such a voyage—a feeling of utter relaxation and peace, and of accomplishment.

Ernle Bradford

It was warm in the cabin and the rain beat a pleasant tattoo overhead. That was one of the good moments—when you were safe in an anchorage, with night coming down and the sea slapping against the side. It gave you a warm feeling to know that a few hundred yards away the water was boiling on the rocks and the wind was too strong for canvas.

The rain had stopped when I went out on deck to hoist our riding light. The wind was still high, though, and the torn edges of nimbus were skating over the headland. I could just make out the lights of Poros gleaming wetly across the bay . . . I was happy to go below again knowing there was no need for an anchor watch. It was fine to get the bunks down and have a night cap, listening to Athens radio, with an old book to read that I had read many times before. Janet's light went out, and I knew by her breathing that she was asleep. I mixed myself another whisky and turned the pages. "At Damme, in Flanders, when the May hawthorn was coming into flower, Ulenspiegel, son of Claes, was born . . ."

When I woke in the small hours the book lay on the floor, with my hand trailed across it. My light was still on. I padded out and opened the hatch. The night was still and there was mist rising off the island. The clouds had gone, and after the rain they would not return. There was no wind, and the sky went on and on, with the stars liquid in its folds. The boat smelled pleasantly of damp cordage and drying teak. I could hear fish rising, farther out in the bay.

Samuel Eliot Morison

The October spring low is something I would not miss. After a day of brisk northwest wind the harbor is glassy calm, reflecting sunset clouds, the brilliant maples on the shore the white hulls of yachts waiting to be hauled out Around the edge of the sand flats, well below the blue mussel beds, is a rod-wide belt of eel grass catching its fortnightly chance to breathe.—Big black-backed gulls walk through the grass with a dignified gait, stalking the tiny crabs and little fishes which normally obtain protection among the grass but are now laid bare to the piercing eye and hungry beak.

E. F. Knight

We landed at the Praya, the ancient and dirty stone quay which stretches along the shore for four miles, a spot of great commercial activity. Here are the great warehouses whence the coffee, sugar, tobacco, cotton, logwood, and the other produce of this rich tropical land are shipped to every quarter of the globe. Here, too, are markets of strange fruits and vegetables, and a bazaar where one can buy gorgeous or voluble parrots, baboons and monkeys of many species, pumas and jaguars too, and, indeed, specimens of nearly all the wild beasts of South America. Grog shops, where poisonous white rum is sold to British seamen, are frequent. Along the quay are ranged the quaint native lighters with their half-naked ebon crews. A jostling, jabbering crowd of Negroes and Negresses with gaudy robes and turbans throngs the Praya, and when one first lands one is oppressed by a bewildering sense of confusion—a flashing of bright colors—a din of Negroes, parrots, and monkeys—a compound smell of pineapples and other fruit, of molasses, Africans, bilgewater, tar, filth, too, of every description; not a monotonous smell, however, but every varying, now a whiff of hot air sweet with spice, then an odor that might well be the breath of Yellow Jack himself.

John MacGregor

Now there is a peculiarity of the French ports which we may mention here once for all, but it applies to every one of them, and has to be seriously considered in all your calculations as a sailing master.

They are quiet enough up to a certain time of night, but as the tide serves, the whole port awakes, all the fishing vessels get ready to start. The quays become vocal with shouts, yells, calls, whistles, and the most stupid din and hubbub confounds the night, utterly destructive of sleep. This chorus was in full cry about two o'clock a.m. Soon great luggers came splashing along with shrieks from the crews, and sails flapping, chains rattling, spars knocking about, as if a tempest were in rage. Several of these lubberly craft mashed against the pier, and the men screamed more wildly, and at length one larger and more inebriated than all the rest, dashed in among the small boats where the *Rob Roy* slept, and

swooping down on the poor little yawl, then wrapped in calm repose, she heeled us over on our beam ends, and after fastening her clumsy, rusty anchor in my mizzen shrouds (which were of iron, and declined to snap), she bore me and my boat away far off, ignominiously, stern foremost.

Certainly this was by no means a pleasant foretaste of what might be expected in the numerous other ports we were to enter, and, at any rate, that night's sleep was gone.

Rex Clements

Christmas Day we spent very quietly, doing no work and having duff for dinner. In the morning it was blazing hot, and we sat and smoked about the foredeck, singing songs to Jimmy's accordion, and making the little penguins we had caught run races along the deck. Thorough little sportsmen they were, and waddled along manfully, the winner receiving a piece of fish as a prize. The old man sent the steward along with a couple of bottles of pisco, so we all had a drink apiece and wished each other a pleasant passage home. The wind freshened at midday, and during the afternoon blew a gale. We looked at the white-lipped seas outside, and hoped for a spell of calm weather when we were loaded, for it would be impossible to get through the northern entrance to the Bay except with a steady, gentle breeze.

Next morning we returned to our unsavory labors, and worked steadily away at the guano through an exceptionally windless week.

Charles Violet

Two hours I waited for the necessary officials to come and give me "free pratique," but I was completely ignored. "To hell with this," I decided, "I'm going ashore." First I sauntered up and down the quay admiring the boats or finding fault, then I got bolder and made for the center of town. Except for the hot sun it could have been an English seaside resort. There were crowds of people dressed in holiday attire, and children carrying buckets and spades; the beach was a blaze of huge colored umbrellas, with many beautiful girls in scanty sunsuits. Not all black-haired with olive complexions, but a good sprinkling of fair heads. It was fun to mingle with the crowd for a little while.

Edward H. Dodd, Jr.

No sooner had we dropped anchor off the Myrtlebank Hotel than we were encircled by a flotilla of decrepit rowboats. The occupants stood up in their boats grasping our rail, and hissed loudly to attract our attention. Polished coral, bits of painted wood, and stuffed blowfish were dangled enticingly. Ponderous Elizabeth, with perspiration shining on her broad black face and through her thin chintz dress, hissed petulantly between gleaming teeth for our laundry. Beatrice, on the other side, sent forth a series of competitive hisses. Both presented their cards with a persistence that could not be denied. A boatload of six richly powdered prostitutes added six cabaret cards to our rapidly increasing store. Unable to rid itself of this motley assemblage, the *Chance* became a veritable arena. As we cleared up the ship, we felt like a group of stage sailors and every glance at the gallery drew more excited hisses.

Rex Clements

How strange the ship looked and felt as we came out on deck after tea for a smoke! After so many days with tiers of bellying canvas above our heads—to see nothing but the naked spars: instead of the unending dip and roll of the hull—to tread a motionless and steady deck: in place of the rustle of wind aloft and murmur of water overside—an uncanny silence. It all seemed very flat.

Joshua Slocum

On the first evening ashore, in the land of napkins and cut glass, I saw before me still the ghosts of hempen towels and mugs with handles knocked off.

Harry Pidgeon

It was good to be on the ground and in the shade of the trees once more.

Rex Clements

When we turned out we were in a better condition to take stock of our surroundings. It was a busy scene that greeted us. The harbor was a wonderful sight by reason of the great number of deep-sea sailing ships then in port. There were no less than a hundred and sixteen of them when we arrived, not counting steamers or coasters, and a grand show they made. Right away from Queen's Wharf, just inside the Bluff, up past the Dyke they lay in an unbroken line as far as Waratah, or "Siberia" as it was called, from its remoteness to everywhere else. In the Dyke, where we were lying, the ships lay three deep and there was a double row of them over on the other side at Stockton. Masts and yards were packed as thick as bristles on a hedgehog. During the day there was as much activity afloat as ashore, in consequence of the tremendous number of steam-launches, ferry steamers, chandlers' boats and ships' gigs dodging about among the shipping.

Ray Kauffman

We had no detailed chart of Surabaya's inner harbor, so we felt our way in past lights and wharfs until the life of the town was all about us, and dropped the anchor, with a silent prayer that we were not in the middle of a shipping lane. We went to sleep on the cool deckhouse, with the sound and smell of Java's second city borne off in the land breeze, wondering what the dawn would unfold; for a strange harbor at night is cloaked in mystery and is without scale or bearings, except for the blinking channel lights, and often a liner alongside a jetty will look larger than the city itself; a dark mass may be a hill, a distant mountain or a rock pile close by. The sounds past midnight are unidentifiable; the subdued throb of a city blends with the metallic sound of the shipping; but there is a thrill in the smell of the land, not heated by a sterile sun, the moist green, the night earth, the warehouses of copra, molasses, cotton and freshly sawn timber; the cordage, tar, oil and damp rusty metal of ships; and, filtering through, is the faint, mysterious smell of the East: spice, joss-sticks, dirty clothes and sewage.

Hilaire Belloc

We ran straight for a point where could be seen the gate to the inland bay; we rounded it, and our entry completed all, for when once we had rounded the point all fell together; the wind, the heaving of the water, the sounds and the straining of the sheets. In a moment, and less than a moment, we had cut out from us the vision of the sea; a barrier of cliff and hill stood between us and the large horizon. The very lonely slopes of these western mountains rose solemn and enormous all around, and the bay on which we floated, with only just that way which remained after our sharp turning, was quite lucid and clear, like the seas by southern beaches where one can look down and see a world underneath our own. The boom swung inboard, the canvas hung in folds, and my companion forward cut loose the little anchor from its tie, the chain went rattling down, and so silent was that sacred place that one could hear an echo from the cliffs close by returning the clanking of the links; the chain ran out and slowly tautened as she fell back and rode to it. Then we let go the halyards and when the slight creaking of the blocks had ceased there was no more noise. Everything was still.

John MacGregor

At night there was a strange sound, shrill and loud, which lasted for hours, and marred the calm eve and the quiet twinkling of the stars. This came from a hundred children collected by a crack-brained stranger (said to be English). These he gave cakes and toys lavishly to by day, and assembled them at night on the quay to sing chorus to his incoherent verses.

Desmond Holdridge

I went into Lunenburg with Randolph, having the intention of making some small purchases, and I saw the Lunenburg fleet back from the "frozen bait" trip and preparing for the summer on the Banks. The harbor was thronged with magnificent schooners, big and fast and handsome, tall topmasts soaring from their lower sticks and all the gear there to swing the clouds of canvas. Through the streets rumbled drays loaded with sails and nets. At the blacksmith's ship, anchors, mast bands, boom fittings, "Yankee jibers," and every manner of ironwork for a vessel were being forged. The oar-makers and blockmakers worked from daylight to dark in a rambling shop where I saw a hundred-year-old model of a frigate made by a French deserter who had died in the local jail. Scores of stout fishermen paraded through the streets in seaboots, jerseys, and (some) berets, for that style was just being introduced by the bootleggers. In the air was the sweet chink of calking mallets, the whir of band saws cutting into new wood, the thump of heavy mauls driving big spikes into the sides of rugged ships. Money was being made and spent and the price of fish was high.

E. A. Pye

They came alongside and fingered the ropes and blocks with many "bonas"; soon boat after boat sailed in till we were the center of a little fleet, and our decks, gear and spars, were lit by many flares. One or two of the men spoke a little English. They said that *Moonraker* had been recognized as a fishing boat, but they were all puzzled as to how she had become a yacht. They examined her in every detail and marvelled at her being so strongly built. An old coil of rope gave them pleasure and we exchanged cigarettes for fish. A dozen sails were hoisted to the breeze, a dozen twinkling lights spread out across the bay: a shout, a snatch of song, and they were gone.

William Robinson

Late at night when we returned to the river landing, *Varua* would be hidden in the drifting mists. The sleeping boatman would emerge from beneath his dripping poncho and row us diagonally upstream to allow for the current. Soon the glow of the masthead light would appear floating unattached in the air, followed moments later by the white masts themselves. Gradually *Varua* would emerge mysteriously at arm's length. The botero would vanish into the mist, oars creaking, his parting words hanging disembodied in the damp night air. "Buenas noches, Senor."

Richard Maury

Climbing aboard, we set sail, and working over a glowing slide of water, secured her amid a fleet of ancient wrecks. Then Dombey and I moved ashore to "Caledonia," the home of my uncle and aunt, leaving the schooner to wait patiently, guarded from wind by useless, wornout hulls, Experience, Hoary Age and Infinite Wisdom lifted high above her: crumbling masts, samson posts and great broadsides of metal, teak, and wormed pine; while old rigging whispered of a lost, of a romantic youth. On a night of southerly winds the fleet could be heard complaining—a groan from a half-filled hold, the creak of an unbraced yard working on a rusted parrel, and less distinct sounds, the "talk" of damaged ships. Morning would find them silent, motionless in sunshine, like a squadron thrown up by a departed hurricane: the French barkentine *Fraternite,* white-boned and broken; a down-East schooner that had turned turtle and drowned her crew; the teak hull of H.M.S. *Ready,* sloop-of-war, Her Majesty's brasswork turned green, almost black; the decommissioned *Gladisfen*—the "Rooster," as she was devotedly called. Beyond, on the glittering harbor lay the most favored of the fleet—one still moving to wind—the beautifully modeled *Duncrag,* once a bark, now a hulk, coal-laden.

Edward H. Dodd, Jr.

The next morning we found the dinghy absent and, after a search with field glasses, discovered it at the other end of the harbor gently pounding itself on the rocks.

Ernle Bradford

Under the lemon-sun of winter the cobbled streets gleamed with water where butchers, flower sellers, and fishmongers wash down outside their narrow-fronted shops and market stalls. The street traders did not fit into narrow distinctions; on one stall there was a mixture of children's toys, sugar animals, plaster statuettes of saints, razor blades, old American army boots, and cotton dresses. At the corner, where the alleys met, there was always a fat middle-aged man, with a face like a glass of red wine, who sold cooked octopus as well as singing birds in cages. The sea smell was heavy around the lower end of the market where most of the fishmongers had their stalls. Lean dogfish lay cheek by jowl with octopus and squid, dappled mullet, prawns, mackerel, the claw of Mediterranean lobsters, and strange scaly monsters with huge heads . . . Layers of bacalao lay on marble slabs, with jets of water playing over the yellow sun-dried flesh. From this sea-world we made our way up another passage bright with fruit and vegetables. Here were piles of oranges, lemons, and mandarins; roots of fennel and fresh herbs from the mountains; figs, grapes, sugary raisins, and the fat-leaved artichokes which grew in the fields outside the city.

"Water, sweet water!" cried one man on whose back was strapped a brass contraption like an old geyser. The water was flavored with anis and cost a penny a glass.

"Lemons! Lemons! Lemons with the most beautiful sugar!" cried another who was pushing a chemist's jar on pram-wheels through the throng. On a hot day a glass of his lemonade was as clean and astringent as a spring among rocks.

Dark doorways and gratings underfoot threw

our warm smells of baking bread or roasting coffee. Cavern-like entrances, lit only by fly-specked bulbs, disclosed the vaulting shadows of wine casks. Sometimes we would sit happily in one of these, the only customers. The padrone was a friend of Gaspare and his wine was good and strong at fourpence a glass. Where the door opened on the street I would watch the passersby like puppets on their miniature stage.

John MacGregor

The harbor here dries bare at low tide, and as seventeen years had elapsed since we had sailed into it, this bad habit of the harbor was forgotten, but more years than that may pass before it will be forgotten again, for as evening came, and the water ebbed, and I reclined unharnessed in the cabin, reading intently, there suddenly came a rude bumping shove upwards as from below, and then another—the *Rob Roy* had grounded. Soon there was a swaying this way and that, as if yet undecided, and at length a positive heel over to *that;* the whole of my little world within being canted to half a right angle, and a ridiculous distortion of every single thing in my bedroom was the result. The humiliating sensation of being aground on hard un-romantic mud is tempered by the ludicrous crooked appearance of the contents of your cabin, and by the absurd sensation of sleeping in a corner with everything askance except the lamp flame, which, because it burns upright, looks most awry of all, and incongruously flares on the spout of the teapot in your pantry.

And why this *bouleversement* of all things? Be-cause I had omitted to bring a pair of legs with me, for a boat cannot stand upright on shore without legs any more than an animal.

Next time the *Rob Roy* came to Margate we made one powerful leg for her by lashing the two oars to the iron shroud, and took infinite pains to incline the boat over to that side, so as to be turned away from the wind and screened from the tide, and I therefore weighed her down by placing the dinghy and heavy anchor on the lee gunwale, and then with misplaced contentment proceeded to cook my dinner. At a solemn pause in the re-past, the yawl, without other warning than a loud splash, perversely turned over to the wrong side, with deck to sea and wind, and every single thing exactly the contrary of what was proper. I had just time to plunge my hissing spirit lamp into the sea, and thus to prevent the cry of "Fire!" but had not time to put out my cabin lamp, and this instantly bore its flame provokingly upright against the thick glass of the aneroid barometer, which duly told its fate by three sonorous "crinks," and at once three starred checks shot through its crystal front.

The former experience of the night as spent when one is thus arbitrarily "inclined to sleep" made me wish to wish to get ashore; but this idea was stifled partly by pride, and partly by the fact that there was not water enough to enable me to get ashore in a boat, and yet there was too much water besides soft mud to make it at all pleasant to set off and wade to bed. The recovery from this unwholesome state, with all the world askew, was equally notable, for when the tide rose in the late midnight hours, the sea-dreams of disturbed slumber were arrested by a gentle nudge, and then by a more decided heaving up of one's bed in the dark, until at last it came level again as the boat floated, and all the things that were right when she was wrong turned over now at wrong angles, be-cause the boat had righted.

E. A. Pye

Our stores ordered, we strolled towards the outskirts of the town, where a schooner lay hove-down by her fore and main halyards, so that her garboard strake was exposed to the calking hammer of the ship-wright as he hammered in the cotton.

Edward H. Dodd, Jr.

Our stay at Bermuda was an ideal one. Coming in from the sea with blisters on our hands and salt on our faces, we fancied that a vacation was deserved, and proceeded to disport ourselves. Work on board was eliminated by the immediate necessity of painting the deck. This was undertaken on the first day, so that it would have plenty of time to dry before we left, and thereafter the wet paint was an excellent excuse to stay on shore.

Joshua Slocum

My vessel being moored, I spread an awning, and instead of going at once on shore I sat under it till late in the evening, listening with delight to the musical voices of the Samoan men and women.

William Robinson

You are busy with anchors, mooring lines, and making things shipshape for a few moments and then you sit on the cabin house and relax, and add one to the lengthening lists of ports made.

Hilaire Belloc

My companion and I sat in the hatch that evening under quiet stars, smoking pipes, watching that most pleasant of sights, the home lights of a little harbor town, and their trembling reflections in the water, the slight swaying of the masts of fishing boats moored by the quay.

Ann Davison

A tourist remains an outsider throughout his visit, but a sailor is part of the local scene from the moment he arrives.

Amos A. Evans

Judging of the females of this place [Boston] by their appearance in the street, the only opportunity I have had of seeing them, I should say they were not so handsome as those in Philadelphia or Baltimore. Their persons are not so neat nor their motions so graceful. Their complexions are rosy and healthy, their countenances, features sprightly and animated, or, in other words, they appear to have more mind and less grace than the Southern ladies. I know nothing of their dispositions, but if permitted to apply the rules of Lavater to their physiognomies should say there is a superabundance of Tartaric acid in them.

John MacGregor

When the lights at Havre hove in sight the welcome flashing was a happy reward to a long day's toil, and as the yawl sped forward cheerily through the intervening gloom, the kettle hummed over the lamp, and a bumper of hot grog was served to the crew. Soon we rounded into the harbor, quiet and calm, with everybody asleep at that late hour; and it was some time more before the *Rob Roy* could settle into a comfortable berth, and her sails were all made up, and bed unrolled, and the weary sailor was snoring in his blanket.

Hilaire Belloc

. . . and I whistled, but no wind came. I sat idle and admired the loneliness of the sea. Till, towards one, a little draught of air blew slantwise from the land, and under it I crept to the smooth water within the stone arm of the breakwater, and there I let the anchor go, and, settling everything, I slept.

It is pleasant to remember these things.

Ernle Bradford

I dried myself on deck, with one of the old yellowing towels, harsh-tongued with salt and sand, that we kept for bathing. Then I went round the boat for the morning inspection.

Anchors and Rum

Anchors and rum are the symbols of that good life, the sailing life. Tenacity, purpose, the quality of seeing it through are among the virtues of a high ethic that are symbolized by a ship's iron finger, her burrowing anchor. For many sailors, however, the anchor is merely the sign of another ended affair with the sea. Rum, on the other hand, is a universal symbol of the zestfullness and good spirits found in every articulate Jack.

Woodes Rogers

Aug. 5, 1702. We saw the Land, and finding we had overshot our Port, came to an anchor at twelve a clock off of the two Rocks call'd the Sovereigns Bollacks. . . .

Desmond Holdridge

. . . the splash of our anchor in the smooth water broke a silence . . .

Hilaire Belloc

The best noise in all the world is the rattle of the anchor chain when one comes into harbor at last and lets it go over the bows.

Richard Maury

We lay off and on the Grand Turk beacon until daybreak, then headed for the low island. When on soundings, a Negro pilot came on board dressed in the attire of a battleship's commander, we sailed toward the open roadstead. The sands of the shore drew nearer, the blue water paled to lime, the sails fell muffled down the spars, and a black anchor making an arc over the bows splashed into the peaceful water.

L. Francis Herreshoff

. . . whether Coridon was alone or had a guest, he would invariably call out: "Down killock!" For coming to anchor seemed to give him a very agreeable sensation, and although he had been doing it for years, it still gave him pleasure.

Alfred Loomis

Once the hook was down in hard sand and weed in three fathoms of water I was, as always, discontented with my choice of anchorage.

John MacGregor

The anchorage on the south of the pier is in mud of deep black color, but not such good holding ground as it would seem to be, and then what comes up on the anchor runs like black paint upon your deck, and needs a good scrubbing to get rid of it from each palm of the anchor. Even after all seems to be cleared away thoroughly, there may be a piece only the size of a nut, but perverse enough to fasten upon the white creamy folds of your jib newly washed out, and then the inky stain will be an eyesore for days, until, for peace of mind, the sail must be scrubbed again. Trifles these are to the yachtsman who can leave all that to his crew, who sees only results, but when the captain alone is the crew, the realities of sea life must be endured as well as enjoyed, and yet surely he is the one to enjoy most keenly the luxury of a white spotless sail whose own hands have made it so.

Charles Violet

. . . I could see . . . the land enfolded in the night, and a joyful glimpse of twinkling lights high up the mountainside. An off-shore breeze brought the scent of wood smoke. All was peacefully quiet and utterly restful. The murmur of the swell on the rocks outside was no longer something to be feared, but a soft bass note from the sea-symphony.

Richard Maury

. . . the accumulation of minor strains that must never be revealed while under way, now flooding to the surface when the sails are furled, when progress has ceased and the very purpose of life seems to disappear with the drowning of the anchors; when that delicate instrument, a sailing craft, that for so long now has registered every rhythm of elements stretching to every shore, is suddenly brought to a stop, to jerk at her chains, to pound indelicately, rolling like a drunken sailor off the new-found port: and invariably, for a moment at least, the crew is overtaken by a feeling of nausea, by a desire to scud to sea—for another submergence, another helping of that windy blue drug.

Joshua Slocum

It was when I anchored in the lonely places that a feeling of awe came over me.

Richard Maury

We raised the mountains of Nuka Hiva, bore in to Ta-o-hae Bay and dropped anchors off the village. The sails fell onto salted decks, leaving the bare masts curiously naked and useless. Mystical scents, warm, tropical, came off shore as we felt something leaving us weak, awkward, slightly breathless; even as we gazed at the green mountains, at the shining coco trees, we knew it was only that another voyage had ended.

Samuel Eliot Morison

And I advise all sound cruisers to anchor properly in a harbor, not tie up at a "marina," the yachtsmen's slum.

William Robinson

We found very poor anchorage in the lee of the island, where I had hoped to stay a day or so, and were deceived into dropping the anchor in 12 fathoms, thinking it to be only half that from the extreme clarity of the water. This meant that we should have to have help in getting it up again, for 12 fathoms of ⅜ chain plus a 75-pound anchor are too heavy for us to get in a hurry, and we should have to have quick work in getting away from the coral heads and back eddies. The currents came around from both sides of the island and met here in the lee, causing a bad swell. I was quite uneasy while on the shore, especially as with the new moon, I feared a change in the weather from the calms and light breezes we had been having. So the stay in this interesting place was cut short to the one day, and we sailed off just at dark.

E. A. Pye

We dropped anchor behind Molasses Reef on a patch of sand, but the bottom was a mass of coral-heads and I was not surprised the next morning to hear Bob say that our chain was round three lots of heads, with the anchor lying useless on its side.

Rex Clements

For a few moments there was the deuce to pay. T'gallants and tops'l halyards were let fly and the yards came down with a run, with the canvas flapping in the breeze.

"Let go!" yelled the old man to the mate on the fok'sle head. Chips sprang to the windlass, while the bosun seized a topping maul, jumped on the cathead and knocked out the pin of the ring-stopper. The anchor went down with a rush and a roar and the cable leapt out so furiously that the windlass brakes caught fire. Old Chips was almost blinded by the flying sparks and dust, but hung on to the brakes and gradually checked the mad rush of the cable. The anchor held and as we clewed up the sails in desperate haste, the barque's way slackened and she came to a standstill within a biscuit's throw of the reef.

The puff of wind only lasted a couple of minutes. It was all over in that time and was succeeded by a dead calm which enabled us to warp the ship into the fairway and moor her properly in the anchorage, with both bowers down and 35 fathoms out on each.

Alan Villiers

I saw steamers approach the Bali roads with caution, dragging an anchor on 60 fathoms of chain very slowly, and fetching up as soon as it touched.

Frank Wightman

. . . the looped and hummocked anchor chain uncoiling as *Wylo* drifted back before the puffs. Its piled links straightened out on the coral bottom, raising little whirlwinds of pink sand that stormed round the writhing chain like eddying mist, until it became a rigid bar. It rose from the bottom sullenly and tugged at the anchor, which spun round and waddled forward for a moment before it suddenly burrowed into the sand like a frightened mole.

Hillaire Belloc

I spent an abominable night once off a shingle bank in heaving water, where the tide ran strong, from having let out too much chain in the dark. The metal lay all along the bottom like the great sea serpent, and the movement of the boat sent a violent wrangling of iron up the chain all night long, so that I was perpetually running up on deck, between poor intervals of sleep, to judge by the distant light whether she were dragging or no. And I had good occasion for anxiety, seeing that not far upon my lee the shoal came right up out of the sea, with the water breaking upon it. You might think that however much chain you had let out, your boat would lie to the end of it; but it is not so. If you have a great deal too much chain let out in shoal water, the weight of it holds the boat like a kind of second anchor, and it grumbles and shifts and moves all the time.

E. F. Knight

We were anchored on a sandy bottom, but we could feel by the grumbling of our chain as the yacht swung, that there were many rocks under us as well. These caused us a good deal of annoyance; for on several occasions, when the vessel was lying right over her anchor, the slack of the chain would take a turn round a rock and give us a short nip; so that when a swell passed under us the vessel could not rise to it, but was held down by the tautened chain, which dragged her bows under, producing a great strain. The rocks must have been of brittle coral formation, for, after giving two or three violent jerks as the sea lifted her, the vessel would suddenly shake herself free with a wrench, evidently by the breaking away of the obstruction. At last all the projecting portions of the coral rock must have been torn off, the chain having swept a clear space for itself all round, for after a time we were no longer caught in this way. These great strains loosened our starboard hawse pipe badly . . .

Alfred Loomis

It didn't take long to find that we had chosen the wrong place for anchoring.

E. A. Pye

If we got the mainsail set while the anchor still held, we had a chance; without it, there was none. And at the back of my mind was the nagging thought that never had the ship been in such danger, and we were not even at sea, just caught in a trap of our own making. We got the mainsail up. Anne brought up the third jib, and both she and John were soaked to the skin (we were still in our pajamas) before they had it set. Tack for tack we sailed her up to her anchor. The green paint on the chain, the 15 fathom mark, came inboard and still she held; one short tack to port, a quick lee-

oh, and, with the foresail set, she sailed the anchor out so sweetly that John never felt the jerk on the winch. She beat off that lee shore like a thoroughbred, and after two tacks I dared to look astern to where the wall was fast receding. Anne took over and put her in the wind, while John and I hauled in the rest of the chain and the anchor.

Erling Tambs

We let go our anchor in the midst of a squall. It looked as though we had dropped it altogether, so fast did we drag. With 50 fathoms of chain and a 180 pound grapnel at the end of it, we traveled quick and lively inshore towards the rocks.

E. A. Pye

The sound of the chain dragging along the bottom brought me to my senses quicker than a bucket of cold water. . . .

Edward H. Dodd, Jr.

That night the wind shifted northward and the full force of it came roaring through the pass and down the bay. With ropes rattling and awnings thrashing the *Chance* tugged at her anchor. Before we had realized the strength of the wind, there was a rasping jerk of the anchor chain in the hawse pipe. She was dragging anchor!

John MacGregor

Nor is the property in boats' anchors quite free from the legal

subtleties which allow but a dim sort of ownership in things that are "attached to the soil."

When, indeed, your boat is at one end of the cable, you will scarecely fear that the anchor should be stolen from the other end. But when necessity or convenience causes you to slip anchor and sail away, you must recollect that though the anchor is the emblem of hope, it does not warrant any expectation that on returning you will find the anchor acknowledged to be yours. It has now passed into the category of "found anchors," and it is not yet decided how the rights to these are best determined.

Francis Brenton

I felt I could do without the barnacles, of which I estimated that I must have had 300 pounds under my hulls. Barnacles were 90 percent water, so their weight was not a tremendous factor, but their feeding cirri, probing before them, acted as thousands of small anchors.

Ernle Bradford

. . . fishermen and men who live in ports can always use a drink. It may be the salt air, or it may be that men who live by the sea like the shared friendliness that wine brings. The peasants and farmers were different. They were closed in against one another, and suspicious of anything like wine that made them lower their guard.

Woodes Rogers

           . . . we had but a slender Stock of Liquor, and our Men but meanly clad, yet good Liquor to Sailors is preferable to Clothing.

Joshua Slocum

           I reached for a bottle of port wine out of the locker, and took a long pull from it . . .

Sir Francis Chichester

           Also, he had on board a keg of his magic brew, raw eggs mixed with rum . . .

Alfred Loomis

           . . . and we spliced the main brace; one has to make a perfect landfall after five days in a tossing yawl to understand just how enthusiastically we spliced it . . .

Richard Maury

           While lacking searoom, a bottle of Demerara, the gift of a concerned friend, was brought on deck, broached, and a toast made to the success of the venture. This one time liquor was permitted on board remains clear in mind: the young three of us wet with spray, tippling a bottle while the *Cimba* smashed a way to sea—a dark waste on which the sunset died, over which winds from the southeast came to redden our wetted faces.

Ernest K. Gann

The time was known as "Bardinet Hour" after the rum of my own devotion, and it was always held on deck. Sometimes we stood in water up to our knees as seas swept across the deck, and sometimes we were at great pains to prevent rain or flying salt spray from diluting our refreshment, and sometimes we had to pause momentarily to hand a sail or come about on a different tack, but *always* the hour of Bardinet was observed.

Sir Francis Chichester

. . . I started celebrating my birthday drinking a bottle of wine . . . sitting in the cockpit with a champagne cocktail . . . full rig, smoking jacket, smart new trousers, black shoes, etc. The only slipup is that I have left my bow-tie behind, and have had to use an ordinary black tie.

Charles Violet

Ahead of me was one small fishing boat, whose crew waved to me and, raising their arms in a drinking motion, invited me over.

Herman Melville

But Mad Jack, alas! has one fearful failing. He drinks. And so do we all. But Mad Jack, he only drinks brandy. The vice was inveterate; surely, like Ferdinand, Count Fathom, he must have suckled at a puncheon. Very often, this bad habit got him into very serious scrapes. Twice was he put off duty by the Commodore; and once he came near being broken for his frolics. So far as his efficiency as a sea-officer was concerned, on shore at least, Jack might souse away as much as he pleased; but afloat it will not do at all.

Now, if only followed the wise example set by those ships of the desert, the camels; and while in port, drank for the thirst past, the thirst present, and the thirst to come—so that he might cross the ocean sober; Mad Jack would get along pretty well. Still better, if he would but eschew brandy altogether; and only drink of the limpid white wine of the rills and the brooks.

Herman Melville

"Rum and tobacco!" said Landless, "what more does a sailor want?"

Ray Kauffman

Rum, lime and brown sugar with ice and water were passed around. They were cool and good and not too sweet; but the Tahitian rum gave me nostalgia for Papeete, and our passage through thirty degrees of longitude passed through my mind in a panorama of islands and faces.

Rex Clements

The Colonial beer though, had a reputation for headiness. "Sheoke" beer it was called and old Australian traders used to spread a net under the gangway, called therefrom the "sheoke net," whose office it was to save mariners who "missed stays" when coming aboard from falling into the dock. Each morning the ends of the net were hauled up and its slumbering occupants bundled out on deck.

A great institution was the sheoke net and saved from a watery end many a mariner whom it would be harsh to call drunk. "Drunk" is an opprobrious term and implies a state of intoxication absolute and irredeemable. What it means to be really "drunk" is well-suggested by a little yarn that often went the rounds.

It is said that late one night in Melbourne, a well-primed seaman returned on board his ship, staggered up the gangway and collapsed on deck, where he lay sleeping peacefully. The mate came on board soon after and, seeing somebody "dead-oh," whistled for the night watchman. "What the hell's this?" said he, "take this man for'ard; he's dead drunk!" The watchman bent over the prostrate form for a moment, then looked up cheerfully, "No sir, 'e ain't drunk" he said, "I saw 'im move!"

Charles Violet

Going up to the town to hunt for some bread, I fell in with three men from whom I enquired the way to the nearest boulangerie. They insisted on taking me to a cafe for aperitifs; alas, I had too many, and when negotiating the gangplank to the barge I stumbled, and the loaf disappeared into the brown flood . . .

Herman Melville

Three of them drank a good deal too much; and when they came on board, the Captain ordered them to be sewed up in their hammocks, to cut short their obstreperous capers till sober.

Sir Francis Chichester

I decided that keeping watch was a waste of time, went below and mixed myself my anti-scorbutic. The lemon juice . . . not only keeps physical scurvy away, but if enough of the right kind of whisky is added to it, mental scurvy as well. *Gipsy Moth* sailed on through the dark.

Boston Gazette, August 12th, 1771:

The beginning of last Week a Fishing Schooner arrived at Marblehead having on board 4 Men and 2 Lads, who gave an Account, that about a Week or Fortnight before they got in, one Saturday Evening, after the Crew had made a Supper of Pork and boiled Dumplins, their Skipper and one Russell, died very suddenly, the former immediately after Supper and the latter the next Morning. Although the Men and Lads agreed in the Circumstance relative to these Deaths, yet the Magistracy tho't proper to make a legal, particular Enquiry into the Affair, which was done last Saturday, when it appeared that Russell, after the Men had finished their Supper, challenged the Skipper, or any other, to drink Bumpers of Rum with him; which being accepted, a Pint Mug was filled and Russell drank it off, and the Skipper then drank the same Quantity. Russell repeated the fatal draught which completed a Quart; before the Skipper had

Time to drink his second Draught he fell and immediately expired. His Champion dropt very soon after, continued in a lethargic State till the next Morning and then died. The 4 Men and 2 Lads agreed to Conceal the unhappy cause of these Deaths; which they did until examined by Authority.

Herman Melville

A man at the fore topsail yard sung out that there were eight or ten dark objects floating on the sea some three points off our lee bow.

"Keep her off three points!" cried Captain Claret, to the quartermaster.

And thus, with all our batteries, store-rooms, and five hundred men, with their baggage, and beds, and provisions, at one move of a round bit of mahogany, our great embattled ark edged away for the strangers, as easily as a boy turns to the right or left in pursuit of insects in the field.

Directly the man on the topsail yard reported the dark objects to be hogsheads. Instantly all the topmen were straining their eyes, in delirious expectation of having their long grog fast broken at last, and that, too, by what seemed an almost miraculous intervention. It was a curious circumstance that, without knowing the contents of the hogsheads, they yet seemed certain that the staves encompassed the thing they longed for.

Sail was now shortened, our headway was stopped, and a cutter was lowered, with orders to tow the fleet of strangers alongside. The men sprang to their oars with a will, and soon five goodly puncheons lay wallowing in the sea, just

under the main chains. We got overboard the slings, and hoisted them out of the water.

It was a sight that Bacchus and his bacchanals would have gloated over. Each puncheon was of a deep green color, so covered with minute barnacles and shellfish, and streaming with seaweed, that it needed long searching to find out their bung holes; they looked like venerable old loggerhead turtles. How long they had been tossing about, and making voyages for the benefit of the flavor of their contents, no one could tell. In trying to raft them ashore, or on board of some merchantship, they must have drifted off to sea. This we inferred from the ropes that lengthwise united them, and which, from one point of view, made them resemble a long sea serpent. They were struck into the gun deck, where, the eager crowd being kept off by sentries, the cooper was called with his tools.

"Bung up, and bilge free!" he cried, in an ecstasy, flourishing his driver and hammer.

Upon clearing away the barnacles and moss, a flat sort of shellfish was found, closely adhering like a California shell, right over one of the bungs. Doubtless this shellfish had there taken up his quarters and thrown his body into the breach, in order the better to preserve the precious contents of the cask. The bystanders were breathless, when at last this puncheon was canted over and a tinpot held to the orifice. What was to come forth? salt water or wine? But a rich purple tide soon settled the question, and the lieutenant assigned to taste it, with a loud and satisfactory smack of his lips, pronounced it Port!

"Oporto!" cried Mad Jack, "and no mistake!"

But to the surprise, grief, and consternation of the sailors, an order now came from the quarter-deck to strike the "strangers down into the main-hold!" This proceeding occasioned all sorts of censorious observations upon the Captain, who, of course had authorized it.

It must be related here that, on the passage out from home, the *Neversink* had touched at Madeira; and there, as is often the case . . . the Commodore and Captain had laid in a goodly stock of wines for their own private tables, and the benefit of their foreign visitors. And although the Commodore was a small, spare man, who evidently emptied but few glasses, yet Captain Claret was a portly gentleman, with a crimson face, whose father had fought at the battle of the Brandywine, and whose brother had commanded the well known frigate named in honor of that engagement. And his whole appearance evinced that Captain Claret himself had fought many Brandywine battles ashore in honor of his sire's memory, and commanded in many bloodless Brandywine actions at sea.

It was therefore with some savor of provocation that the sailors held forth on the ungenerous conduct of Captain Claret, in stepping between them and Providence, as it were, which by this lucky windfall they held, seemed bent upon relieving their necessities; while Captain Claret himself, with an inexhaustible cellar, emptied his Madeira decanters at his leisure.

But next day all hands were electrified by the old familiar sound—so long hushed—of the drum rolling to grog.

After that the port was served out twice a day, till all was expended.

Richard Hughes

Captain Jonsen, however, had his own idea of how to enliven a parochial bazaar that is proving a frost. He went on board, and mixed several gallons of that potion known in alcoholic circles as Hangman's Blood (which is compounded of rum, gin, brandy, and portar). Innocent (merely beery) as it looks, refreshing as it tastes, it has the property of increasing rather than allaying thirst, and so, once it has made a breach, soon demolishes the whole fort.

Leonard Wibberley

St. Vincent and Barbados rums are dry—Trinidad rum is semi-sweet; Jamaica rum is heavy and sweet, like liquor. Venezuela rum is passionate!

Desmond Holdridge

. . . and, what was more, he had the fastest vessel on the coast and the only cargo that ever went in it was raw, red, Demerara rum. He said that when he felt the need of extra money he poured water into the rum and added cayenne pepper . . .

Farley Mowat

By this time I was soaked, depressed, and very cold, but the Hallohan brothers and their ancient mother, who now appeared from a back room, went to work on me. They began by feeding me a vast plate of salt beef and turnips boiled with salt cod, which in turn engendered within me a monumental thirst. At this juncture the brothers brought out a crock of Screech.

Screech is a drink peculiar to Newfoundland. In times gone by, it was made by pouring boiling water into empty rum barrels to dissolve whatever rummish remains might have lingered there. Molasses and yeast were added to the black, resultant fluid, and this mixture was allowed to ferment for a decent length of time before it was distilled. Sometimes it was aged for a few days in a jar containing a plug of niggertwist chewing tobacco.

However, the old ways have given way to the new, and Screech is now a different beast. It is the worst conceivable quality of Caribbean rum, bottled by the Newfoundland government under the Screech lable, and sold to poor devils who have no great desire to continue living. It is not as powerful as it used to be, but this defect can be, and often is, remedied by the addition of quantities of lemon extract. Screech is usually served mixed with boiling water. In its consequent near-gaseous state the transfer of the alcohol to the bloodstream is instantaneous. Very little is wasted in the bloodstream.

This was my first experience with Screech and nobody had warned me. Harold sat back with an evil glitter in his eye and watched with delight as I tried to quench my thirst. At least I *think* he did. My memories of the balance of that evening are unclear.

Edward H. Dodd, Jr.

Towards evening all hands combined intellects to compose a punch. Prescribed ingredients were not available, but there was plenty of Galapagos rum, a liquor which, in spite of its innocuous cloudy white color, was a capable base. Fruit juices from vari-colored bottles, water and lime juice were all mixed in experimental cups. The final composition was quite palatable, even though it did leave a delicate stain on Sandy's porcelain saucepan.

Dennis Puleston

There is a very fine native rum made in Tahiti, and when we learned that we could buy some in bond as ship's stores at a very low price, we decided to lay in a stock of it. But we were dismayed to find that, buying it in bulk this way, the least quantity we could take would be a 220 liter barrel. Two hundred and twenty liters of rum! That meant about two hundred and forty quarts. It seemed ridiculous . . .

Rockwell Kent

. . . first dinner; then the charts; and then, on board, the commonest, most vulgar, strong Jamaica rum.

Humphrey Barton

At dusk—about 8 p.m.—I mixed a good stiff drink. Equal parts of rum, gin and orange juice.

Erling Tambs

He broke off and dived down into the cabin. I looked below and saw him emptying the remainder of our liquors, whisky, brandy, and rum, into a saucepan. With a cupful of this potent brew for each member of the crew he presently returned on deck proposing a drink to the *Teddy*.

"Skal!"

Francis Brenton

Later my financial position improved, and I bought rum, which solved most of my drinking problems. It also made my cooking taste better.

Farley Mowat

. . . black coffee made with rum as a substitute for water is a drink of exceptional authority.

Vito Dumas

On board the motionless *Lehg II* more than ten persons were celebrating her success in rum that had crossed the Atlantic. The bottles passed from mouth to mouth; we drank and drank again.

Rockwell Kent

. . . that night of story telling over beans and rum . . .

Leonard Wibberly

I visualize my friends very clearly as I drink their health. As if they were present I can even hear their voices. Imagination seems to have a fourth dimensional quality at sea, especially when sailing singlehanded, and can conjure up scenes and people in a manner unknown ashore.

Herman Melville

"Drink and pass!" he cried, handing the heavy charged flagon to the nearest seaman. "The crew alone now drink. Round with it, round! Short draughts—long swallows, men; 'tis hot as Satan's hoof. So, so; it goes round excellently. It spiralizes in ye; forks out at the serpent-snapping eye. Well done; almost drained. That way it went, this way it comes. Hand it me—here's a hollow! Men, ye seem the years; so brimming full life is gulped and gone. Steward, refill!"

E. F. Knight

. . . also our rum, which was the only alcoholic beverage on board; it certainly is the most wholesome spirit for sea use, especially within the tropics.

Ernest K. Gann

Because the *Henrietta* was totally dependent on her ability to sail, I had envisioned dreary delays, waiting in some isolated port for more wind or less wind. I had therefore taken the precaution of stowing a modest-sized keg of rum alongside our water barrels and in the evening when all was secure, I drew upon it. The rum was not of medal-winning caliber, but the color was pleasing and the bouquet not objectionable. In body it could not compare with Bardinet, but it did have a certain integrity. Unfortunately my appreciation of it was a lonely affair.

Farley Mowat

Happy Adventure puttered blindly on into the dark and brooding murk and I was soon fog-chilled, unutterably lonely, and scared to death. Since rum is a known and accepted antidote for all three conditions I took a long, curative drink for each separate ailment. By the time Jack appeared on deck I was much easier in my mind.

Herman Melville

Hark! the infernal orgies! that revelry is forward! mark the unfaltering silence aft! Methinks it pictures life. Foremost through the sparkling sea shoots on the gay, embattled, bantering bow, but only to drag dark Ahab after it, where he broods within his sternward cabin, builded over the dead water of the wake, and further on, hunted by its wolfish gurglings.

Edward H. Dodd, Jr.

Jonsey . . . had mixed a rum punch for the occasion—one half rum, one half white wine and fruit juice. But he had forgotten cocktails. Rising to the occasion,

however, he poured some of his famous punch into the shaker, added an equal amount of gin and redeemed himself.

Ralph Stock

It is a delightful, healthful drink composed of the very best rum, bitters, syrup, fresh lime . . .

Dennis Puleston

The manufacture of coconut toddy, a fiery distillate of fermented coconut water, is forbidden in the French islands . . .

Alfred Loomis

. . . we made the acquaintance of Mr. Tom Collins . . .

Dennis Puleston

Kava is a strange drink, slightly pungent in flavor, with a very smooth effect on the throat. Made from the pulverized roots of a small shrub belonging to the pepper family, it has no alcohol content and can be taken in large doses without muddling the senses. On the body, however, its effect is disastrous. After my first kava party I was amazed to find that I had lost control over my legs.

Ray Kauffman

"I tol' him to bring a bonito an' fix us all a mess o' raw fish. It's de best thing for a hangover."

K. Adlard Coles

My wife produced the bottle of vodka purchased at Riga, so, as I was anxious to find out how it was drunk, I placed it on deck together with a jug of water, signing them to help themselves. The eldest took the bottle and emptied most of the contents into a large mug, then added water and, with the assistance of a friend, finished the lot. Next he drained the remainder of the bottle. Thus in my method of learning the fashion in drinking it I lost all the vodka I possessed.

Samuel Pepys

. . . and so we came to an anchor, and to supper mighty merry, and after it, being moonshine we out of the cabin to laugh and talk, and then as we grew sleepy, went in and upon velvet cushions . . . fell to sleep.

Baggywrinkle

Bits and pieces of worn rope, small stuff or any piece of line having no further use aboard ship, were formerly picked apart, strand by strand, by the frugal sailor to make chafing gear called baggywrinkle. Their shaggy shapes are still seen today aboard larger, often older sailboats, high up in the shrouds. The term is used here to suggest bits and pieces, a nautical pot-pourri of scenes and aphorisms dear to the heart of any sailor.

Alan Villiers

"No, no, sonny," said the mate. "That won't do. Only criminals and foolish people hide in boats."

Herman Melville

With anxious grapnels I had sounded my pocket . . .

Warwick Charlton

"People forget that it all began . . . with a damned acorn."

Unknown

Harbors and ships rot men.

John Masefield

A WANDERER'S SONG

A WIND'S in the heart of me, a fire's in my heels,
I am tired of brick and stone and rumbling wagon-wheels;
I hunger for the sea's edge, the limits of the land,
Where the wild old Atlantic is shouting on the sand.

Oh I'll be going, leaving the noises of the street,
To where a lifting foresail-foot is yanking at the sheet;
To a windy, tossing anchorage where yawls and ketches ride,
Oh I'll be going, going, until I meet the tide.

And first I'll hear the sea-wind, the mewing of the gulls,

The clucking, sucking of the sea about the rusty
hulls,
The songs at the capstan in the hooker warping
out,
And then the heart of me'll know I'm there or
thereabout.

Oh I am tired of brick and stone, the heart of me
is sick,
For windy green, unquiet sea, the realm of Moby
Dick;
And I'll be going, going, from the roaring of the
wheels,
For a wind's in the heart of me, a fire's in my
heels.

Alan Villiers

               Apple pie, ship-
shape and no damned Irish pennants!

Joshua Slocum

              Commenting on
coast-hugging mariners: "Briny sailors of the
strand."

Alan Villiers

            An old, old scene,
this—the violinist playing on the capstan head to
the crew, while the anchor was tripped and the
ship turned her graceful head to the seas.

Joshua Slocum

            Vignette: Captain
Slocum selling canvas souvenirs of the *Spray's*
mainsail.

Thomas Fleming Day

WHEN
When western winds are blowing soft
Across the Island Sound;
When every sail that draws aloft
Is swollen true and round;
When yellow shores along the lee
Slope upward to the sky;
When opal bright the land and sea
In changeful contact lie;
When idle yachts at anchor swim
Above a phantom shape;
When spires of canvas dot the rim
Which curves from cape to cape;
When sea-weed strewn the ebbing tide
Pours eastward to the main;
When clumsy coasters side by side
Tack in and out again—
When such a day is mine to live,
What has the world beyond to give?

Unknown

            Spritsail yards:
term loosely used by early sailors to describe
bones piercing the nose gristle of natives.

James Tazelaar

THE LAUGHTER OF WATER
The water laughs off the loo'ard bow
Displaced by wooden kiss, shakes its brow
Swollen faced, spews Hydra's tongue—thin
dollops—
From broken head—sassy, taunting trollops!

The water laughs off to loo'ard now
Beheaded, as it were, it (I vow)
Lisps Castilian and with mocking laugh
Lips the limbs of our heeling craft.

The water laughs and, passing, unravels
Mingles with the wake's anemone (lacy nemesis)
And its splintered, splendored body revels
To find and kiss a wind'ard face with emphasis!

Alan Villiers

            "Don't let the
books fool you, my boy. There's no sailor writing
them."

References and Acknowledgements

Thanks are due to the following publishers, authors, agents and owners of copyright for permission to reprint the selections for this book.

The numbers in parentheses after each reference refer to pages in this volume.

HUMPHREY BARTON, *VERTUE XXXV,* 1950, Adlard Coles Ltd., London. Published in New York by W. W. Norton & Co. as *Westward Crossing.* Reprinted by permission of Humphrey Barton and Rupert Hart-Davis Ltd. (3, 4, 58, 62, 98, 99, 157, 159, 177)

RICHARD BAUM, *BY THE WIND,* 1962, Van Nostrand Reinhold Co. Reprinted by permission of Richard Baum. (20, 63, 74, 138)

HILAIRE BELLOC, *ON SAILING THE SEA,* 1951, Rupert Hart-David Ltd., London. Reprinted by permission of A. D. Peters & Co. (3, 8, 9, 12, 20,

22, 25, 26, 28, 32, 33, 35, 36, 40, 41, 42, 43, 44, 45, 46, 50, 51, 52, 58, 61, 62, 63, 65, 67, 70, 73, 75, 86, 98, 110, 128, 140, 144, 145, 146, 148, 158, 164, 168, 170, 171)

BIBLE. (63, 64)

ALAIN BOMBARD, *THE VOYAGE OF THE HERE-TIQUE,* 1953, Simon & Schuster Inc. Reprinted by permission of Simon & Schuster Inc. (43)

THE BOSTON GAZETTE (175)

ERNLE BRADFORD, *THE WIND OFF THE IS-LAND,* 1960, Harcourt Brace & World. Reprinted by permission of Harcourt Brace Jovanovich, Inc. and Brandt & Brandt. (19, 36, 58, 61, 62, 151, 157, 162, 166, 168, 172)

FRANCIS BRENTON, *LONG SAIL TO HAITI,* 1965, William Heineman Ltd., London. Reprinted by permission of William Heineman Ltd. and Margot Johnson Agency. (27, 61, 63, 88, 103, 122, 129, 130, 138, 157, 172, 177)
THE VOYAGE OF THE SIERRA SAGRADA: ACROSS THE ATLANTIC IN A CANOE, 1969, Henry Regnery Co. Reprinted by permission of Henry Regnery Co. (50)

RACHEL CARSON, *THE SEA AROUND US,* Oxford University Press, Inc., New York. Copyright 1950, 1951, 1961 by Rachel L. Carson. Reprinted by permission of Oxford University Press, Inc. and Marie Rodell. (68, 116)

Warwick Charlton, *THE SECOND MAYFLOWER ADVENTURE,* 1957, Little Brown & Co. Reprinted by permission of Little Brown & Co. (18, 135, 180)

SIR FRANCIS CHICHESTER, *GIPSY MOTH CIRCLES THE WORLD,* 1969, Coward McCann Inc. Reprinted by permission of Coward McCann & Goeghegan Inc. and Hodder & Stoughton Ltd. (4, 9, 59, 85, 124, 130, 135, 174)
THE LONELY SEA AND THE SKY, 1959, Coward McCann Inc. Reprinted by permission of Coward McCann & Goeghegan Inc. and Hodder & Stoughton Ltd. (37, 124, 133, 173, 175)

REX CLEMENTS, *A GIPSY OF THE HORN,* 1924. Reprinted by permission of Rupert Hart-Davis. (2, 4, 19, 21, 23, 25, 27, 28, 29, 34, 51, 52, 58, 59, 65, 70, 73, 75, 76, 79, 84, 89, 91, 92, 97, 101, 106, 107, 109, 120, 121, 122, 123, 124, 125, 128, 129, 130, 131, 138, 148, 162, 163, 164, 171, 174)

K. ADLARD COLES, *CLOSE HAULED,* 1926, Seeley Service & Co. Ltd. Reprinted by permission of K. Adlard Coles. (54, 135, 137, 156, 178)

JOSEPH CONRAD, *THE MIRROR OF THE SEA,* 1906, J. M. Dent & Sons Ltd. Reprinted by permission of J. M. Dent & Sons Ltd. and the Trustees of the Joseph Conrad Estate. (17, 32)
PLANTER OF MALATA from *WITHIN THE TIDES,* 1924, J. M. Dent & Sons Ltd. Reprinted by permission of J. M. Dent & Sons Ltd. and the Trustees of the Joseph Conrad Estate. (61)
RESCUE, 1920, J. M. Dent & Sons Ltd. Reprinted by permission of J. M. Dent & Sons Ltd. and the Trustees of the Joseph Conrad Estate. (20, 21, 25, 38, 40, 58, 64, 68, 71, 78, 104, 145, 151)
THE SHADOW LINE from *TYPHOON AND OTHER TALES,* 1963, J. M. Dent & Sons Ltd.

Reprinted by permission of J. M. Dent & Sons Ltd. and the Trustees of the Joseph Conrad Estate. (33, 63, 64)

RICHARD HENRY DANA, *TWO YEARS BEFORE THE MAST.* (18, 65, 98, 159)

THOMAS FLEMING DAY, WHEN from *SONGS OF SEA AND SAIL,* 1898, Rudder Publishing Co., N. Y. Reprinted by permission of Rudder Magazine. (181)

ANN DAVISON, *MY SHIP IS SO SMALL,* 1956, Peter Davies Ltd. Reprinted by permission of A. M. Heath & Co. Ltd. (6, 33, 54, 168)

HANS C. DE MIERRE, *THE LONG VOYAGE,* 1963, Harold Stark Ltd. Reprinted by permission of Harold Stark Ltd. (59, 132)

EDWARD H. DODD, JR., *GREAT DIPPER TO SOUTHERN CROSS,* 1930, Dodd Mead & Co. Reprinted by permission of Dodd, Mead & Co. (18, 19, 21, 25, 28, 42, 43, 59, 62, 63, 67, 69, 74, 76, 78, 79, 87, 88, 89, 90, 94, 96, 98, 99, 100, 102, 108, 109, 119, 120, 123, 129, 133, 135, 139, 140, 151, 158, 159, 163, 166, 167, 172, 177, 178)

VITO DUMAS, *ALONE THROUGH THE ROARING FORTIES,* 1960, Adlard Coles Ltd. Reprinted by permission of Granada Publishing Ltd. and John de Graff, Inc. (4, 9, 26, 37, 43, 70, 84, 94, 102, 103, 122, 133, 177)

RALPH WALDO EMERSON, *ENGLISH TRAITS,* Hurst & Co., New York. (2, 36, 54, 92)

AMOS A. EVANS, *JOURNAL KEPT ON BOARD THE FRIGATE CONSTITUTION,* 1967, Sawtells of Somerset, Lincoln, Mass. Reprinted by permission of the Historical Society of Pennsylvania. (119, 168)

ERNEST K. GANN, *SONG OF THE SIRENS,* 1968, Simon & Schuster, Inc. Reprinted by permission of Hodder & Stoughton Ltd. and Simon & Schuster, Inc. (6, 14, 15, 19, 20, 22, 23, 25, 26, 28, 32, 33, 37, 46, 50, 65, 70, 73, 85, 103, 110, 119, 134, 138, 140, 141, 152, 153, 158, 174, 177)

ALAIN GERBAULT, *THE FIGHT OF THE FIRECREST,* 1926. Reprinted by permission of Anthony Sheil, Associates, London. (3, 4, 9, 37, 42, 70, 71, 78, 91, 107, 125)

M. EDWARD HAIE, *HAKLUYT'S VOYAGES,* 1907. (63)

BRIDGET A. HENISCH, *MEDIEVAL ARMCHAIR TRAVELS.* (8, 22)

HERODOTUS. (95)

L. FRANCIS HERRESHOFF, *THE COMPLEAT CRUISER,* 1956, Sheridan House Inc. Reprinted by permission of Sheridan House Inc. (42, 170)
YACHTS, 1967, Poseidon Publishing Co. Reprinted by permission of Mrs. Boris Lauer-Leonardi. (19)

JOHN HERSEY, *A SINGLE PEBBLE,* 1956, Alfred A. Knopf Inc. Reprinted by permission of Alfred A. Knopf Inc. and Hamish Hamilton Ltd. (2, 87, 90, 92)
UNDER THE EYE OF THE STORM, 1967, Alfred A. Knopf Inc. Reprinted by permission of Alfred A. Knopf, Inc. (13, 20, 36, 37, 40)

THOR HEYERDAHL, *KON-TIKI,* 1950, Rand McNally & Co. Reprinted by permission of

Rand McNally & Co. and George Allen & Unwin Ltd. (41, 50, 69, 70, 73, 96, 107, 115, 121, 131, 146, 156)

DESMOND HOLDRIDGE, *NORTHERN LIGHTS,* 1939, Viking Press, Inc. Reprinted by permission of McIntosh and Otis, Inc. (2, 28, 29, 35, 41, 42, 45, 54, 64, 65, 74, 79, 85, 109, 110, 132, 139, 152, 157, 165, 170, 176)

RICHARD HUGHES, *A HIGH WIND IN JAMAICA,* 1929, Harper & Row, Publishers. Reprinted by permission of Harper & Row, Publishers and Chatto and Windus Ltd. (12, 19, 65, 176)

RAY KAUFFMAN, *HURRICANE'S WAKE,* 1940, The Macmillan Co. Reprinted by permission of Ray Kauffman. (2, 11, 13, 14, 15, 29, 34, 50, 54, 58, 64, 94, 95, 97, 122, 129, 130, 131, 134, 137, 144, 145, 146, 148, 151, 152, 157, 158, 161, 164, 174, 178)

ROCKWELL KENT, *N BY E,* 1930, Brewer & Warren. Reprinted by permission of The Rockwell Kent Legacies. (29, 75, 95, 177)

RUDYARD KIPLING, *CAPTAINS COURAGEOUS.* Reprinted by permission of Mrs. George Banbridge, Macmillan of London and Doubleday & Co. Inc. (20, 59, 67, 95)

E. F. KNIGHT, *CRUISE OF THE ALERTE,* 1890. Reprinted by permission of Mrs. Arthur Ransome. (130, 132, 146, 162, 171, 177)

CHARLES LANDERY, *WHISTLING FOR A WIND,* 1952, J. M. Dent & Sons Ltd. Reprinted by permission of J. M. Dent & Sons Ltd. and Curtis Brown Ltd. (2, 3, 9, 12, 13, 15, 18, 20, 25, 32, 50, 58, 59, 74, 84, 85, 94, 95, 103, 104, 119, 137, 138, 140, 144, 145, 151, 156, 157)

DAVID H. LEWIS, *THE SHIP WOULD NOT TRAVEL DUE WEST,* 1961, St. Martin's Press, Inc. Reprinted by permission of the Hamlyn Publishing Group Ltd. (4)

JACK LONDON, *THE CRUISE OF THE DAZZLER,* 1902, The Century Co. Reprinted by permission of Irving Shepard. (22, 75, 131, 148)

THE CRUISE OF THE SNARK, 1911, The Macmillan Co., New York. Reprinted by permission of Irving Shepard. (8, 19)

DWIGHT LONG, *SAILING ALL SEAS IN THE IDLE HOUR,* 1938, Hodder & Stoughton Ltd. Published in U.S.A. as *10,000 Leagues over the Sea,* Harcourt Brace. Reprinted by permission of Anthony Sheil Associates Ltd. (2, 14, 55, 95, 130, 132, 145, 152, 159)

ALFRED F. LOOMIS, HAPPY ENDING from *THE BEST FROM YACHTING,* 1967, Charles Scribner's Sons. Reprinted by permission of Mrs. Alfred F. Loomis. (90)

HOTSPUR'S CRUISE OF THE AEGEAN, 1931, Harrison Smith, New York. Reprinted by permission of Mrs. Alfred F. Loomis. (11, 17, 98, 139, 170, 172)

CRUISE OF THE HIPPOCAMPUS, 1922, The Century Co. Reprinted by permission of Mrs. Alfred F. Loomis. (14, 18, 36, 61, 84, 100, 173, 178)

JOHN MACGREGOR, *THE VOYAGE ALONE IN THE YAWL ROB ROY,* 1868, Sampson Low,

Son & Marston, London. (12, 25, 27, 35, 36, 40, 41, 43, 44, 52, 78, 86, 87, 104, 128, 134, 135, 152, 163, 165, 167, 168, 170, 172)

JOHN MASEFIELD, *THE BIRD OF DAWNING,* 1933, The Macmillan Co., New York. Reprinted by permission of The Macmillan Co. and Society of Authors as the literary representatives of the Estate of John Masefield. (34, 62, 68, 89, 104, 106) A WANDERER'S SONG from *THE POEMS AND PLAYS OF JOHN MASEFIELD,* 1919, The Macmillan Co., New York. Reprinted by permission of The Macmillan Co. and Society of Authors as the literary representatives of the Estate of John Masefield. (180)

RICHARD MAURY, *THE SAGA OF CIMBA,* 1939, 1972, John de Graff, Inc. Reprinted by permission of Adlard Coles Ltd. and John de Graff, Inc. (3, 15, 20, 22, 23, 26, 27, 32, 35, 41, 42, 51, 52, 62, 65, 67, 69, 70, 71, 76, 78, 86, 87, 90, 94, 97, 98, 99, 100, 101, 102, 103, 104, 106, 107, 108, 132, 134, 144, 146, 151, 157, 160, 166, 170, 173)

HERMAN MELVILLE, *BILLY BUDD AND THE ENCANTADAS,* (114, 123) *MOBY DICK* or *THE WHALE.* (6, 17, 51, 52, 62, 64, 65, 71, 74, 90, 95, 106, 108, 114, 177, 178, 180) *WHITE JACKET.* (2, 51, 58, 75, 79, 84, 87, 89, 103, 107, 109, 128, 159, 174, 175)

EDNA ST. VINCENT MILLAY, INLAND from *COLLECTED POEMS,* 1948, Harper & Row, Publishers. Reprinted by permission of Norma Millay Ellis. (32)

CARLETON MITCHELL, MEREDITH CREEK, from *THE BEST FROM YACHTING,* 1967, Charles Scribner's Sons. Reprinted by permission of Charles Scribner's Sons. (6) *THE WIND'S CALL,* 1971, Charles Scribner's Sons. Reprinted by permission of Charles Scribner's Sons and Nautical Publishing Co. Ltd. who published as *The Wind Knows No Boundaries.* (114, 160)

SAMUEL ELIOT MORISON, *SPRING TIDES,* 1965, Houghton Mifflin Co. Reprinted by permission of Houghton Mifflin Co. and Curtis Brown Ltd. (22, 50, 69, 109, 114, 128, 132, 140, 162, 171)

FARLEY MOWAT, *THE BOAT WHO WOULDN'T FLOAT,* 1969, 1970, Little, Brown and Co. Reprinted by permission of Farley Mowat and Little, Brown and Co. (3, 14, 137, 176, 177, 178)

SAMUEL PEPYS, *DIARY.* (178)

DOUGLAS PHILLIPS-BIRT, *REFLECTIONS IN THE SEA,* 1968, Nautical Publishing Co., Lymington, England. Reprinted by permission of Nautical Publishing Co. (2)

HARRY PIDGEON, *AROUND THE WORLD SINGLEHANDED,* 1932, Appleton-Century, Crofts. Reprinted by permission of Appleton-Century-Crofts. (35, 44, 68, 79, 91, 96, 110, 121, 128, 134, 164)

MARCO POLO, *THE TRAVELS OF MARCO POLO,* ed. Manuel Kofroff, Liveright Publishing Co., New York. (12)

DENNIS PULESTON, *BLUE WATER VAGABOND,* 1939, Rupert Hart-Davis. Reprinted by permission of Rupert Hart-Davis and Dennis Puleston. (6, 17, 18, 46, 61, 64, 71, 120, 123, 128, 137, 138, 144, 145, 149, 161, 177, 178)

E. A. PYE, *RED MAINS'L*, 1952, Rupert Hart-Davis. Reprinted by permission of Dodd Mead & Co. and Rupert Hart-Davis. (12, 15, 18, 20, 26, 35, 40, 41, 42, 43, 44, 46, 62, 81, 86, 90, 96, 98, 99, 106, 107, 119, 129, 132, 133, 134, 141, 159, 161, 166, 167, 171, 172)

ARTHUR RANSOME, *RACUNDRA'S FIRST CRUISE*, 1928, Jonathan Cape Ltd. Reprinted by permission of the Executrix of the Arthur Ransome Estate and Jonathan Cape Ltd. (15, 19, 22, 37, 40, 43, 58, 59, 75, 91, 129, 140)

JOE RICHARDS, *PRINCESS*, 1973, David McKay Co., Inc. Reprinted by permission of Joe Richards. (128, 151)

WILLIAM ROBINSON, *TO THE GREAT SOUTHERN SEA*, 1956, John de Graff, Inc. Reprinted by permission of Nannine Joseph. (3, 8, 36, 52, 65, 70, 84, 87, 97, 109, 110, 138, 157, 166)
TEN THOUSAND LEAGUES OVER THE SEA, 1932, Brewer & Warren. Reprinted by permission of Nannine Joseph. (3, 17, 33, 41, 50, 52, 61, 63, 64, 67, 74, 78, 89, 97, 99, 100, 103, 104, 107, 108, 119, 120, 121, 130, 135, 139, 140, 144, 157, 159, 162, 168, 171)

WOODES ROGERS, *A CRUISING VOYAGE ROUND THE WORLD*, 1969, DaCapo Press Inc. (18, 51, 84, 108, 109, 130, 170, 173)

SIR ALEC ROSE, *MY LIVELY LADY*, 1969, David McKay Co., Inc. Reprinted by permission of

David McKay Co., Inc. and Nautical Publishing Co. (73)

JOSHUA SLOCUM, *SAILING ALONE AROUND THE WORLD*, 1899, The Century Co., 1927, Henrietta M. Mayhew; 1954, Sheridan House Inc. (4, 8, 9, 11, 13, 17, 25, 32, 35, 40, 44, 46, 54, 58, 62, 63, 64, 67, 69, 70, 71, 73, 84, 85, 86, 88, 90, 94, 97, 102, 104, 106, 132, 133, 134, 144, 152, 164, 167, 170, 173, 181)

STANLEY SMITH and CHARLES VIOLET, *THE WIND CALLS THE TUNE*, D. Van-Nostrand & Co., Robert Ross Ltd. (6, 15, 50, 51, 65, 67, 70, 85, 88, 102, 159)

WILLIAM SNAITH, *ACROSS THE WESTERN OCEAN*, Harcourt Brace & World. Reprinted by permission of Harcourt Brace Jovanovich, Inc. and Macmillan, London and Basingstoke. (8, 15, 23, 26, 42, 138)

ROBERT LOUIS STEVENSON, CHRISTMAS AT SEA from *THE HARRAP BOOK OF SEA VERSE*. (6)

RALPH STOCK, *CRUISE OF DREAM SHIP*, 1921, Doubleday & Co., Inc. Reprinted by permission of Doubleday & Co. Inc. (26, 27, 35, 36, 94, 96, 107, 152, 178)

ERLING TAMBS, *THE CRUISE OF THE TEDDY*, 1949, Jonathan Cape Ltd. Reprinted by permission of Erling Tambs. (23, 26, 38, 43, 44, 64, 65, 68, 74, 76, 91, 92, 95, 98, 114, 130, 134, 172, 177)

JAMES TAZELAAR, *SEA VERSE IN A SAILOR'S LOCKER*, 1973, Tidewater Publishers, Cambridge, Md. Reprinted by permission of Cornell Maritime Press. (181)

MARK TWAIN, *LIFE ON THE MISSISSIPPI,* Harper & Row, Publishers, Inc. Reprinted by permission of Harper & Row, Publishers, Inc. (80)

ALAN VILLIERS, *BY WAY OF CAPE HORN,* 1953, Charles Scribner's Sons. Reprinted by permission of Charles Scribner's Sons and Hodder & Stoughton Ltd. (27, 42, 115)
THE CRUISE OF THE CONRAD, 1937, Charles Scribner's Sons. Reprinted by permission of Charles Scribner's Sons and Hodder & Stoughton Ltd. (6, 114, 145, 158, 171)
FALMOUTH FOR ORDERS, 1953, Charles Scribner's Sons. Reprinted by permission of Charles Scribner's Sons. (33, 94, 114)
THE SET OF THE SAILS, 1949, Charles Scribner's Sons. Reprinted by permission of Charles Scribner's Sons and Hodder & Stoughton Ltd. (180, 181)
SONS OF SINBAD, 1969, Charles Scribner's Sons. Reprinted by permission of Charles Scribner's Sons and Hodder & Stoughton Ltd. (17)

CHARLES VIOLET (See Stanley Smith, co-author.)
SOLITARY JOURNEY, D. Van-Nostrand. (2, 44, 61, 71, 91, 108, 132, 134, 156, 157, 163, 170, 174)

ALEC WAUGH, *HOT COUNTRIES,* copyright, 1930, 1958 by Alec Waugh. Reprinted by permission of Brandt & Brandt. (73, 84)

E. B. WHITE, THE SEA AND THE WIND THAT BLOWS in *AN E. B. WHITE READER* edited by W. W. Watt and Robert W. Bradford, copyright 1963 by Ford Times. Reprinted by permission of Harper & Row, Publishers, Inc. (50, 114)

LEONARD WIBBERLEY, *TOWARD A DISTANT ISLAND,* 1969, Ives-Washburn Inc. Reprinted by permission of David McKay Co., Inc. and McIntosh and Otis Inc. (103, 140, 176, 177)

FRANK WIGHTMAN, WYLO SAILS AGAIN, 1957, Rupert Hart-Davis Ltd. Reprinted by permission of Granada Publishing Ltd. (3, 8, 19, 20, 22, 25, 26, 28, 32, 33, 35, 38, 40, 44, 45, 51, 52, 58, 61, 63, 64, 73, 75, 78, 79, 97, 103, 106, 107, 108, 120, 122, 123, 128, 137, 138, 140, 149, 152, 157, 160 161, 171)

THE WIND IS FREE, 1949, Rupert Hart-Davis Ltd. Reprinted by permission of Granada Publishing Ltd. (4, 22, 41, 42, 46, 59, 64, 65, 67, 68, 69, 74, 76, 85, 86, 95, 102, 107, 110, 132, 144, 145, 156, 159, 162)